SIX years ago I wrote a book about marketing churches. Church leaders reacted quite strongly to the book. At one end of the spectrum were pastors who wrote me off as a young, aggressive heretic who did not understand or accept God's omniscience and omnipotence. At the other end of the continuum were church leaders who were excited that someone had articulated some of the struggles they faced in growing a church while offering some practical solutions to their dilemma.

The most common response, though, was fear. In writing about the relationship between ministry and marketing I had unwittingly touched a sensitive nerve. What made the matter even more uncomfortable was that upon reading the book and understanding marketing more clearly, many pastors had to acknowledge that *they were already practicing church marketing*. Although they did not describe their actions with that much-despised term, they were certainly doing their best to market the ministry to which God had called them.

This book is meant to help all church leaders go beyond acknowledging their marketing activity to facilitating more sophisticated and effective church marketing. Realize that church marketing is never meant to be an end in itself, but is a means to an end. That end, of course, is the delivery of truth and love, in God's name and for Christ's glory, to our gospel-resistant culture. Without compromising one iota of the gospel, we are challenged to serve God by cultivating our ministry fields for a full spiritual harvest. Marketing is simply one of the tools we can employ to maximize the harvest that God has prepared.

Few church leaders have taken graduate-level courses in marketing. This book is not a substitute for such training. However, I pray that this book will inspire, encourage, and better prepare you for the marketing opportunities that you will encounter today, tomorrow, and every day in your ministry.

George Barna

GEORGE BARNA

AUTHOR OF *THE FROG IN THE KETTLE* AND *USER FRIENDLY CHURCHES*

A Step-by-Step Guide to

CHURCH MARKETING

Breaking Ground for the Harvest

HOW TO IMPLEMENT SUCCESSFUL MARKETING STRATEGIES IN A BIBLICALLY-BASED, CHRIST-CENTERED WAY

HOW TO RECOGNIZE YOUR CHURCH'S UNIQUE IDENTITY AND USE THAT KNOWLEDGE TO MEET YOUR COMMUNITY'S NEEDS

HOW TO RUN THE BUSINESS SIDE OF YOUR CHURCH WITHOUT COMPROMISING YOUR SPIRITUAL INTEGRITY

Regal Books
A Division of Gospel Light
Ventura, California, U.S.A.

Published by Regal Books
A Division of Gospel Light
Ventura, California, U.S.A.
Printed in U.S.A.

Quotes used in this book and not otherwise identified are from *Simpson's
Contemporary Quotations*, compiled by James B. Simpson, Houghton Mifflin
Company, Boston, 1988.

Library of Congress Cataloging-in-Publication Data
Barna, George.
    A step-by-step guide to church marketing: breaking ground for the harvest /
George Barna.
        p. cm.
    ISBN 0-8307-1404-9
    1. Church management. 2. Pastoral theology. 3. Church growth.
I. Title.
BV652.B32 1992   92-13748
254.4—dc20   CIP

4 5 6 7 8 9 10 11 12 13 14 15 16 17 18 / 00 99 98 97 96 95 94

Rights for publishing this book in other languages are contracted by Gospel
Literature International (GLINT). GLINT also provides technical help for the adap-
tation, translation, and publishing of Bible study resources and books in scores of
languages worldwide. For further information, contact GLINT, Post Office Box 4060,
Ontario, California, 91761-1003, U.S.A., or the publisher.

TABLE OF CONTENTS

APPENDICES

ACKNOWLEDGMENTS

A long list of people have been instrumental in enabling me to get this book into print. Although a token mention of their names is clearly inadequate as a means of expressing appreciation, I hope they realize that this acknowledgment is reflective of a heart of gratitude for their support.

At Barna Research, my absence has been well covered by Cindy Coats, Keith Deaville, Gwen Ingram, Vibeke Klocke, Paul Rottler and Ron Sellers. At Regal Books, the support of Kyle Duncan, Bill Greig III, Bill Greig, Jr. and Mark Maddox has been consistent and influential. Gary Greig composed the inductive Bible study that appears in the appendix; his assistance with this critical dimension of this project is warmly appreciated. At home, my wife, Nancy, and daughter, Samantha, have been bulwarks of support and encouragement. May there never again be a book I write that will tear me away from them in the same manner. Dean Swartz and Rod MacIlvaine, elders at my church, have shown continued interest and support in this work. The numerous pastors who have provided me with materials and ideas are also gratefully—albeit anonymously—acknowledged.

If you don't like what is in these pages, lay the blame at my feet, not theirs. If you do like what is in here, use it and give the glory to God.

ONE
MARKETING CAN HELP YOUR CHURCH GROW

WHICH one of these scenarios best describes your present circumstances?

- You work with a church that is seeking to grow numerically, but you don't have any formal training in disciplines such as marketing and advertising.
- As the spiritual leader of your church, you are relying upon the talents, experience and enthusiasm of the people in your congregation to facilitate the growth of the church. However, since you are ultimately responsible for the health and direction of the overall ministry you want to have at least a working knowledge of what marketing in the church context is all about. Then you can provide your people with more responsible input and leadership.
- You have read about church marketing and remain skeptical of it. In the interests of truly serving the church, though, you want to explore the theory and practice objectively before making a decision either to embrace or dismiss the practice.
- Your ministry has decided to engage in marketing, and you are "doing your homework"—striving to learn all you can about effective techniques and strategies so that you can refine your efforts.

- Perhaps you, personally, are skilled in the art of church marketing, but you are working with people who have little or no experience in this realm. Rather than continue to bear the brunt of the marketing burden alone, you are interested in finding resources that will help you transfer some of your marketing insights and skills to your assistants.

- As a layperson committed to your church's ministry, you are anxious to invest your energy in helping the church impact numerous lives. Aware that effective marketing is a key to enlarging the scope of the church's ministry, you are seeking to learn as much as you can about the church marketing process so that you can take on more responsibility in the church's growth efforts.

This book is written for people engaged in ministry who have learned that God *is* sufficient for all of our needs, and that *part of His sufficiency has been to gift us with the resources and means to do ministry effectively.* And in most cases, that means doing more than saying a hopeful prayer and waiting for Him to do the rest. He calls upon us to use what He has given us in the most intelligent, efficient and productive ways.

Ministry is not an either/or proposition in which you either trust God to do it all (the "stand back and let God be God" approach), or you take it upon yourself to do the entirety of ministry on His behalf (the "He *needs* me" perspective). True Christianity is *balanced* ministry, a combination of trust in God and commitment to action. It is allowing God to use you to accomplish those ends He deems important, through the application of the special gifts, talents and resources He has entrusted to you for the purpose of building His Kingdom and bringing glory to His name.

Can He accomplish His desired ends without you? Absolutely. *But apparently He chooses not to.* Instead, God uses believers, His Word and His Spirit in a transaction that meets people's spiritual needs. That's not a bad definition of *marketing* (see chapter 2). And in that sense *God uses marketing to build His Church.* He doesn't need to. But He clearly does so.

Lessons from the Past

Several years ago I wrote a book about marketing churches.[1] The response to that book was fascinating. Many pastors wrote me off as a heretic, a young, aggressive, worldly fellow who did not truly believe in God's omniscience and omnipotence. Some Christian bookstores "banned" the book, refusing to expose their customers to a volume filled with such scandalous thoughts. For the first year or so after the book's release, I was certainly a persona non grata in many places.

But an interesting phenomenon has developed over the course of the four years following the publication of the book. I have witnessed a parting of the ministerial seas. Many older pastors (the "old school," as some call them) rejected the book and its concepts without a second thought, but many younger pastors (the "new school") were willing to evaluate the potential for introducing marketing principles into a congregational ministry.

Today, much of the early furor over church marketing has died. Of course, a few well-known ministry leaders still protest the use of marketing practices in churches, and cry "foul" when they catch wind of a church that attempts to be user friendly. The typical concern is that consciously engaging in church marketing causes us to place our trust in something other than God to accomplish ends other than His. Sometimes the concern revolves around compromising biblical beliefs in the interest of attracting large numbers of people to the church. Sometimes critics say that attending to people's felt needs is mere pandering undertaken at the expense of sticking to an undiluted, unembellished proclamation of the gospel.

How interesting it is that when these critics promote the anti-marketing message they are guilty of deploying the very tactics they worry the church will utilize to promote the gospel and the expansion of the church! When they promote their views in books, advertising is used, media interviews are conducted, the book cover is designed to appeal to the target audience. When they take to the road to share their message in guest sermons or conference presentations, their appearance is heralded through radio commercials, direct mail solicitations, special product promotions. Visit the churches of these leaders and you will find well-conceived and carefully executed procedures related to the treatment of visitors, the assimilation of newcomers, efficient fund-raising, and communications about the various ministry activities sponsored by the church. In short, they prudently market their church and its ministry.

For the most part, the debate is over. Although the need is always there to be held accountable for our actions and our motives, and to conscientiously avoid compromising any portion of biblical truth, the church is better off in every way when it blends good marketing practice with unswerving commitment to the call of Christ. There are ample examples of churches who have creatively marketed their ministries without compromising their mission or beliefs, to prove that marketing can be a significant benefit to the church.

May the thousands of floundering churches in America today realize they can move a step closer to achieving their ministry goals by adding effective marketing to the other skills they already utilize in their daily operations.

Getting Beyond the Theory

Marketing the Church was conceptual in nature. It outlined a seven-step approach for marketing, but did not really delve into the nitty-gritty mechanics of how a ministry-minded person or team might apply those elements to church marketing. For many pastors, simply understanding and buying into the basic concepts of marketing and how these concepts relate to what we do in churches was a major step. It was difficult to come to grips with the fact that they were already doing marketing, even though they did not call it by that name or realize that some of their routine efforts qualified as marketing.

In retrospect, perhaps *Marketing the Church* achieved its purpose: to confront, head-on, the church-marketing controversy and to get church leaders to understand and accept marketing as a viable component of ministry. To immediately expect pastors and other church leaders to blast forward with cutting-edge ministry strategies and tactics, based upon a newly-embraced, marketing-driven mind-set may have been expecting too much. Why? Because knowing the theory behind an approach is very different from understanding and implementing the actions that make the approach work in the real world.

Today, many churches in our country need to take the next step and address the how-to's of the marketing process. Few pastors have formal training in business disciplines, and even fewer have any training in marketing. This book cannot substitute for a full-scale, graduate-level education in marketing. I hope, though, it can provide enough insight into some of the key marketing procedures, described in relation to church ministry, to enable you to be more confident and capable in your ability to market your church. We will also point out some essential differences between church marketing and secular aspects of marketing.

This One Is for You, If...

I have written this book with pastors, church staff and active lay leaders in mind. During the past decade I have worked with enough churches and parachurch ministries to know that the laity will ultimately have to be involved in the marketing process if the church is to increase its influence. However, it is also a reality that an "official" leader from the upper strata of the church hierarchy must champion the process on behalf of the church. Having the sanction of the church leadership is essential to seeing the process catch on and make a difference. Thus, this book is intended for those in professional ministry who lack formal background in marketing, but wish to be conversant in the techniques and to implement them in an effective, noncompromising ministry.

If you wish to market your church effectively, you will involve a variety of people from within the congregation. This book may prove to be a source of common ground, too, between those who are in full-time ministry and those who volunteer their time and energy to make the church effective. By sharing a mutual understanding of the procedures involved in church marketing, and jointly deciding how to forge ahead in your own ministry context, this resource may help eliminate much of the miscommunication, misguidance and lack of know-how that so often plagues churches as they strive to grow.

For the Sake of Continuity

Because this is a how-to type of resource, and given that marketing is a multistage, continuous-loop process, you may not need to read the chapters in the order they appear. You may not need to read some of these chapters at all, if you have already undertaken some of the steps outlined in those sections or have significant skills and experiences in those areas.

I recommend that you read through all of the next chapter. It provides an overview of church marketing along with a description of the multistep process. It is an important chapter to make sure you and I are operating with the same perspectives and assumptions about ministry and marketing.

I also ask a favor of you. Please read the chapter on vision for ministry (chapter 9). (Also see *The Power of Vision,* Regal Books, 1992.) I am convinced that effective ministry cannot happen in the absence of God's vision. I am also aware, through our research with numerous churches across the land, that *many church leaders do not have God's vision for ministry.* They may have *mission,* but that is not vision. They may have *their own* sense of vision, but they need *God's.* Mission and vision statements are provided in the chapter to help you understand the difference between these elements, and to see how other churches have attacked the issue.

I ask you to read chapter 9 because vision is so critical to bringing the entire marketing process together. Here, again, I think the time you devote to the chapter on vision will be well-spent, regardless of what stage of marketing you are currently at, or how much experience in church marketing you have gained over the years.

As for the other chapters in this book, move through them as suits your purposes. Concentrate upon the aspects of marketing in which you are currently engaged. You may choose to read them out of order and possibly come back to the sections you skipped at a later date. (Then, again, you may not!) As long as you understand the process, have done your homework, created viable strategies, and are successfully implementing and revising a plan containing these strategies and tactics, you are in good shape.

This book also includes a number of appendices. These are not "filler" sections created to make a plump text. Each appendix has been included because it is an integral supplement to what appeared earlier in the book, providing samples, examples and other key information. Here is what you will find in the back of this manual:

- Samples of questionnaires used to survey a community or a congregation;
- Examples of church news releases, ideas on how to structure your communication with the media;
- Names and addresses of organizations that provide valuable materials, or services for hire;
- A brief marketing plan created by a growing church;
- A listing of other published resources you may wish to consult for deeper or different perspectives on a given topic.

If you are like me, you only read one-third of each book you pick up, lament not having the time to complete the rest, and move on with life. The rear sections of the book never see the light of day. I hope you will make use of the valuable resources provided in the appendices of this volume.

The Challenge

Never lose sight of the fact that we are not seeking to replace our confidence in God's leadership and blessing with man-made wisdom and techniques. Neither are we "selling Jesus," for we do not own Him. God remains the Lord of all creation, the only One capable of creating positive change in people. As we experience success in ministry it will be through our commitment to His sovereignty and His purposes, through His guidance and empowerment that such gains are made. We are simply His vessels.

Although we must humbly recognize our position we need not be ignorant, foolish vessels. My prayer is that God will use the information in this volume to enable you and other committed servants to achieve a broader and deeper influence in the lives of people, for His glory.

Already Seeking Compassion

Please understand that throughout this book, I will be using masculine pronouns in reference to leaders and marketers. This is not to imply that women have no role in the church or that they are incapable marketers. Some of the greatest marketing lessons I have learned were from women I have worked with or whose careers I have observed. Sadly, the English language does not permit us to write in a flowing, personalized manner without appearing "sexist." Forgive me for using this convenience of language; it is not intended to omit or offend anyone.

Note
1. George Barna, *Marketing the Church: What They Never Taught You About Church Growth* (Colorado Springs: NavPress, 1988).

TWO

CAN MARKETING AND MINISTRY PEACEFULLY COEXIST?

B EFORE we get into the specifics of how to market a church, let's cover some of the basics to make sure we are operating with a common perspective.

What Is Marketing?

Marketing is a broad term that encompasses all of the activities that lead up to an exchange of equally valued goods between consenting parties. In other words, activities such as advertising, public relations, strategic planning, audience research, product distribution, fund-raising and product pricing, developing a vision statement, and customer service are all elements of marketing. When these elements are combined in a transaction in which the parties involved exchange items of equivalent worth, the marketing act has been consummated.

Marketing is not simply a synonym for "selling." For instance, the creation and communication of a good image for an organization is part of marketing. In developing an image, a product or service is not necessarily exchanged. Instead, the image is developed to help the company sell its products or services.

Similarly, even though strategic planning in itself does not involve the exchange of goods, the process enhances the full scope of marketing. Such planning prepares the way for more efficient management of limited resources in anticipation of the most mutually beneficial exchange of resources.

Thus, all marketing is somehow related to exchanges or transactions. A number of activities, however, may precede the actual transaction; these actions are considered to be part of the marketing world.

Further, realize that marketing is not necessarily associated with money. Many marketing transactions occur without any money changing hands. Trades or barter deals qualify as marketing transactions even though no currency is involved.

It surprises some church leaders to hear that evangelism is a form of marketing. To leaders who hold a negative view of marketing, that certainly sounds heretical! We do not generally think of sharing our faith with other people as an adventure in marketing, but think about it. A believer engages a nonbeliever in dialog with the intention of seeing some type of active response to the shared information. After some discussion, both parties attempting to understand the needs and expectations of the other, the listener decides, either to accept or not accept Christ as Savior at that point in time. Regardless of the outcome, a marketing event has transpired. And when one individual leads another to accept Christ as Savior, a marketing transaction has occurred.

Let's not get sidetracked by theological diversions here. I recognize that *we* do not convert people. The conversion is done by God, through His Holy Spirit. In that process He uses us as a conduit for communicating truth to those who need to hear that message.

What is exchanged in an evangelistic encounter? The nonbeliever has committed his time to hear your message. If he decides to embrace Jesus as his Savior, he gives up worldly freedom and a sinful nature and agrees to commit himself to following Jesus Christ. In return, he gains the assurance of eternal life with God.

Believers play the role of middleman in the transaction. Charged by God to serve as representatives of His Kingdom, we explain the meaning of a relationship with Christ in obedience to God's command to His people. When a nonbeliever accepts Christ as Lord and Savior, the remuneration to us, as evangelists, is the spiritual and emotional satisfaction of seeing another soul enter God's Kingdom and knowing that we have been obedient to God's call to service. By making the effort to build a relationship with the nonbeliever, modeling a Christian life-style, explaining the meaning of a relationship with Christ, praying for (and, perhaps, with) the unsaved person, we will sometimes witness the fruits of an effective marketing effort.

> **"There is no such thing as a 'soft sell' and a 'hard sell.' There is only 'smart sell' and 'stupid sell.'"**
> Charles Brower, former president of advertising agency BBD&O

You, the believer, are the middleman; the Holy Spirit is the other party invisible to, but necessary for, the closure of the deal.

Marketing works well when the objective of both parties is fairness and mutual satisfaction. Fairness means that the exchange is completed with full disclosure by both parties, and that both parties are pursuing a reasonable deal. Mutual satisfaction is generally achieved by attempting to understand and fulfill the needs of the other party, while seeking some response from the party that will fulfill your needs.

Ministry, in essence, has the same objective as marketing: to meet people's needs. Christian ministry, by definition, meets people's real needs by providing them with biblical solutions to their life circumstances.

Will You Lose Your Salvation if You Market a Church?

Despite the apparent parallel between marketing and ministry, many Christians wonder if a bolt of lightning will strike them if they attempt to introduce marketing into the world of church ministry. This concern may be because marketing is not taught in seminaries or the term marketing never appears in the Bible. Or because marketing has been broadly misunderstood to mean *selling people something they don't really want, don't really need or can't really afford.* This makes many Christian leaders fearful of marketing a church.

Yet, the reality is that every church *is* engaged in marketing. The only real questions are, (1) what a church will call its marketing efforts, (2) and how good a job the church will do at marketing.

To circumvent the first challenge, churches have invented a series of innocuous or sanctified terms to describe their marketing endeavors. When you hear church leaders use these words, recognize that they are probably talking about marketing:

- Church growth;
- Church dynamics;
- Congregational development;
- Strategic ministry;
- Community outreach;
- Membership drive;
- Kingdom building.

When we hear such terms, we feel comfortable. Churches engaged in such activities are probably the types of churches you commend for being cutting edge, aggressive and forward thinking. These expressions and many others like them, however, actually refer to the process of church marketing.

Do you doubt that your church does marketing? Consider each of the following marketing activities. Our research reveals that most of America's Christian congregations engage in one or more of these efforts. How many of these characterize your church?

- Newspaper advertising;
- Display advertising in the Yellow Pages;
- A sign on the lawn or attached to the church building, listing the name of the church (and, maybe, the name of the pastor), the church's telephone number, times of the worship services, and perhaps the title of next Sunday's sermon;

- A brochure describing the mission of your church and some of its key programs and ministries;
- Posters or signs on bulletin boards around the church;
- A newsletter sent to church participants concerning the activities of the church;
- A membership drive of some sort, such as Friends Day or a community-wide mailing.

Naturally, involvement in marketing does not justify it biblically. But if we study the Bible, we can discover the fathers of our faith engaging in marketing practices. Although the Bible never uses the term "marketing," it is filled with examples that show the importance of marketing principles.

The faithful part of King Uzziah's reign was partly because "his fame spread far and wide" (2 Chron. 26:15). Before Ezra could begin the task of restoring the Temple in Jerusalem, he had to make a survey of his resources and of the skills of available people (Ezra 1 and 2). Barnabas successfully tackled a tough marketing or "PR" assignment when he overcame the early disciples' fear of Paul, convincing them he was no longer a persecutor of the church (Acts 9:26,27). And word of mouth—the world's most effective advertising—helped spread the word about Jesus Himself (Mark 1:28).

Examples of every aspect of the seven-step marketing process (described later in this chapter) are listed throughout the Old and New Testaments. (For a more complete discussion of the biblical support of these elements, consult the first appendix.)

How Church Marketing Is Unique

When secular professionals engage in marketing, their product is generally a tangible object: a car, a candy bar, an insurance policy, a jacket. Evaluating the purpose, appeal and accuracy of their pitch is relatively straightforward. The essence of their call to action is consistent: They want you to acquire the object they represent in return for a specified sum of money. Their marketing generally takes place in a store or office dedicated to finalize such transactions. You discover the availability of the product, attractive features or benefits of the product, by various types of promotional efforts made by the marketer. Perhaps you learned of the product from advertising, from discount coupons you received in the mail, or even from words of praise spoken by friends who previously purchased the product.

CHART 1
The Four "P's" of Marketing for the Local Church

Product	Relationships
Price	Commitment
Place	Presence of Believers
Promotion	Word-of-Mouth

These four key marketing considerations—(1) the *product* itself, (2) the *price* of the product, (3) the *place* in which the transaction happens, (4) and the *promotional* activities leading to the transaction—are called the "marketing mix."[1] Every product has a marketing mix. The effective organization consciously dictates the nature of that mix.

What about a church? Does your church operate with a discernible marketing mix, even though it does not exist to sell products or make a financial profit?

Absolutely.

Granted, the church is in a different situation. We do not have such a tangible product. As we said, we are not selling Jesus. Nor are we selling the Bible, because that is not what God called the church to do. We are not focused on promoting our worship services or programs. Ultimately, *we exist to move people into a relationship with Jesus Christ.* That relationship *is* our product. Once a person has built that life-saving bond, then we seek to make easier a variety of secondary relationships. We encourage relationships between the person and other believers for the purpose of encouragement, accountability, support and edification. We encourage relationships with nonbelievers for the purpose of introducing them to Jesus Christ and to the church.

Rather than ask people to provide monetary payment for the privilege of being in relationship with Christ, or to be part of His family, *the price exacted for this exchange is an intellectual and emotional toll: commitment.* The person's income makes no difference; his/her ability to give to the church is not of primary importance. The bottom-line requirement for the relationship to flourish is that the believer commit his life to that relationship. As the bond grows and the believer becomes more deeply committed to Christ, giving financial support to a church and other ministries is a natural and probable outgrowth. But no financial fee is required for a person to become part of His family.

Sometimes we get caught in the mentality that "church" is something that happens—an event that occurs, probably on Sunday, probably at a building we know as "the church." Biblically speaking, though, every person who confesses Jesus Christ as Lord and Savior is the Church. Once we embrace Jesus as our Redeemer we then become the living Church—24 hours a day, 365 days a year. Thus, although a secular marketing professional might require a showroom, an office or a store to market his product, the Christian has a whole different challenge. We are always on display, constantly representing the God of eternity, always being the Church, wherever we are, whatever we are doing. *The place in which we do our business as Christians—following Him and serving Him—is wherever we happen to be, at any time of the day or night.*

When it comes to promoting the product, *we are the best promotion there is,* simply speaking the truth in love to others, sharing the knowledge we possess of the true meaning of life. Yes, we can use advertising, direct marketing, public relations, events, and all types of other activities to create interest in what we, as a church body, are doing to share the gospel and influence lives. In the end, though, the research consistently shows that the best form of promotion is one-on-one, human interaction, one friend telling another about what is so important and significant in his life.

In summary, we have a product very different from those usually marketed. Ours is exchanged for a nonmonetary fee. We strive to complete a transaction that can occur at literally any time or place. The transaction itself is most effectively facilitated by nonmedia promotions. Nevertheless, we have a clear mandate to market the church, using our clarified understanding of the product, price, place and promotional elements of the process.

Grasping the Proper Technique

We can fine-tune our insight into the marketing process a bit more by recognizing a key difference between those organizations that succeed and those that fail.

Studies of businesses that go bankrupt generally find one of a handful of conditions in place. The failed companies generally began their operations without sufficient start-up capital; were led by individuals who had inadequate experience; or suffered from a warped view of how to generate the desired revenues. It is this last problem that relates to our interest in church marketing.

If you study how organizations market their products and services, you quickly learn the two basic types of organizations: *product-driven* and *market-driven*. It is the product-driven firms that typically declare bankruptcy. It is the market-driven firms that become the case studies of how to run a successful business.

A product-driven firm is usually launched by people who have a particular expertise or special interest. Their primary interest is to satisfy their own needs and desires by doing what they enjoy, or what they believe they are particularly skilled at accomplishing. The usual belief is that if they produce a good product, there will be a market for it somewhere, and the market will eventually discover the product.

A market-driven firm is generally launched by people who have a desire to meet people's needs, believing that their own personal needs (e.g. profit, influence, providing opportunities for people) will be met in the process. Toward this end, then, the market-driven person seeks to understand gaps in the marketplace—needs that have not been addressed or that have been insufficiently met. The products and services offered by these firms are geared to meeting those needs. The task of marketing is one of alerting people to the

CHART 2
Marketing Orientation

	Product-driven	Market-driven
Focus:	On what you produce	On what you produce it for
Motivation:	Doing what you desire	Providing what people need
Goal:	Personal satisfaction	Customer satisfaction
Motto:	Take it or leave it	How can I serve you?
Target:	Whoever wants the product	Specified niche

availability of the goods that the marketplace has desired but lacked.

This distinction is a vital one for churches to understand. Frankly, most of America's churches today are product-driven churches. This is fine, insofar as they want to "market" God's will and God's way. But the problem is that most church leaders have a model in mind of what a church should be like, and doggedly implement that model, regardless of whether or not it addresses the real needs of people. When people reject the model, certain leaders complain that the people are secularized, unspiritual, worldly or insensitive.

Most adults in this country do not regularly attend church worship services. This is interpreted by people in the product-driven school of marketing as a condemnation of the values and life-styles of our society, rather than a reflection of a church that has ceased to understand and respond to the needs of that society.

Our research generally reveals that the churches making a difference in their communities and attracting more and more people are market-driven. The typical rap on such churches, of course, is that they supposedly compromise the gospel to attract people or to focus on felt needs. The critics of such churches contend that these new models of Christianity are not valid, and are not true Christianity at all.

The facts often do not support these claims, though. Certainly, there are examples of large, fast-growing churches that soft-sell the gospel, or add elements of their own theology to make the faith more appealing. But the problem in these situations is not that attention to people's needs and trying to market a church is wrong, but that the people entrusted with the responsibility of leading God's people and presenting Him to an inquiring world have chosen to compromise what they believe or how they behave.

In other words, the problem is the technician, not the technique.

There are countless examples of authentic, Christ-serving churches that use marketing without apology. They proclaim the gospel, they facilitate relationships between people, they serve the community and they do basic marketing activities to enable such ministry to continue and to flourish.

American society is no longer effectively reached through mass marketing. Successful marketers these days are *niche marketers*—they target a particular segment of the population, not everyone in general. Two decades ago, the idea was to treat everyone as if they were part of a desirable reference group, and market the same products and services to everyone at the same time, in the same ways. From the mid-'40s through the mid-'70s Americans took pride in being part of a larger group of people and wanted to "keep up with the Joneses."

Today, people celebrate their individuality and go to great lengths to be recognized for who and what they are. People avoid group identification in favor of personalized attention. It is considered more blessed to be unique than to be common. Americans no longer care what the Joneses are doing; what they *do* care about is whether a marketer has adequately understood them to be the

---

CHART 3
The Marketing Process

Collect Information

↓

Capture the Vision

↓

Identify and Marshal Resources

↓

Create the Plan

↓

Implement the Plan

↓

→ Gain Feedback on the Process

Revise and Implement ←

---

unique and important people they believe themselves to be, and that such recognition is reflected through some type of customized or personalized marketing effort.

In previous decades, successful products were marketed by television network advertising. Today, if television is used it is increasingly likely to be cable TV, to reach a specific population niche. Even when network television is used, the programs chosen for ad placement are not necessarily those that deliver the largest audiences. The key is having your product seen by the right audience, which may require airing during a low-rated show.

In the '50s, '60s and '70s, successful products emphasized uniformity of ownership; you were not complete unless you, too, owned the product. In the '90s, the focus is upon having a unique, personalized product that meets your peculiar needs.

The implication for church leaders is this: If you want your church to be successful, respond to people personally, not as if they constitute a single, massive, undifferentiated audience. Segment the population in such a way that you can determine who is your target audience, and what it will take to satisfy their needs.

Previous research has shown us convincingly that no matter how large your church is, how talented the pastor may be, or how diverse the needs of the nearby population are, you cannot be all things to all people. Focus is critical. This means developing a mindset of meeting the needs of a specified population niche.

Does such a strategy minimize the possibility of reaching the world for Christ, as we have been commanded by Scripture? Absolutely not. In fact, niche marketing enhances the process. Why? Because it allows you to focus, prioritize and have a greater effect on a smaller group of people. Hence, the hundreds of thousands of churches that exist in America can each focus on a particular segment they have uniquely been called to reach, and have the type of influence they desire. Niche marketing enables a church to specialize and achieve excellence in ministry, rather than being spread too thin and accomplishing comparatively little. (Chapter 10 provides a deeper discussion of strategic thinking in a niche-based marketing environment.)

The Seven-Step Solution

Marketing is an organized, orderly process. To understand that process, think of marketing as a seven-step procedure.

Briefly, here is an explanation of each of the seven steps in the marketing cycle.

1. Collect Information

If you want to make intelligent decisions, or understand the context of your ministry, you must have accurate information. You can use secondary information along with primary data to form the basis of key decisions about what you will do, and how you will do it, in ministering to the world around you.

2. Capture the Vision

Once you have a good grasp on objective reality, you will be in a position to seek God's vision for your ministry. People cannot truly move the church forward without strong leadership. Strong leadership requires the determination of God's vision for the church, and the effective communication of that vision.

3. Identify and Marshal Your Resources

Before specifying the details of the ministry the church has been called to, it is necessary to determine what resources are available to the church, and how they can be activated for ministry. It makes no sense to create grandiose plans that cannot be fulfilled.

4. Create a Marketing Plan

Spontaneous activity may lead to a few short-term gains, but the secret to consistent, long-term progress is to develop a well-conceived plan and to carry it out. The plan should reflect all that has been gleaned through the early stages of the process: the ministry context, the ministry calling, the ministry resources and the ministry opportunities.

5. Implement the Marketing Plan

The best plan in the world is of no value until it is put into action. Even a great plan can fail miserably if it is not implemented with care, commitment and sensitivity. What often differentiates organizations is not the quality of their plans or the strategic insight they possess, but the ability to make their plans come to life in the real world.

6. Gain Feedback

Once the plan is put into practice, the marketer must evaluate how well the plan is working. That feedback should be constantly collected and examined so that improvements can be made, and greater ministry influence can be achieved.

7. Revise the Plan and Reimplement It

Knowing whether or not the plan is working is only part of the task. When shortcomings are discovered, and potential enhancements are conceived, the ministry ought to shift gears to reflect the suggested improvements.

The marketing process then becomes a continual loop. As new research uncovers strengths and weaknesses in both plans and performance after the plans have been developed and implemented, attempts can be made to shore up the weaknesses and change the plans accordingly. As changes are implemented and studied, new research will reveal other effects and opportunities, again requiring changed plans and activities. This process continues indefinitely, occasionally resulting in major shifts such as a revised information base, revisiting the vision for ministry, reassessment of the church's resource base, or creating an updated marketing plan.

What Is Coming

In the chapters that follow, we will examine the crucial marketing procedures in greater detail. Our goal is to enable you and your team to market your church with greater efficiency and impact. By understanding the tasks involved more completely, I hope you will achieve greater ministry productivity.

Note
1. E. Jerome McCarthy and William Perreault, Jr., *Basic Marketing* (Homewood, IL: Richard D. Irwin Books, 1987), pp. 37-40.

THREE

A Sea of Facts: What You Need to Know

IT has been said that we live in the Age of Information. Indeed, we have more information available to us today than ever before, and futurists are predicting that within the next 20 years the amount of data available to us will increase by more than 33 times. The problem, then, is not a lack of information. The real challenges are determining what information you really need, knowing where to find it and determining how to use it once you have it.

You can take either of two approaches to gather the information you need. One approach is to seek out what is known as *secondary information*. This is information that has already been collected by someone else for their own purposes, but has been made available for your use. This is known as secondary data because once the originator of the information (i.e. the primary user) offers it for broader use, you become its secondary user.

The other approach is to conduct your own fact-finding mission and generate what is called *primary information*. In this case, you dictate the entire information process: the group of people in whom you are interested; what types of facts will be gathered; the means of gathering them; how to tabulate and interpret the information; and eventually deciding if and how to disseminate the information to others (i.e. to secondary users). At some point, should you decide to release the information to others, your primary data become their secondary data.

In this section we will focus on how to apply secondary data to church marketing. Subsequent chapters will address primary information and data analysis.

What Information Do You Need?

Collecting, packaging, interpreting and disseminating information has become its own industry. This year alone, more than $10 billion will be spent on acquiring information for corporate decision-making. Depending upon what you need to know, the chances may be good that you are not the first person or organization to desire that information. Possibly someone has already collected that information and is willing to make it available to you—at a cost.

In the complex world of information services, you will not get very far until you satisfactorily answer some basic questions.

Identifying Your Information Needs

The initial question to answer is *what information do you need?* The worst thing you can do is simply launch out to find "interesting and potentially usable facts," as many well-intentioned but misguided people have done. In the research industry, this is generally known as a fishing expedition: Put down your line and see what you bring up.

Should you take that naive approach, you will soon find yourself overwhelmed by the volume of sources, much less the sea of facts, that reside in the marketplace. To make effective use of your time and resources you must pursue information with a strategy in mind.

Foreseeing the Applications

As you ponder your many options you will realize that before you can determine exactly what information you need, you must grapple with a second basic question: *why do you need this information?* One of the most important steps in the process is determining ahead of time how you will use the information you think you need. Once you have identified the potential application, you are in a better position to determine the actual importance and value of the information.

Debating the Value of Information

Some church leaders consider the process of incorporating information into their planning and wonder why they should bother. Why not just "do our best and pray that it's blessed"? If you arrive at this point, you may wind up wrestling with a few questions like those listed below. (I have taken the liberty of answering these questions on the basis of our past experience with corporate and church clients alike.)

Q. I am an expert in my field. Can't I simply operate on the basis of my experience and instinct?

A. Yes, you can, and many do. Some people are gifted with sharp instincts—but these instincts have been honed by exposure to the right information. This information, then, provides the keen insights that lead to what looks like effortless, intuitive decisions. Their intuition is invariably based on information gleaned in uncanny ways. Be aware that relatively few people have such abilities. The evidence suggests that success is a direct function of the accuracy and inspired use of targeted information.

Q. Why spend the time and money on gathering information? Can't I simply do my best and learn from my mistakes?

A. You certainly can—and you increase by more than tenfold the chances of running your organization out of business within five years! Trial and error, as this approach is commonly known, is the most costly form of collecting and analyzing information. Often, the people who make the errors on which new insights are based are not in business long enough to benefit from their adventure in seat-of-the-pants marketing research.

Q. I am running a church, not IBM—how can we afford to buy information? Besides, this is not a for-profit company.

A. In actuality, you can't afford *not* to collect and analyze pertinent information about your ministry. Although there are many reasons why we have so many lethargic, inert churches in America, one of the key reasons is that the principals in the ministry are not adequately attuned to the environment these churches are seeking to influence. These leaders mean well, but they are out of touch with the hearts and minds of the people they wish to change. Without that sensitivity they have a severely reduced potential for creating great ministry strategies that make a difference.

Whether you are running a for-profit or not-for-profit organization, you spend your hours on the job using God-given talents in His service. As such, you should make the best possible decisions and strive for the most efficient use of your limited resources. The value of information is that, when properly applied, it will enable you to make better decisions.

Q. *Isn't it improper for a minister of the gospel to rely upon anything other than God for guidance?*

A. Absolutely. But recognize that He provides guidance in myriad forms—including information that can be gathered and evaluated through your God-given talents and resources. To simply rely upon Him to implant ideas, strategies, tactics and insights in your mind, without your taking any of the initiative or making any real effort, is irresponsible and borders on the mystical. He calls you to use the abilities and real-world information He has provided to arrive at logical, reasonable conclusions.

What Type of Information to Pursue

Assuming you conclude it is wise to obtain objective information for making more efficient and effective ministry decisions, you must determine if you are better off using *primary* or *secondary* data. In some cases, you may wish to use a blend of both types, perhaps using secondary data to give you insight into what has been known before, but then using primary data to expand and update your knowledge base. In other circumstances, you may desire the use of secondary data but find none available. Or you may prefer to lean on primary data but find the process or cost beyond your capabilities.

Each type of information has its advantages and disadvantages. Chart 4 offers a brief comparison of some of the major considerations.

CHART 4
A Comparison of Primary and Secondary Data

Comparative Measure	Primary Data	Secondary Data
Cost	Varies by scope of project methods, but generally in the thousands of dollars	Varies, but usually lower than primary data; from free to thousands of dollars
Acquisition speed	Varies: 1-3 months on average	Varies: may spend time searching for nonexistent data, or may find what's needed immediately
Information accuracy	If conducted well, very reliable; if sloppy, not worth doing	Wide variation; some is impeccable, some is garbage
Needs and interests applicability	Since you decide what is done, it should be a perfect fit	Since it was done by others for their purposes, it might fit well or it might not fit at all; has little flexibility
Data currency	Fresh and current	Could be recent data or could be so aged as to have dubious value
Source objectivity	If you choose to do it right, you can ensure data objectivity	You never really know for sure; you must make educated guesses about the purposes of the data gatherers

Calculating Data Reliability

One of the most difficult aspects of using secondary information is to determine whether a particular body of information is reliable. Here are some clues to pursue as you attempt to determine reliability.

- Did the organization that conducted or analyzed the data have a vested interest in the outcome? If so, you may wish to pass by the information: better to have no information than misleading information.
- Is the research methodology for the study described in sufficient detail to build up your confidence in the information? If not, the organization may have something to hide. Alternatively, a lack of information about method may be a clue as to their lack of sophistication and reliability. Check any description of the methodology carefully to make sure they have used reasonable procedures.
- Is the research methodology reliable? Check the nature of the sample, the size of the sample, how the sample was drawn, the means of data collection, the survey response rate (if it was a survey) and any other facts that might help you determine if the project was done in a defensible manner.
- How old are the data? Information may be valuable even if it is 10 years old—if it relates to an aspect of people's lives that does not change much or if it is to be used as one point in a time-series (i.e. longitudinal or tracking) study. With the rapid pace of change in today's world, however, the life of information is ever shorter. If you have reason to believe that the factors measured may have changed substantially since the data were collected, then the information may not be of high value to you.
- Is the cost worth the insight received? Sometimes, syndicated studies of specialized groups sell for several thousand dollars. They are well worth every penny if the party buying the information has a research budget sufficient to absorb such a cost. Or if the organization can make decisions of a magnitude that justify such expenditures. Also, if the insights

CHART 5
Value of Secondary Data:
Assessment Worksheet

Consideration regarding the data

Your assessment of the data

1. What organization collected the data originally?

2. When did they collect it?

3. What was their original reason for collecting the information?

4. What data collection methodology did they use?

5. How well does the focus of their data match your information needs?

6. How satisfactory are the research parameters and procedures they used, given your needs?
   a. sample size?

   b. type of sample used?

   c. sample population?

   d. response rate?

7. What is your budget for the information they can provide?

8. How much does their information cost?

9. In what format will you receive the data?

10. Are there alternative sources for the same information that is accessible to you?

gained are so unique that the organization would not have acquired them from some other source for less money. Information can be seductive, but you have to know the true value of information to avoid being sucked into the vacuum.

- What is the reputation of the researchers? Some organizations are known for doing shoddy research, or as being "hired guns"—i.e., conducting research by reputable methods but influencing the outcome in other ways that shade the findings to the liking of the researchers or their clients. You will do best by relying upon the work of reputable firms.

As you decide whether to use primary or secondary data, realize that no matter what choices you make, you rarely operate under perfect conditions. If you use either secondary or primary information exclusively, or use a combination of both procedures, there will be tradeoffs inherent in your choices. Your responsibility is to make the most efficient choice and then move on with the project.

Typical Uses of Information

The applications of information in the decision-making process are nearly infinite. From a church marketing standpoint, here are some of the most common applications. Think through the potential uses of information in your ministry before you create any type of plan to collect information. Some productive uses of such information for church ministry have included the following:

- Identify prime locations for a new church.
- Understand the background characteristics of the people within a ministry area.
- Predict the demographic changes in the community that will occur in the next few years assuming that the current trends continue unabated.
- Describe the life-styles and daily preferences of the people living in the community.

- Project expected church growth to prepare for the facilities, programming and personnel needs of the future.
- Understand the background characteristics of the people who are currently in the congregation.
- Test new ideas or materials to be used for church marketing, outreach or fund-raising.
- Evaluate existing levels of awareness and image of your church, and of the others in your community.
- Determine why some churches have achieved growth in your community while others have plateaued or declined.
- Identify the personal felt needs of the people you will minister to.
- Determine the financial capacity of your church.
- Measure the impact of the church on people's lives.
- Evaluate the different elements of the church's ministry: preaching, teaching, worship, music, facilities, relationships, programs and so on.

Some of these interests can be served through the acquisition and application of secondary data; others almost always require you to conduct primary research. Perhaps those for which secondary data sources are most available and reliable are the first four items mentioned in the preceding list.

What Secondary Data Are Available?

Having decided that you wish to explore the secondary data available to your church to meet its marketing and ministry needs, your next task is to outline your information objectives.

Information objectives are simply statements that tell what information you want to know. Here are a few examples from some churches we have recently worked with.

- What is the demographic profile of adults living within five miles of your church?
- How many households in your community have children under the age of 13?

- What percentage of people in your community have lived there for more than 10 years? For less than three years? Moved out within the past year? Moved in within the last year?
- Which section of town is experiencing the fastest population growth?
- How do residents in the community spend their free time?
- How many people attend church services at churches located in your community?

Before you start searching data bases for interesting or useful clues about the nature of the people to whom you'll be ministering, be sure you outline, as specifically as possible, your information objectives. (Use the worksheet on the next page to facilitate this process.)

A useful related step is to state how acquiring the information listed in each objective will influence what the church will do. The purpose of this step is to make sure that you don't wind up spending your limited resources acquiring data that is interesting but of little (or no) practical value. For instance, knowing how many people were married at a church in the community is interesting, but what difference would it make in your marketing plans?

Once you have identified your information objectives, and are satisfied that they are worth pursuing and promise to provide you with actionable insight, determine the types of information for which you will search. Here is a listing of the key varieties of secondary data commonly accessible.

Demographics. These are the elements of personal or household background information that give a broad sense of a population group. Typical demographics you might wish to understand are how the population is divided by age, gender, household income, occupational status, educational achievement, marital status, presence and age of children, racial or ethnic group identity, and location (region, state, community, zip code and so on). More than five dozen different demographic variables could be studied. Those listed here are the ones we have found most beneficial in church marketing activities.

CHART 6
Information Objectives Worksheet

Specify the exact description of the desired information.	Explain why that information is necessary for your church marketing.	Explain how you will apply such information.

Population counts. It is often useful to know the size of a population. If you are operating a ministry within a community, you may wish to know both the total community population and how that population is divided among zip codes or perhaps census blocks. If your church focuses upon a wider geographical area, you may wish to get population figures for several communities, as well as counts for smaller designated areas.

Attitudes. Sometimes you can locate studies conducted by other organizations in which people were interviewed about their attitudes toward specific realities and potentials. Realize that such information is relatively fluid: People's attitudes can change overnight. However, knowing their thinking can help you predict their behavior, or establish a means of ministering to them more effectively given their mind-set.

Behavior. Understanding how people act is critical toward effective ministry. Knowing key aspects of how they spend their leisure time, what types of products they buy, where they shop, the allocation of their time to various activities, and the like can help you design a more effective and appealing ministry. Even studies that show how much money people spent on various products can create a profile of the population, which helps you understand them better.

Values. What people value often drives their attitudes and resulting behavior. On occasion you may encounter studies that attempted to identify the value systems of people.

Voting data. Not only is it sometimes helpful to know how many people voted, or what parties local residents are registered under, but how they voted on special issues that appeared on the ballots, or in reference to distinctive candidates. For instance, you might learn something by discovering how the populace voted on referenda related to public education, crime, rights for special populations, or how they reacted to "single-issue candidates" (e.g. people whose primary reference point was opposition to abortion, or championing of gay rights).

After determining just what information you want, where do you go to get it? We'll show how to answer that question in the next chapter.

FOUR

HOW TO FIND THE INFORMATION YOU NEED

J UST as the *amount* of available information may overwhelm you with overchoice, so the number of outlets offering various kinds of data may surprise you.

Where Can You Find This Information?

Creativity and chutzpah (the Yiddish word for unabashed determination) are decided pluses if you will be searching for secondary data. In a world filled with information, the only problem is that you are more likely to be overwhelmed by the volume of facts and the energy it takes to get them, than by the sophistication of the networks in place to put such information at your fingertips.

Naturally, a logical starting place is the best-known dispensary of information: the library. Public libraries, especially in major metropolitan centers, have vast information capabilities, and usually employ competent people who are well-acquainted with what is available. College and university libraries are another possible source to check with in the early stages of a fact-finding mission.

Depending on what information you are pursuing, your denomination (if you are a denominational church) may have what you need. Many denominations have research departments who can conduct the information search for you; provide a custom report based on in-house data bases or obtain such information through relationships with reliable suppliers; or advise you on how to attack your information need.

Beyond these initial sources, you can turn to a number of tried and true places for a profitable investment of time and energy (and, sometimes, money). If the local, inexpensive data sources described above are not available or unable to meet your needs, you might consider the following sources of secondary data.

Census Data

The Census Bureau, Department of Commerce
The decennial census conducted by the federal government every 10 years is undertaken by the Census Bureau and made available in various formats for anyone willing to pay the relatively minimal costs involved. You may contact the Bureau directly (in Washington, D.C., or at one of their regional offices). In addition to the national census, the Bureau also makes available a variety of other reports based on its vast pool of continual research studies. (See appendix 2 for the addresses of the Bureau's offices.)

State Data Centers
Every state in the union has a government office whose responsibility it is to provide population and commerce data to other government offices and to state residents. Some of the information is from federal sources, some of it is from studies funded or directed by the state (and sometimes by county or community governments). Often, the information can be provided for specified geographic areas (e.g. counties, communities, zip code areas, SMSAs [Standard Metropolitan Statistical Area], etc.), as well as on a statewide level. (Appendix 2 contains the latest available addresses of the state data centers for all 50 states.)

Private Vendors
Slicing and dicing census data has become a multimillion dollar industry. Some of the vendors provide very sophisticated analytical

tools for making sense of the sea of numbers available. The follow-ing organizations represent those that offer such services:

- Urban Decision Systems (Los Angeles, CA)
- CACI Marketing Systems (Fairfax, VA)
- NPA Data Services (Washington, D.C.)
- Donnelly Marketing Information Services (Stamford, CT)

Government Data

The United States government is the world's largest research organi-zation. Through its various departments, it either conducts or sub-contracts for the conducting of hundreds of millions of dollars of primary research. Studies are conducted regularly by departments whose foci are health, commerce, transportation, education, jus-tice, agriculture and immigration. The decennial census is just the tip of the iceberg.

One way to identify what the federal government has available is by contacting the U.S. Government Printing Office (202-783-3238) and requesting the catalog of reports and papers they publish for the public. This catalog, which must be purchased, is a compre-hensive listing of all the documents the government produces for sale. Among a myriad of other offerings, you will find information about the following areas:

- housing and population transience;
- health measures and health care trends;
- marriage and divorce;
- interstate and intrastate commerce and trade;
- educational achievement levels and dropout rates;
- crime statistics;
- immigration patterns.

A widely overlooked means of getting needed information is to call upon your elected officials. Congressmen and senators employ staff to handle such requests made by the voters of their districts. They probably cannot acquire the information you want for free (although that sometimes happens), but they may be able to identify sources you are not aware of, or to expedite the acquisition process on your behalf.

Life-style Information

Several organizations focus on providing a combination of data bases to help you understand the life-styles that typify an area's residents. Called "life-style segmentation data," these companies offer packaged information that clusters people into different life-style segments to help you understand both the demographic traits and the life-style preferences and behaviors of these people. Because each company is using different data on which to base their judgments, and has created different ways of clustering attitudes, behaviors and demographics, the services offered are similar in nature but each organization provides a unique body of information.

For example, Claritas provides a life-style system known as PRIZM. In that system, they classify every household in America as belonging to one of 40 different segments. Another supplier of life-style data, Donnelly Marketing Information Services, calls its proprietary system ClusterPlus, and divides households into 47 disparate segments. Although there are similarities between the ClusterPlus and PRIZM categories, they are clearly distinct.

In comparing what each company has to offer, you will probably find that the most economically efficient approach is to select a single firm and use its output exclusively, rather than attempting to buy the services of two or more of these firms to compile the most comprehensive body of data. In the end, the additional insight gained from this extra expenditure of time and money will probably not be worth the investment.

The life-style data market has become increasingly competitive. To survive, suppliers have added their own bells and whistles to make its package attractive. Before you enter this arena and are overwhelmed by the many alluring and sometimes confusing options, determine what is and is not valuable to you. You will be faced with choices of what you will receive: data tables, mapped data, data on diskette, data commentary, periodic updates, combinations of demographics with life-style information, on-line data bases, consulting services, etc. Know what you need, why you need it, and how much you can realistically afford to spend before you get tempted by the varieties of cluster packages.

The organizations named below offer such services, and include a brief, subjective note about the experience our church clients have had with these organizations. If you plan to use such services, contact them all to determine for yourself how valuable their services might be, and the relative costs involved. Their addresses are listed in appendix 2.

- CACI. System: ACORN. This service, although preferred by some of the larger denominations, is somewhat limited in scope and inflexible.
- CIDS. System: MicroVision. CIDS is a value-added supplier of the Equifax MicroVision data base. They concentrate on working with churches.
- Claritas. System: PRIZM. High-powered system, now available through Barna Research Group.
- Donnelly Marketing Information Services. System: Cluster-Plus. Somewhat cumbersome, used by relatively few churches. Most useful if you purchase mailing lists from Donnelly, since those lists are ClusterPlus coded for better targeting.

On-line Data Services

Because of increasing sophistication of the data industry, more and more data services offer on-line access to a variety of data bases. To make use of these bodies of information, you will need a personal computer, a modem and a password to access the data base (which subscribers to the system are given). You can then call up the system any time of day or night, access a particular data base, and examine its contents (and, if desired, create a hard copy of the information). In addition to a membership and monthly service fee, you generally pay an on-line charge for the amount of time you spend accessing the data base.

The identity of the data bases in these systems changes periodically; contact them directly and determine which ones would be most beneficial for your needs. Some of the on-line services you might evaluate are the following:

- CompuServe (Columbus, OH)
- DIALOG (Palo Alto, CA)
- Dow-Jones News Retrieval (Princeton, NJ)
- FIND/SVP (by Knowledge Industries, New York, NY)
- POLL (by the Roper Center, Storrs, CT)
- Nexis (Mead Data Control, Dayton, OH)

Data Archives

A less high tech but useful resources are the existing data archives. These are essentially libraries for research studies. They vary in size, but each contains hundreds—if not thousands—of surveys and polls conducted for a variety of organizations by reputable suppliers on a wide range of topics.

The archives provide several services. You may use them like a public library, having access to studies that are housed in the archives. (You may be charged an annual user fee to gain such access.) Several of the archives allow you to call in data requests from the research librarians and receive the information for a fee. Several of them also sell the data bases on tape or diskette, enabling you to tabulate and analyze the information in whatever way suits your needs.

Listed below are the archives that provide a balance between breadth and reliability of data.

- The Roper Center, University of Connecticut, Storrs, CT.
- Institute for Social Research, University of Michigan, Ann Arbor, MI.
- National Opinion Research Center, University of Chicago, Chicago, IL.
- Louis Harris Archives, University of North Carolina, Chapel Hill, NC.

Research Organizations

More than 2,500 marketing and public opinion research companies operate in America. Some of these organizations provide special services to churches, others simply provide services that churches might find applicable to their needs.

For instance, companies such as Barna Research and The Gallup Organization conduct research for churches; syndicated studies pertaining to religious and life-style issues, which may then be purchased for a nominal cost; and other nationwide research that might be available in other formats (e.g. news releases, newsletters, books, audiotapes).

A list of the organizations that have a special focus upon the church market are listed below. Contact them to identify what resources they make available to churches.

- Alban Institute (Washington, D.C.)
- Barna Research Group, Ltd. (Glendale, CA)
- Gallup Organization (Princeton, NJ)
- Glenmary Research Center (Atlanta, GA)
- MARC, Division of World Vision (Monrovia, CA)
- Search Institute (Minneapolis, MN)

Professional Associations

One of the major purposes of professional associations is to provide members with useful information about the state of the industry and the marketplace the members seek to serve. Often these groups commission primary research that can be obtained for a small fee or sometimes no charge. Although their findings are generally national in scope, and focus on the performance of professional duties by members, such research may offer insight into the population you wish to serve.

More than 1,000 professional and trade associations exist in America today. The names provided below are but a small sample of those available, but include those that provide some level of research to their members and may have some value to churches.

- American Association of Public Opinion Researchers (Princeton, NJ)
- American Marketing Association (Chicago, IL)
- Christian Booksellers Association (Colorado Springs, CO)
- International Christian Video Association (Euclid, MN)
- National Association of Evangelicals (Wheaton, IL)

- National Religious Broadcasters (Morristown, NJ)
- World Future Society (Bethesda, MD)

Interest Groups

As our nation becomes more and more divided into population niches and into segments that are ardently committed to single issues or to clusters of public issues, a growing number of special interest groups are arising. Be careful when using the information gleaned from these organizations, for they generally have a specific point of view, a vested interest in their cause and tend not to release information that conflicts with their perspective and therefore might damage their pursuits. The value of contacting them, however, is that they have probably scoured the nation in search of relevant information and may be able to provide you with such information, or give you valuable leads that will help you get the information on your own.

Published Resources

It is almost impossible to keep up with the proliferation of newly-published resources flooding the marketplace these days. Many of these publications have great insights to offer the church market. More than 20,000 new books are published every year in America; literally hundreds of these contain facts and figures that can help your ministry. As well, more than 10,000 magazines and other periodicals are produced each year, frequently offering the most current information in a given subject area. Syndicated reports (i.e. studies conducted by a sponsoring organization and made available to any entity that wishes to pay for a copy of the report) are also increasingly common.

How can you find out about these resources? One way is to keep in contact with the organizations most likely to produce such reports or resources. Ask to be placed on their mailing list so you will be notified of new product releases. A second way is to get connected to organizations that market a variety of such resources to church leaders. For instance, a number of organizations produce and/or sell catalogs, books, reports, tapes and other resources related to the life of the local church. Some of these organizations are:

- Alban Institute (Washington, D.C.)
- American Institute of Church Growth (Monrovia, CA)
- Barna Research Group, Ltd. (Glendale, CA)
- Charles E. Fuller Institute (Pasadena, CA)
- Church Growth Institute (Lynchburg, VA)
- Church Resource Ministries (Fullerton, CA)
- Princeton Religious Research Center (Princeton, NJ)
- Willow Creek Association (South Barrington, IL)

About 100 periodicals geared to the interests of Christians and church leaders, plus others, contain great potential value to church leaders. Generally, if you are not a subscriber but request a sample issue, you may receive one to help you better evaluate the viability of the publication. Some of the periodicals church leaders tell us about and prove to be helpful are named below.

- *American Demographics,* monthly magazine, published by American Demographics, Inc., Ithaca, NY.
- *Christianity Today,* biweekly magazine, published by CTI Publications, Carol Stream, IL.
- *Church Growth,* quarterly magazine, published by The Sunday School Board, Nashville, TN.
- *Emerging Trends,* newsletter, 10 times annually, published by the Princeton Religious Research Center, Princeton, NJ.
- *Leadership,* quarterly magazine, published by CTI Publications, Carol Stream, IL.
- *Ministry Currents,* quarterly newsletter, published by the Barna Research Group, Ltd., Glendale, CA.
- *National and International Religion Report,* biweekly newsletter, published by Wike & Associates, Roanoke, VA.
- *The Public Perspective,* quarterly report, published by the Roper Center, Storrs, CT.
- *research alert,* monthly newsletter, published by Alert Publishing, Long Island City, NY.

Maintaining Your Information

Two additional considerations are involved in working with data, whether you are handling secondary or primary information. First, think through how you will keep your data base up to date. Once you begin to use information for decision-making, you will probably find it helpful—and addictive. Many pastors have wondered, after we helped them initiate a data collection system for their church, how they had conducted ministry in the past without such vital information at hand. But the value of the data base decreases as the data age. Having current, reliable information at your disposal is a benefit that warrants a well-conceived maintenance or continuity plan.

> **"In decision-making, the only thing worse than no research is bad research."**
>
> George Barna

Second, you must develop an efficient means of cataloging and accessing the information you collect. Having information is of no use unless you can readily determine what you have and then access it quickly and easily. Simply throwing it all in a box for future reference won't do. Information is a critical and valuable resource. It must be treated as such, especially as you make new decisions that will influence the outcome of your church's aggregate ministry.

When it comes to keeping the data base current, you have a number of options. Here are some approaches that other churches have used to their benefit. Choose the option—or options—that best fits your culture and needs and implement it as soon as possible.

- Have college or seminary interns examine a prescribed list of information sources on a regular basis and provide you with the fruits of their labors.
- Utilize detail-oriented volunteers from the congregation who will perform the data collection function, following your explicit instructions.
- Subscribe to an on-line data base and have a staff member regularly examine the latest additions to the files and obtain

pertinent information for your own church's data base.
- Carve a specified period of time out of the pastor's schedule (if it is a single-staff church) to allow for such updating.
- Ask members of your church who are in information-driven businesses if they have access to data bases that might be useful to your church. Assuming that accessing these files does not break ethical barriers, and that the individuals can do such work on personal rather than company time, have them regularly provide specified updates from those data bases.

Once you have this wealth of information, how can you maintain control of it? You absolutely need to develop a system that will:

- provide you with easy and rapid access;
- be understood easily by other people;
- take little time for maintenance;
- have sufficient flexibility to allow you to use it in different ways.

Once again, the experience of other ministries provides some clues as to the options available to you.

- Make copies of all documents; assign a code to the document copy; file the copies so the subject matter is referenced (on an index card, or on a computer file) and can be easily located by that code once the subject matter has been selected as being of interest at some time in the future.
- Enter the key facts from a resource into a computerized data file that can be accessed by a word search, chronological search or other indexed search. This can be done simply through a good word processing program.
- Place copies of all documents into a file folder designated for resources related to that subject area. Simply maintain a card catalog of the different subjects for which folders are kept.
- Maintain a notebook, listing the sources of useful information on given subject matters. When you need information on that topic, consult the notebook, determine where poten-

tially usable information can be found, then search out the source itself.

Whatever method you use to label and file your collected information requires you to (1) know your needs, (2) know your resources and, (3) know how to work creatively. We know of no single "right" way to proceed.

FIVE
QUALITATIVE INFORMATION: TAPPING INTO PEOPLE'S PASSIONS

I F you decide to supplement your secondary information with primary data, you can follow two distinct approaches. One approach is to conduct *qualitative* research; the alternative is *quantitative* research. What is the difference?

Qualitative research is mainly concerned with understanding *how and why* people think and act, rather than how many people think or act that way. The idea behind such research is to grasp insight into the quality of their thoughts and actions: the intensity of feelings, the breadth of understanding, the depth of importance. The methods through which qualitative information are derived emphasize the character of people's beliefs, opinions, attitudes and values, not simply the basic content of these elements.

Quantitative research, on the other hand, emphasizes *how many* people think or act in a prescribed manner. The census God ordered in the book of Numbers was to determine how many Israelite males age 20 and older were available for military duty (Num. 1:1-3). Today, through the use of random sampling techniques, quantitative studies allow the data to be projected to the population from which the sample was drawn. (Qualitative information, lacking the same rigorous sampling and data collection requirements, cannot be projected.) Conducting a quantitative study may require greater technical expertise in research, but it also provides "hard data" that are useful as a cornerstone for planning and marketing efforts.

Which is better, quantitative or qualitative information? Although this question is posed often, the answer depends upon the types of decisions you are making and upon what stage in the decision-making process you are at. Each research approach yields different types of insight. The choice of a methodology must be made accordingly.

Qualitative research, in general, is not necessarily information that truly reflects the thinking or behavior of the population you are studying. Because of the ways people are selected to participate in qualitative research, you can never assume that the individuals involved are a valid sample of the total audience.

Qualitative research usually draws information from small samples of individuals who were *not* chosen by a random selection procedure. The information collected may suffer from weaknesses in the collection process (particularly in "focus groups," which often rely on an open-ended discussion format). Because such studies typically provide nonstatistical information, the resulting analysis of the information tends to be more subjective than is true in quantitative studies. Although such subjectivity is not necessarily detrimental, it does reduce the scientific nature of the process and may be a weakness.

Nevertheless, churches have made effective use of qualitative research. Don't reject the approach until you have considered the potential.

The Potential Uses of Qualitative Research

Qualitative research can give you useful information in at least eight ways. Here is a brief description of these applications.

Idea generation. Some churches have used qualitative procedures as a creative prod, encouraging people to provide input into the church's ministry by conceiving new ideas or strategies. This is a form of brainstorming; the moderator of the process guides participants through a predetermined procedure aimed at sparking new thoughts or creating novel responses to a given situation.

Testing a questionnaire. Qualitative processes are sometimes used to evaluate the validity of a questionnaire that will be used in a quantitative study. By exposing qualified respondents to the questionnaire before it is administered at large, problems can be identified and rectified.

Concept testing. Because effective church ministry involves such a breadth of activities and the consideration of a wealth of creative ideas, some churches have used qualitative research to test these concepts before spending huge sums to implement them. The product of the research might be the rejection of all ideas; the refinement of one or more ideas for further testing or implementation; or the discovery of new ideas resulting from the testing process. In addition to results related to the opportunities at hand, the research provides insights useful for future ministry decisions by exposing not only how people might respond to new concepts, but why they respond in those ways—facilitating better concept designs in the future.

Quantitative explication. Often, qualitative data can help explain what is behind the numbers derived by a quantitative study. Although the latter form of research informs us of the size of a population, it overlooks why people respond as they do, or the connection between people's answers to various questions. Qualitative research can lift the veil and offer insights into the thinking behind the numbers.

Problem/opportunity conceptualization. A major benefit of conducting research is to determine the problems and opportunities that exist in the marketplace. Marketing is geared to meeting people's needs, but is unlikely to be effective at that task unless the needs themselves can be determined. Qualitative methods can enlist people's thoughts about what barriers to growth and impact might beset a ministry, as well as enumerate some of the more inviting opportunities that await a ministry's response. Sometimes these ministry options are revelations for the church: options that were previously overlooked but which represent new avenues of reaching people.

Capture language. Advertising agencies are the most common users of qualitative research, and a frequent reason is to hear the words and expressions used by consumers to describe a product or service. That language is then used in communications with the target population concerning the product or service, conveying a more natural and comfortable discussion of the entity being marketed. Churches have used focus groups to the same effect, especially with people groups they do not interact with often: the unchurched, non-Christians, unwed mothers, ethnic adults, the homeless, teenagers and so on.

> **"Good research is not a panacea, but it does reduce the risk in decision-making."**
>
> George Barna

Emotional depth. In a quantitative survey, the usual output is a statistic. That figure communicates no depth of emotion or intensity of feeling. Qualitative data, on the other hand, provide no statistics but convey the emotional contours of people's responses to stimuli. Comprehending how deeply people feel about a topic is a critical dimension to making a good marketing decision—especially in an age when commitment, loyalty and tradition are less important to people.

Extended boundaries. Because these methodologies encourage people to let loose with their thoughts and emotions, they provide a better depiction of the outer limits of people's thought patterns. Although quantitative research is good at telling us the central tendencies (i.e. the most common answers), qualitative methods are better at detailing the boundaries of people's attitudes and how they arrived at the outlying places on the opinion map. This is quite useful when attempting to foresee unexpected problems (i.e. the unusual behavior that can really foul up an event or interaction).

Qualitative research is sometimes employed for one other reason, although the purpose is unrelated to information. Bluntly put, churches may use such studies to enhance the image of the church or its leadership. By informing the congregation that small discussion groups or personal interviews with a small sample of people will take place, many individuals feel that the church and its leaders care about the people, are investing in the ministry, and will respond to the heartbeat of the people once they have the full picture of what is going on. Thus, research becomes a means of portraying the church leaders as people who are well connected to the congregation and will adequately represent everyone's interests.

This is to be discouraged if the process becomes a matter of politics and opinion manipulation rather than true marketing. Note, too, that if the church leadership gets involved with focus groups and is exposed to people's true feelings, then conscientiously ignores a ground swell of concern related to a given topic, the resulting image may become negative rather than positive.

Types of Qualitative Research

Several forms of qualitative research are available to the church.

Depth interviews are lengthy, open-ended, one-on-one interviews in which a small number of people are led through a sequence of predetermined questions and encouraged to speak exhaustively about the topics raised. The purpose of such interviews is to gain a comprehensive understanding of how individuals process information and apply insights to their own opinion, belief and attitudinal development procedures.

The greatest challenge in depth interviewing is to create a thorough interview guide and to know when and how to probe for more complete answers from people.

Depth interviews are based on quantitative research strategies and have qualitative elements built in. The process is partly scientific, partly art.

Observation techniques (commonly known as participant observation or nonparticipant observation) are methods in which trained researchers enter a situation with the purpose of noting the interaction among people and systems. In a church context, the observer may be studying the web of interactions between people attending the church: (1) the language and behaviors they commonly (or infrequently) use, (2) the endeavors that seem to create satisfaction, (3) those that appear to create discomfort and (4) other discernible patterns of behavior. The distinctive value of observation methods is that a well-trained researcher may be able to identify patterns and conditions of the people being observed. These conditions could not be identified through direct questioning because the people being observed may not be aware of the nature or effect of their actions or words.

In observation methodologies, the dominant challenges are in knowing what to observe, how to accurately record the observations, and understanding the aggregate framework of the social system so that some sense can be made of the many inputs that are available to the observer.

Observation methods are mostly art with a few scientific factors bearing on the process.

Focus Groups

The most common form of qualitative research is focus groups. Increasingly, churches are turning to focus groups to help clarify issues and opportunities, or to uncover the hidden thought processes of the congregation as they relate to ministry. Let's explore focus groups more thoroughly.

Understanding Focus Groups

A focus group is simply a planned group discussion. It is named a focus group because the idea is to take a topic or series of topics and focus on them in a concentrated manner. The coverage of the topics is meant to be more intensive than extensive. Although the discussion itself is unrehearsed, the discussion is guided by a facilitator, generally called a moderator, who has a carefully developed set of guidelines for how the discussion should proceed.

The key concept of focus groups is for people to be made totally comfortable in the group setting. They must feel that whatever they have to say, as long as it is on the topic being discussed, is important and valid. A pastor may have to make a conscious effort to "change hats" at this point. One legitimate role of the pastor is to warn against sin and error. But a focus group is not an appropriate context for this pastoral function. Another important pastoral role is to *really hear* what people think—and that is what focus groups are for. Here we are not as interested in right or wrong answers as in people being open and honest.

Focus groups are meant to include everyone in the discussion: it is to be more of a group conversation than a series of questions directed from the moderator to one individual after another. Good focus groups involve each person so that they do not feel like they are under the "research microscope" but are simply having a good time sharing their thoughts and feelings with others who are doing the same.

Recruiting the Participants

Ideally, focus groups consist of 8 to 10 qualified adults who have been invited to come together for a group discussion. The people are generally recruited by telephone one to two weeks in advance of the discussion session. They may be chosen at random from the community, from a congregational member list, from other lists available—it depends on the types of people you wish to hear from.

The initial telephone call is designed to screen people to make sure they qualify. When they are contacted they are asked to answer a few questions to determine if they fit the profile of the people you wish to study. People whose answers meet the desired criteria are then asked to attend the discussion session.

Because these discussions usually last between 60 and 120 minutes, it is generally conceded that people need a tangible incentive to give up that time. The typical incentive these days is cash. Depending on who you are inviting and your location, the amount varies. Members of your church may be willing to participate for as little as $10 or $20 a person. Outsiders with busy schedules and a limited interest in the subject matter—for instance, non-Christian, unchurched adults who are being asked to attend a session about attitudes toward churches may have to be persuaded by larger sums (e.g. $50 each). Cost of living also enters into the picture: Rural communities can usually pay lesser amounts than major cities. The incentives are usually higher in the Northeast and in California than in other areas of the nation.

The screening process is important. If you do not have people with the desired profile in the group, it will be awkward for them, difficult for the moderator, and a waste of your time and money because their presence has added nothing to your knowledge base. The screening questionnaire and interview must therefore be carefully thought through and created with your needs in mind.

For instance, if you desire to learn how effective the singles ministry in your church has been for young adults who have never been married (as opposed to divorced or widowed singles), you should develop a screening questionnaire to reflect those limitations. Questions might ask if they have participated in the activities of the singles group during the past year; if they attend the church regularly; their age; and if they have ever been married. Assuming they meet the predetermined specifications of the people you are seeking (e.g. active in the singles group, attend church twice or more a month, are under age 30, and have never been married), you would then finish the telephone interview by inviting them to participate in the discussion group.

If, instead, you wanted to know what it would take to reach the unchurched adults in your community, your screening questionnaire (known as a screener) might ask about their church attendance patterns; their openness to attending some type of Christian church within the coming year; and whether they have ever visited your church. If the people with whom you speak meet the desired profile, they would then be told of the group session, the incentive, and be invited to participate. (For an example of such a screener, see appendix 3.)

During the screening process, people generally are told only in vague terms what the discussion session will be about. The reasons for this masking of purpose are to avoid people dropping out because they are not interested (they may be the very people whose opinions are most important), and to preclude preparation for the discussion (unless the topic merits such premeditation).

When it comes to how many people to include in a focus group session, preferences vary. It is generally conceded that because of the nature of group dynamics, having 6 or fewer people in a session is problematic; 7 is marginally acceptable; 8 to 10 is ideal; 11 or 12 is difficult; 13 or more is untenable.

My experience has been that having more than 10 people participate at a time makes it difficult for everyone to feel comfortable speaking, and to hear from each person a sufficient number of times to understand their perspective. Should more than 10 people recruited for the group actually show up, it is common practice to decide which 10 would be the best to involve, and to simply give the remaining people the incentive they had been promised and let them leave without participating in the session.

When recruiting people, realize that for every 14 people who say they will show up to the sessions about 10 will normally do so. Thus, if your goal is to have 8 people participate (which is about the fewest that you would want to have), count on recruiting 11 or 12 people; if you are seeking 10 to show up, try to get commitments from 13 or 14 people.

When the recruited people show up for their session, you might wish to "rescreen" them. This means that they would fill out a one-page survey, which contains the same questions they were asked by telephone during the recruitment process. It is amazing how many people give different answers during the rescreening process than they did over the telephone. If the discrepancies disqualify them from participating, the common practice is to ask them about the discrepancy. If they indicate that some type of error was made in the telephone survey (meaning that their real answer would disqualify them), thank them and pay them the incentive. Tell them that because of the error, they will not be able to participate in the group.

It is imperative to reconfirm people's agreement to participate in writing. Immediately after recruiting the person send a confirmation letter stating the time, date and place of the session, and the incentive they will receive. Also confirm by telephone the night before they are scheduled to attend. Our experience has shown that confirming attendance the night before the session can increase attendance by as much as 50 percent. Put differently, failure to confirm participation 24 hours ahead of time may cause a disastrous turnout and a useless research exercise.

The Moderator

The importance of having a talented moderator cannot be overstated. A good moderator can overcome a number of deficiencies in the focus group process; a bad moderator will negate the value of the entire process.

The moderator is more than just the person who sits at the head of the table and directs the course of the conversation. The moderator is responsible for working with you to develop the recruitment screener; for creating a discussion guide or outline; for rescreening all of the participants before they enter the session; for leading the actual discussion; and for providing an analysis of the sessions (either in writing or verbally, as agreed upon).

Depending upon your requirements, the moderator may be required to arrange for a suitable facility for the discussions. He may also need to arrange for related activities, such as providing the incentives to people, taping the discussions, overseeing the confirmation of the recruits, providing the food or snacks for the group participants and so forth. If the moderator is not expected to make these arrangements, you or another person or organization you designate must do so.

What makes a moderator effective? This is a key question. Even if the recruiting goes smoothly, everyone shows up, the room is comfortable, and the participants are talkative, a group can be negatively swayed by the direction (or lack of direction) provided by a moderator. You might examine potential moderators to see if they have the following qualities:

- nonjudgmental, able to be accepting of all honest responses;
- articulate, without being verbose, pedantic or overly intellectual;
- flexible enough to allow and follow up useful divergences in the discussion to a logical conclusion, before returning to the predetermined track;
- sensitive enough to distinguish between a useful divergence and a useless sidetrack—and capable of gently but firmly

guiding the discussion back to the main track without an excessive loss of time or focus;

• experienced enough with group dynamics to understand how to quiet a loudmouth without being insulting or scaring the others in the group from saying whatever comes to mind; and how to draw out the thoughts of those who are quiet, reluctant or otherwise uncommunicative;

• capable of following people's lines of thought over the course of the session and understanding their thought processes;

• knows when to probe answers for greater depth and when to leave superficial answers untouched because they will yield little of real value;

• able to translate the discussion into a series of insights that make your decision-making process better.

Where do you find such a person? You may hire them from market research companies; psychologists often have these skills; and many pastors and other people-oriented, marketing-savvy people may possess the requisite characteristics.

If the people participating in the group sessions are from your church, it is best *not* to have the pastor or staff members moderate the groups. People will be less likely to give honest feedback in front of the pastor, especially if the discussion turns to matters related to the pastor's performance or the aggregate effect of the church and its programs. Sometimes it is best to have a total stranger lead the groups; someone who is competent, sympathetic but not biased, and with whom the participants will feel comfortable to speak their mind.

If you or someone else you work with closely will be moderating the sessions, here are a few tips on how to more successfully guide the group discussions.

• *Managing loud people.* Invariably, every group has someone who wishes to emerge as the leader. They talk louder than others, they talk more frequently than the rest, they speak more extensively. The task you have is to quiet them without scaring everyone else into silence. Some ground rules should be shared at the outset: "We want to make sure that everyone has opportunity to participate.

There may be times when I will have to remind you of this. This will enable everyone to have opportunity to share."

A method that works is to avoid looking at people as you look around the room. Refuse to look at them as they give their answers. When asking for responses, if they begin to answer, politely cut them off and say "I've heard from you quite a bit, (name), let me hear from someone else on this one"; or prefacing a question with a statement like "I think I'm getting a sense of how (name) feels, let me hear from some of the rest of you on the matter of...."

• *Separating friends.* In most cases, it is advisable not to have people who know each other in the same group. If you are conducting a group of people from the church, though, this is virtually impossible. The best thing to do when the session begins is to arrange people's seating so that those who are most friendly with each other are not tempted to be nudging each other all session long, passing notes back and forth, or sharing whispered comments.

• *Simultaneous responses.* How frustrating it gets when everyone speaks at the same time. You miss most of what is going on, and if you are relying upon the tapes to capture all of the information, what you will wind up with is a garbled, unintelligible mess. At the very beginning of the session, take three minutes to lay down the ground rules: one person speaks at a time, feel free to disagree with others, do not engage in attempts to convert people to a particular perspective, no one monopolizes, etc. If the group breaks into a spontaneous outburst, quiet them and ask the people, individually, to share what they were saying.

• *Group involvement.* You have 8 to 10 people present because you want interaction, and because you want everyone involved. Actively encourage such engagement. Have people react to what other group members have said. When only one or two people are consistently answering, use silence as a means of drawing people out of their reticence. You can also call on people, but must do so cautiously: some people will be frightened into further silence by this approach.

• *Losing control.* Even the best moderator occasionally encounters a group that gets out of control. It is critical to quickly reestablish leadership of the situation. Some ways of doing so are to stand

and hold up your hands, indicating the need for silence, enabling you to remind them of the ground rules, and return the session to normalcy. Alternatively, you might simply ask outright for people to be more courteous and controlled in their participation.

• *Affirmation without confirmation.* To encourage people to continue to provide honest feedback, it is important to provide affirmation of what they have to say. At the same time, though, be careful not to come across as suggesting that you agree with or otherwise embrace their position. The moderator must remain neutral if a valid discussion is to take place.

• *Use humor.* Sometimes the tension in the room builds, due to the positions taken by people, the sensitive nature of the topic discussed, or people's fatigue with the topic. A good moderator is able to use humor to break the tension without undermining anybody's position. Be careful not to rely too much on humor, lest the group become an amateur comedian's night and people try to get a laugh with their responses.

• *Paper and pencil.* Sometimes you may fear that once someone provides a socially desirable answer to an inquiry, people who hold less fashionable or socially desirable opinions may be apt to clam up. By having everyone write their responses on paper before they verbalize any answers, then going around the room and asking everyone to share their responses, you get a more complete set of options. Further, it is more likely that people will not change the opinion they share with the group after they hear what other people say; they are more likely to feel obligated to read what they wrote.

• *Use visual aids.* People can respond to concepts, but they are much better equipped to react to tangible stimuli such as drawings, videos or products. If you want them to describe colors, give them samples of colors: red means different things to different people. If you want them to design a logo, provide them with a chalkboard or easel and allow them to sketch out what they have in mind. If you are delving into a corporate image, give them copies of the organization's print advertisements to respond to. The more tangible the stimulus, the more precise their response—and, often, the more you learn.

• *Play devil's advocate.* Sometimes people give answers you believe are simply the responses they think you want to hear. Confront this head-on, by playing the devil's advocate role and having them defend their stated position. If the discussion becomes too predictable, this type of soft confrontation can bring out nuances and insights that might have been missed otherwise.

• *Role-playing.* On occasion, it might be advantageous to ask people to play divergent roles. If conducted properly, everyone can get involved, not just the handful of role-players. Suggest points the characters overlooked or did not adequately develop. This approach enables you to understand perceived strategic weaknesses of positions, untapped image points and the like.

The Discussion Guide

The discussion guide is a critical piece to the entire puzzle. This outline takes your objectives (i.e. the reasons for conducting the research) and converts them into a nonthreatening, logical, flowing road map for the discussion.

Before asking a moderator to prepare the guide, it is the responsibility of the people sponsoring the research to provide the moderator with a detailed list of the types of information desired from the process, and how it will be used in the marketing process. Armed with that insight, a skilled moderator can then develop a guide that will contain the needed information.

Moderators each have their own style, and the guides may well reflect these different approaches. Some provide guides in which they write out the questions they intend to ask word for word. Others write down the order of the concepts they will pursue, but leave the exact language to be determined by the nature of the group discussion. Other moderators offer a combination of these two varied styles.

Regardless of the approach used by your moderator, be sure you see and approve the guide before the groups meet. You should receive the guide a week or so in advance of the sessions, and provide changes and eventual approval of the guide at least two days ahead of time. (A sample discussion guide also appears in appendix 3.)

Expect the discussion to require that the moderator jump around a bit from the plan outlined in the discussion guide. In a freewheeling discussion, this is unavoidable. A good moderator, however, will keep the discussion focused and will eventually hit all of the topics that were originally designed for examination.

Location of the Meeting

The most professional approach is to have the groups meet in a room designed specifically for focus groups. These facilities generally have two adjoining rooms, separated by a wall that has a one-way mirror. To preserve the discussion, microphones are built into the ceiling, the table, or other unobtrusive areas. Such focus group facilities are available in all metropolitan areas and in some smaller markets. Look in the Yellow Pages under "Marketing Research" and contact the companies listed to determine if they have such a facility. Such companies will also make moderators and recruiting services available to you, for a price.

While the participants conduct their discussion in the larger room, the people who are commissioning the research may sit in the adjoining room and watch the discussion from behind the special mirror. Ethically, the moderator has a responsibility to tell the group members before the discussion starts that they are being watched and, if appropriate, audiotaped. This circumstance may cause a bit of discomfort for people for a few minutes, but once they get into the discussion they tend to forget about the observers and concentrate on the ideas being shared.

If this arrangement is not feasible or desirable, you may hold the discussion meeting in a conference room at a nearby hotel or business center. Although the one-way mirror for unobtrusive observation is not available, a suitable setting with adequate parking and facilities is provided. Other viable options include using classrooms at local schools or a small auditorium or theater.

Alternatives that have been used, but not recommended, are holding the sessions at a restaurant—too many distractions during the discussion, may be hard to hear everyone's answers and very difficult to cleanly tape the discussion. A church setting brings too much emotional or perceptual baggage with the discussion, possibly influencing people's answers and giving misleading information.

How Many Groups Are Needed?

Ideally, you should schedule groups in pairs until you have conducted enough sessions so that you are no longer learning anything new related to your objectives. This strategy, of course, requires a considerable budget and an open-ended time frame.

In the real world, these two resources are rarely available in sufficient quantities to allow the ideal approach. The more practical approach, then, is to conduct a minimum of two sessions with people from the same group, but hopefully at least four.

Why at least two sessions? Because it is possible that one of the sessions was somehow biased, or that the group itself was not sufficiently representative of the area from which they were drawn to provide reliable insights. Four sessions are preferable because this allows for some repetition of information, giving the analyst a better sense of the dominant emotions, viewpoints and considerations for people.

If your research is designed to understand the thinking of more than one people group—say, for instance, baby busters, baby boomers, pre-boomers, and senior citizens—you need at least two groups for each separate segment. In the example listed here you need at least eight sessions, two for each of these group segments.

Strategically, you are frequently better off keeping the groups homogeneous. In other words, rather than spread people from each of the four people groups evenly across the eight sessions, you gain greater clarity of insight by separating them into the age groups suggested.

When to Hold the Discussions

Be sensitive to the life-styles of your audiences when you set the schedule. If you are speaking with young people (e.g. teenagers or elementary school kids), you have to meet the schedule needs of the kids (who attend school, have homework, should be at home for dinner) and the parents (who must drive them from school or home to the session).

For adults, the usual meeting times are weeknights at 6:00 or 8:00. The best nights tend to be Tuesday through Thursday. Monday is possible; Friday is least desirable. Saturdays can work okay, but Sundays generally are not advisable.

Remember that if you have the groups meet during a time when meals are usually served (e.g. 6:00 P.M., or around noon), you are responsible for providing some type of meal. (A sandwich or deli platter are popular options, served with chips, cookies, sodas and coffee.) At other times, you should provide light refreshments (cookies, cake, soda, coffee).

What to Expect from Focus Groups

You should emerge from this discussion process with two or three products.

First, if your recruiters keep good records of their interviews in the screening process, you should be able to tell *the proportion of the people contacted who met your criteria.* This is known as the "incidence level": the percentage of people from the target population who fit the profile you were seeking. This figure, in itself, can be very helpful information.

Recently we conducted research for a ministry that wanted to know how many people in a specified area were Christian; gave money to charities other than churches; and held specific opinions on a prescribed set of current issues. Finding these people for the qualitative research was more difficult than expected. After we had recruited all of the people we needed, we went back to all of the screening questionnaires we had used, tallied the answers, and found that only about 1 out of every 10 adults had been qualified, by our predetermined criteria, to participate.

Be forewarned that not everyone who is qualified for involvement in your research will agree to participate. There is no standard expectation for the proportion who will ultimately participate. In some people segments, we have had near-perfect acceptance; in other groups, the acceptance rate has been less than 25 percent. In the study I mentioned above, about half of the qualified people agreed to be involved in the research.

Think about these ratios for a moment, because they may greatly influence your willingness to do all the focus group recruiting in-house. In our study for the above ministry, for every adult we successfully recruited for our research, we actually contacted about 40 adults: 15 to 20 refused to be interviewed (i.e. screened); 18 were screened but did not qualify; 1 was screened and qualified, but declined the invitation to the session; and our 1 adult was screened, qualified and agreed to participate. To conduct 2 focus groups with adults meeting these criteria would require that more than 1,000 adults be contacted, drawn from a list of at least twice as many potentially qualified names and numbers!

In this case, it was an expensive and time-consuming process just to find and recruit qualified participants. Not all projects require locating such a small incidence population, though. That ministry was seeking a group with a 10 percent incidence. If you are after the unchurched, the incidence might be from 25 percent to 60 percent, depending on your definition of unchurched and the area of the country. If you are seeking people who attend your church, you ought to be able to provide a list that provides 90 percent to 100 percent qualified people.

The point, however, is that by keeping track of the outcome of each screening interview and tabulating the results, we then had a better idea of just how large (or, in this case, how tiny) the group of people was who shared the heartbeat of this particular ministry. Notice that the qualitative research process has provided us with a bit of quantitative insight.

Second, you might wish to have audiotapes (or, possibly, videotapes) of the session for future reference. Especially for key people who were not able to attend the sessions live, hearing the tapes can be instructive.

Third, have a written summary or analysis of what was learned. The written product might be a simple "top line analysis," which summarizes the key findings. It might be a comprehensive analysis, which includes verbatim quotes from participants as needed to shed light on a discussion point, along with recommendations for action as a result of the discussions. Another option is to have a typed transcript of the discussions, without any type of formal analysis. Our experience has been that the top line analysis, if properly developed, proves to be the most efficient use of everyone's resources. (An example of a top line analysis is included in appendix 3.)

If you have someone prepare an analysis, what should it include? The purpose of the research was to explore (1) how people think, (2) why they have drawn certain conclusions, (3) the breadth of the conclusions that have been drawn, (4) the intensity of people's feelings, (5) new ideas that people offered, or (6) the potential for motivating people to respond in desired ways. The analysis should keep these types of objectives in mind and tie all discussion references to such ends.

The analysis should also conclude with ideas related to the relationship between these insights and the marketing plans or opportunities of the church. Research conducted for its own sake is a waste of precious resources. Research tied to concrete conclusions regarding how to enhance the efforts of the ministry is good stewardship.

What should the analysis *not* include? *First,* be sure it does *not* contain percentages of people who gave specific responses: "30 percent of the participants said they had heard of Calvary Church." To convey the same idea, the report might indicate that "a minority of the participants" or perhaps "roughly one-third of these adults" had heard of the church. Because this is not quantitative information, it should not be treated as such.

Second, the conclusions drawn from the research should be neither dogmatic nor too broad-based. The value of qualitative information is its ability to open our eyes to new ways of understanding people's perceptions and reactions. However, because we do not have any idea how representative these new insights are, we cannot justify recommendations that are overly ambitious or that are stated with excessive confidence. Instead, this research should lead to suggestions for further study; to ideas that might be considered in marketing planning; and warnings about potential consequences of specific decisions or directions.

Determining the Budget

Primary research is rarely inexpensive, although given the amount of time and money that can be saved by having the right information and preventing serious mistakes as a result, such money is often well-spent.

If you undertake all aspects of the focus group process with in-house personnel for recruiting, conduct the groups in donated facilities. Possible facilities may be a nearby school that allows you to use their rooms and equipment, or a hotel managed by a member of the congregation who donates its conference room. Utilize a talented moderator who lives in the area and wants to offer his services for free. Your expenses would be minimal when you take advantage of these free services. Incentives, food, telephone line charges, confirmation postage, and audiotapes for a high-incidence pair of groups might run in the neighborhood of $800 for the two sessions. (The vast majority of that—about $600—is for incentives.)

If you subcontract the project to a marketing research organization, and have them do the entire process, from recruiting through analysis, the cost is likely to be in the area of $2,500 to $3,000 a session.

CHART 7
Which Approach to Choose:
Quantitative or Qualitative

Characteristic	Quantitative	Qualitative
Dominant question answered	How many	Why
Generally accepted minimum sample size	200 people	2 groups
Projectable data	Yes	No
Typical project duration*	4-6 weeks	3-4 weeks
Average project cost*	$6,000	$5,000

*For quantitative study assume 200, 10-minute telephone interviews with a 90 percent incidence population. For qualitative research, assume two, 10-person focus groups, lasting 90 minutes each, giving $30 incentives, at a focus group facility.

SIX

GETTING NUMBERS WITHOUT GETTING NAUSEATED

A FTER God's people, Israel, had served their time in captivity because of their unfaithfulness, the scribe and priest Ezra was charged with helping restore them to their homeland. Among other ways God's covenant had been ignored was the matter of marriage. Instead of preserving a pure lineage for the coming of the Messiah, the Jews had intermarried. But which ones? And who had they married? Thousands were involved. How could Ezra set things straight?

Why, by doing quantitative research, of course! Some 2,500 years ago Ezra used this "modern" marketing tool to determine the precise nature of the marital situation of those Jews who were returning to Jerusalem. His work yielded specific names, tribal heritage and numbers (see Ezra 10).

In chapter 5, we noted that quantitative research emphasizes *how many* people think or act in a prescribed manner. The focus is on determining numbers that can ultimately be used to make statements about the aggregate population. Quantitative research generally produces what is known as "hard data"—numbers that are reliable enough for marketers to use as a foundation for their thinking and planning.

Whether you find yourself in need of information from your

congregation or your community at large, the procedures involved in quantitative research are the same.

Sample or Census: Which Is Best?

Gleaning information from a population can be done in two ways. You can either conduct a census or a sample survey.

A census means that you will ask your questions of all the people in that group. When we use the term census, we naturally think of the decennial census conducted by the federal government. That census, the largest research study of its kind, involves responses from more than 240 million people, at a cost of tens of millions of dollars. The Department of Commerce also conducts a regular census of business firms, involving hundreds of thousands of businesses, again with a multimillion dollar price tag. Other, less ambitious census research exist, too.

Every year, the Southern Baptist Convention conducts a census of its churches to compile its annual statistics on the state of its denomination. This involves information from nearly 40,000 churches. Smaller groups of people—e.g. state legislators, pastors belonging to a particular synod or district, teachers employed at a given school, a board of directors of an organization—occasionally are asked to complete a survey form of some type. In complying with that request, they are participating in a census: The aggregate population is asked to take part in the information gathering process.

The benefit of a census, of course, is that it provides the most complete and reliable quantitative information possible. By asking everyone to participate, the chance of gaining a realistic picture of current circumstances is heightened. The downside of the census approach, though, is the resources the process consumes. Conducting a census may take a prolonged period of time, due to the necessity of following up on those who did not provide the requested input. The money spent collecting and tabulating the information is also significant.

The alternative to a census is to take a sample of the whole target population and gain information from them. If a probability sample is used, the results can then be projected to reflect the answers of the target group. If, however, a nonprobability sample is utilized, the answers not only cannot be projected to the population, but are of relatively little value for any purpose.

Understanding Probability Sampling

If you intend to use sample surveys, you ought to rely exclusively on probability samples. The notion behind a probability sample is related to two key concepts: probability theory and the law of large numbers. To draw a probability sample, three conditions must be satisfied.

1. All members of the target population must have a chance to be included in the sample. This means that the resulting sample has precluded bias based on nonrepresentative selection procedures. It is the bias from unequal selection procedures that would render the results of a survey misleading.

   Practically speaking, for all units in the target population to have a chance of being selected means that when you select names or telephone numbers from a list it must be up-to-date and complete. Otherwise, bias has been introduced since all of the qualified elements in the target population did not have a chance of selection.

   Using lists such as a telephone directory or a reverse directory are inadequate because not everyone in the community is listed in such directories, and those directories are woefully out of date by the time they are published. Sometimes, in an effort to locate a hard-to-find segment, such as evangelical Christians, a list is used that includes a high proportion of such people—such as the subscriber list to an evangelical magazine. Again, the problem is that not every Christian is on the list, so bias has been introduced into the sampling process, which makes the resulting research data unreliable.

2. The chance of inclusion must be known; in other words, we must be able to determine the probability of any one person

being selected from all the people on the list. Ideally, each member should have both an equal and known chance.

3. The selection of each person or entity to be part of the sample must be made independent of all prior selections within the sample. Choosing one element from the target group should neither guarantee the selection nor rejection of any other member of the group. For the sample to truly provide every unit with a chance of being included, each selection must occur as if it is the first pick in the process, untainted by any choices made previously.

The law of large numbers helps us to understand why a sample can be reliable. Assuming probability procedures have been used, we know from testing that the more cases chosen for a sample, the closer the results of the sample will be to the actual population proportion.

Say, for instance, we base a survey on a sample of 1,000 adults in your community. You know from the census data that 75 percent of the adults in your community are married. If we draw a sample of four people, two might be married and two might be single. This does not accurately reflect the true population proportion. But by using probability selection methods, the more people you select, the closer to the actual population proportion you will come. By the time you have selected the 1,000th individual, chances are good that you will have a sample within 2 or 3 percentage points of 75 percent married adults and 25 percent single adults.

In every sample there is likely to be some degree of *sampling error*. This is due to the reality that not everyone was included, but instead a relatively small proportion of people were chosen to represent the larger target population. The differences between what you find by taking a census and what you learn by a probability sample are attributable to chance, and called sampling error. The larger the sample, the lower the sampling error. The lower the sampling error, the higher the reliability of the resulting information.

Perhaps the hardest reality for people to grasp is that a sample of 1,000 can accurately reflect the behaviors and beliefs of a nation of 190 million adults. The key is being certain that the sample was chosen by probability selection methods, and that the group itself is relatively homogeneous. Statistical testing has continually shown that when the sample is properly drawn, the results are within a few percentage points (depending on the sample size) of the true population condition, regardless of the population size.

Theoretically, if everyone in the target group behaved and thought exactly alike, you would not need a sample, but could simply interview one person. Whichever person you selected would perfectly represent all of the others. If there were some variation among the people in the population—i.e. they are similar, but not exactly identical—you could draw a small sample of those people and know that the variation within the population group, overall, would cause a slight difference between the sample measures and the true population outcome. If you have a target population in which there is little in common from person to person, the sample drawn should be large in order to compensate for the distinctiveness of the population units.

Types of Probability Samples

Five types of probability samples are commonly used: simple random, systematic, stratified, cluster and quota. For the purposes of research conducted by churches, let's explore the three methods you are most likely to use.

1. Simple random samples are the most pure of the sampling procedures. In a simple random sample (SRS), every element on the list (known as the sample frame) has an equal and known chance of being selected. This might be done by assigning every person (known as the sample unit) a number and then randomly selecting numbers until the entire sample has been picked. The point is to be certain that the choices are totally unpredictable, and that everyone has the same likelihood of being chosen.

This process has many variations. For instance, you could write the name of each sample unit on a piece of paper, put all of those pieces of paper in a barrel, thoroughly mix the papers, then randomly pull as many sample units as needed from the barrel. Other variations on this approach are readily imaginable.

One variation that requires special mention is the *random-digit dial* sample (aka RDD samples). This has become the most widely used form of random sampling in telephone surveys. In this process, all existing area codes and prefixes are programmed into the computer, along with the working blocks (i.e. last four digits). The computer then randomly selects area codes, prefixes, and a working block in which two or more of the digits in that block have been randomly generated by the computer. In essence, it has created a totally random sample frame based upon telephone numbers.

This procedure gives all households with a working telephone (over 90 percent of America's homes) an equal chance of selection, even if the household has an unlisted or unpublished number or has just had the telephone installed that day. Several companies specialize in providing such samples for you if you wish to conduct a telephone survey using the RDD sample. (One of the most reliable suppliers is Survey Sampling, located in Fairfield, Connecticut.)

2. Systematic random samples require that all of the sample elements be listed in an orderly, but random fashion, and the names are then systematically chosen. This is sometimes referred to as an "n-th name sample" because sample units are drawn according to a predetermined interval. This process is deemed a random sample procedure because each name is listed in a nonbiased order, the initial selection is random, and the units drawn afterwards were chosen without any intentional bias.

For example, if you have a list of 20,000 names and wish to draw a sample of 1,000 names, you might take every 20th name. (That interval was chosen by dividing the number of names desired into the universe of sampling units: 20,000/1,000=20.) To make the sample truly random, though, start the process by randomly choosing the first name from the first 20, then applying the skip interval (i.e. every 20th name) after that.

Caution! One of the most popular approaches used by amateur researchers is to take a telephone book or other listing and start from the first page and select every n-th name to pull a community sample. It is cheap, easy, quick, accessible and may have the appearance of randomness. What is wrong with this approach?

For starters, by beginning with the first name listed, instead of a random initial selection, the randomness of the sample is removed.

Second, using a telephone book as the sample frame is a problem because it is outdated and incomplete. Growing numbers of households do not allow their numbers to be published, introducing bias by reliance upon those people who do have a published number. (In Los Angeles, as an example, about *half* of the households have unpublished or unlisted numbers!) Further, on the day the new telephone book first hits the street the numbers included in it are outdated. Months have passed from the time of collection, inputting and checking. Hundreds of new numbers are not in it; hundreds of disconnected numbers are included.

A similar difficulty is reliance upon comprehensive lists of community residents that have to be "number matched." This is a process in which a list of names and addresses is available for your use, but the telephone numbers of those households are missing. The solution is to provide the list on a computer-readable format (i.e. tape, disk, diskette) to a supplier who compares your list with their master data base of all names, addresses and telephone numbers for the community. Whenever one of the names and addresses on your list is also located on their list, the telephone number of the household is appended to your list.

Although this process is laudable, the difficulty is that the match rate is generally around 40 to 50 percent. In other words, the majority of people who ought to qualify for selection within the sample will be excluded because of an incomplete master data base. This process provides sufficient cause for concern that if you are able to procure a more complete sample from other methods, even if more expensive, it would likely be in your best interests to do so.

3. Stratified random samples call for a random selection—either using simple random or systematic random procedures—within identifiable, specified strata of the target population. Each stratum represents a particular segment within the aggregate sampling frame that can be separated from the rest of the list.

For instance, if you know that your community has 8,000 men and 12,000 women, you might pull two independent, random samples, one for each gender. The value of doing so is that you are ensured of pulling a sample that will have a fair representation of the population by gender, drawing 400 men and 600 women.

Avoid Garbage Samples

So far we have examined probability samples. Many surveys, though, are based on nonprobability samples. Such research is based on selection procedures that do not ensure the results can be deemed representative of the target population. Various kinds of nonprobability samples are used and they go by a variety of names: convenience, haphazard, accidental, nonrepresentative, snowball, quota. The data resulting from such sampling techniques is not projectable and the sampling error cannot be estimated. Avoid reliance on such sampling strategies.

Among the most common forms of nonprobability sampling are mall surveys; the man-on-the-street interviews that appear in newspapers or in television newscasts; and the questionnaires that appear in publications (e.g. magazines) or are sent with fund-raising appeals or "junk mail" to households. The results of these surveys should be recognized for what they are from a scientific point of view: garbage.

How Many People to Sample

The size of the sample you need depends upon two items: your budget and the level of confidence you want to have in your results. Realize, too, that there are statistical boundaries below which the data are useless, and above which an increase in the sample size is a waste of resources.

Confidence levels refer to the degree of confidence you can have in the results of your survey. The most common confidence level used in practice is the 95 percent level. This means that in 95 out of every 100 cases, we can be confident that our research will be reliable to within a prescribed degree. That degree is based upon two numbers: the sample size and the responses to a given question. Three rules of thumb are:

1. The larger the sample size, the smaller the sampling error, and the greater your confidence in the accuracy of the results.

2. The closer the response percentages are to 50 percent (e.g. 48 percent said yes, 52 percent said no), the greater the likelihood of distortion in the findings.

3. The size of the total population has no real bearing on the sample size, if the population is more than 10,000 units. Thus, if the sample is properly drawn, a sample of 200 people taken from a community of 20,000 people is just as accurate as a sample of 200 people from a population of 20,000,000.

Statisticians have worked out a series of figures that estimate the error amount that may be present to produce a reliable probability sample. (See chart 8.) These statistics give us the time-honored expression, popularized by the media, "these data are deemed accurate to within plus or minus (x) percentage points, at the 95 percent confidence level." In English, this means that because we used a probability sample, we can be 95 percent sure that the results for this survey are within (x) percentage points of what we would have found if we asked the same questions of the entire population (i.e., done a census).

Subgroups

This brings us to another key point: the importance of the subgroup sizes. Although a sample of 1,000 people may have a confidence interval of plus or minus 4 percentage points, the error range is larger for the subgroups we may examine, such as men, people 18 to 21 years old or blacks. In analyzing the tabulated data, the information from each of those subgroups must be treated as a separate sample, and the error figures appropriate to the number of people interviewed who fell within the subgroup.

This means that when you are designing your research project, if you decide to interview 400 people in your community, and if you can use census data or other information to estimate the proportion of people who fit key subgroup definitions, you can also estimate how many people, among your 400 interviews, will be from those segments. For example, if the census data indicate that

52 percent of community residents are women and 48 percent are men, your sample might be expected to produce about 208 women and 192 men. If the census figures suggest that among adults in your area 35 percent are ages 18 to 34, 58 percent are 35 to 64, and 7 percent are 65 or older, your sample might be expected to produce 140 of the youngest segment, 232 of the middle group, and 28 seniors. If whites comprise 95 percent of the adult population in your area, blacks are 3 percent and Hispanics are the remaining 2 percent, your sample might provide 12 blacks, 4 Hispanics and 384 whites.

Are these figures helpful? Yes, especially if you have a special

CHART 8
Estimated Maximum Sampling Error at Various Sample Sizes at the 95 Percent Confidence Level

Sample size	Maximum error
10,000	1 percentage point
2,500	2 percentage points
1,000	4 percentage points
600	5 percentage points
400	6 percentage points
250	7 percentage points
200	8 percentage points
100	14 percentage points
50	18 percentage points

*NOTE: These error figures relate only to inaccuracies caused by errors due to use of a random sample. They do not provide any allowance for nonsampling errors (such as improper measurement practices) and they do not address errors associated with nonprobability samples.

interest in subgroups that have a relatively low incidence. In the example cited above, you would not have enough blacks, Hispanics or seniors to analyze. Since you need a minimum of 40 people to analyze (and even with that many people the margin of error is large), you could not draw any conclusions about the people in those segments, even though you interviewed a small number of them.

Thus, as you examine your budget and think about the accuracy required for your information, keep in mind the confidence level for the total sample; the likely numbers of people that sample would provide within key subgroups, and whether the resulting error for data within those subgroups is acceptable; and the cost of conducting additional interviews to reduce the error figure.

Cost

Cost must be handled carefully. Realize, for example, that if your research costs are $30 an interview, a survey of 200 people would cost $6,000 and provide a total sample for which the sampling error would be ±8 points, at the 95 percent confidence level. If you double your sample size, to 400 interviews, your costs would roughly double (to $12,000), but your sampling error would decrease by only two points, to ±6 points. If you again increase your sample size, this time by two-and-one-half times (i.e. to 1,000 interviews), you decrease your sampling error to just ±4 points, at the expense of another $18,000. Thus, for 1,000 interviews, you drop the error to plus/minus 4 percentage points, but the research now costs $30,000. Although a case can be made for such an increase in sample, part of your responsibility is to be sure you have considered the value of the information at a given cost level.

In general, it is unwise to utilize samples of fewer than 200 people to represent the aggregate population you are researching. It is also unusual to need more than 1,000 interviews for any given research project. Sample sizes of 400 to 600 are generally the most cost efficient for churches, depending upon subgroups of importance and their incidence within the population. Also remember that you cannot analyze the answers of fewer than 40 people in any population subgroup and maintain any type of statistical confidence.

What About Your Community?

Suppose you want to examine the aggregate life-styles, beliefs and attitudes of adults in your community. How large a sample should you use?

If you can live with a rather basic, stripped-down look at the community, interview 200 people. You will have data accurate to within 8 percentage points at the 95 percent confidence interval. The disadvantage of this size is that you won't be able to do much analysis of subgroups: maybe men compared to women, or other two-category segments, but nothing beyond such dichotomous groupings.

If you are seeking a more sophisticated analysis, perhaps breaking the community into key demographic segments and seeing how they compare, you might have to interview 400, 500 or even 600 people. For the aggregate sample, you gain little accuracy by increasing the numbers, but by increasing the overall sample, you also increase the subgroup sizes of the key comparison groups. That, in turn, increases the confidence you can have in those statistics (by dropping their error levels). For example, if you interview 600 adults, your base sample will be accurate at the ± 5 percentage point mark. Key subgroups, such as men and women (checking in with about 300 respondents each) would be accurate to within ± 7 points. Ethnic groups would vary: whites (in a random, national sample about 450) would be ± 6 points; blacks (about 75) at ± 14 points; Hispanics (approximately 50) at ± 18 points; Asians, about 25 people, could not be analyzed separately.

Assuming that this kind of numbers game hasn't made you nauseated, let's look in the next chapter at the tricky business of asking the kind of questions in a survey instrument that will tell you what you want to know.

SEVEN
THE ART OF THE SURVEY

YOU have decided to search out your own information, perhaps using your own staff and/or members in a survey. Doing some careful planning at this stage can make the difference between obtaining information that is reliable and useful in your desire to serve Christ, and wasting the Master's time and money.

Preparing to Write Survey Questions

Questionnaire design is an art. Thousands of studies have been conducted on the impact of question wording, placement, context and the like. All of these studies concur: the way the questionnaire is designed will influence the resulting responses.

The best way to start developing a good questionnaire is to define your information objectives. Once you have articulated for yourself what you want to learn, the chances of designing a survey instrument that will facilitate that process are immensely improved. Remember that your resources are limited (time, money, people's patience, etc.), so attempt to specify your needs as tightly as possible, to minimize the resources expended in gathering information. No fishing expeditions!

Having identified the information you need, proceed to group those needs into categories. The advantage of putting questions in subject modules is that it helps respondents follow a train of thought, answer more insightfully and take less time to do so.

From a design point of view, it is also much easier to determine if you have covered all the necessary ground when the questions related to the same topic or pertaining to a common set of objectives are closer together.

If you will be comparing your results to the data derived in prior surveys, know that you can only compare data across surveys when the questions asked were worded identically. Even minor changes in wording can be responsible for shifts in the responses given. To compare across surveys, also make sure that the groups interviewed are similar, or at least acknowledge the differences in the samples as you evaluate the results of these research efforts.

Newcomers to the research process sometimes assume that you can only ask a handful of questions. One myth perpetuated by a well-used marketing textbook is that you can ask no more than seven questions in a survey (ah, the tragedy of scholars writing books about fields in which they have no practical experience!). The typical telephone survey these days runs in the 15 to 25 minute range, which enables you to include between 15 and 100 questions, depending on how the survey is designed.

By the same token, realize that respondent fatigue is a real concern. Studies have shown that after about 15 minutes respondents get tired of the process and the quality of their answers begins to deteriorate. If you can keep your surveys from 10 to 15 minutes, everyone comes out a winner.

Wording the Questions Just Right

The wording of the questionnaire is tremendously important. It will affect the validity of the information, the willingness of people to participate in the study, and even the ability to learn enough from the research to make the types of decisions you need to make.

Before we address the actual words and phrasing of questions, consider different ways of asking the same question. Suppose you are interested in knowing if a person is a church attender. Here are three approaches in getting that information.

1. Did you attend a worship service at a Christian church last weekend? (Response options: yes, no.)

2. On any given weekend, how likely is it that you will attend worship services at a Christian church? Is it very likely, somewhat likely, not too likely, or not at all likely?
3. In a typical month, about how often would you probably attend weekend worship services at a Christian church? Would you probably attend once, twice, three times, four or more times, or not at all?

All of these questions provide some useful information and could be used for your decision-making benefit. However, given the choices, the first question is the least helpful because it provides the most limited data. The question asks for a simple yes or no response, revealing only the presence or absence of a condition. You can do relatively little with that information. This information is known as *nominal level data:* It tells us that a condition either does or does not exist.

The second question is more helpful, because it provides more sophisticated information. Not only do we learn whether or not the person attends church, we can determine the relative commitment of the individual to such attendance. This type of data is called *ordinal level data,* because the response options have a discernible ordering to them, from high to low. We can use this information to greater advantage since we can then rank the answers, combine categories for different effect, and so forth.

The third question is the most helpful, though, because it gives the most detailed data, enabling you to do a more precise analysis of the person's church attendance tendencies. This form of information is called *ratio data,* because it not only can be ordered from high to low, but also has a true zero point and the responses refer to measurement gradations that are mathematically equidistant. That is, going to church two times is exactly twice as often as one time; going four times is exactly four times as often attending once, and so forth.

Notice that the second question employed a scale to gauge the nature of the respondent's behavior. Scales provide a good comparative mechanism for evaluating people's answers. Many types of scales are available for use in surveys. The most common are:

- *Likert scales:* these are questions that ask people to select a point on a scale where each point on that scale has an adjective associated with it. Example: agree strongly, agree somewhat, neither agree nor disagree, disagree somewhat, disagree strongly.
- *Verbal frequency scales:* when people are asked how often they engage in some activity, a scale that ranks their involvement might be used. Example: always, often, sometimes, seldom, never.
- *Forced ranking scales:* often you will want people to evaluate their choices and provide a ranking of the relative appeal of those options. In these questions, each of the options would be given to the respondents, who in turn would be asked to assign a ranking to each one.
- *Numerical scales:* when people are confronted with a listing of various options, they may then be asked to assess where, on a multipoint scale, they would place each option. The end points of this scale ought to be described for people. Example: a seven-point scale, where one means you are extremely satisfied, seven means you are extremely dissatisfied.
- *Adjective checklist:* you may read a list of words or phrases to interviewees and ask them to select all those they believe are an accurate description of the item in question. They may choose none of the adjectives, all of them, or any number of them.

Many other scales are used. Your duty is to select the scale most appropriate for your information needs. However, it is important to balance your information needs with the needs of the respondent. Specifically, remember that they are doing you a favor by answering your questions, and are not nearly as committed to the topics and process as you are. To maximize their involvement, (1) keep your scales simple and easy to understand, (2) include items that move quickly, (3) try to get the most precise data possible (you can always group it into broader categories later, but you cannot break data that were collected in categories into more precise data), (4) avoid making it too simple for respondents to choose a neutral point on a scale.

The questions themselves must be carefully worded. You may be surprised when you start formulating your questions just how difficult it is to craft questions that effectively communicate to a broad spectrum of people. Generally, designing a good questionnaire is not a one draft proposition; a 10-minute questionnaire could easily take a dozen hours to outline, draft and revise in preparation for pretesting.

Questionnaire design is one of those activities in which people tend to improve with experience. As you try your hand at designing a questionnaire, you might evaluate your effort in light of the following checkpoints.

Brevity. If you are long-winded, chances are you will struggle with questionnaire design. Get to the point when writing survey questions. The shorter the question, the less likely the chance of error by either the respondent or the interviewer. Write short, simple sentences; use two simple sentences in place of one long, convoluted sentence.

Poor—In attempting to locate a church that seems suited to your needs, but maintains a clear commitment to the preaching of the gospel, you may encounter a vast spectrum of church options. After having experienced a number of those alternatives, what are some of the most significant factors which you would search for if you were to seek a church home?

Better—If you wanted to find a church to attend on a regular basis, what would be the most important characteristics for that church to possess?

Clarity. You get what you ask for. If your question is hard to understand, people will either give a nonanswer ("I don't know"), or an inaccurate answer because they are not sure what is really being asked. Clarity is imperative so that when you are examining the results, everyone has responded to the same stimulus with the same thoughts in mind.

Poor—Given people's obsession with self and their reluctance to accept an absolute standard, is it your belief that there is a problem with sin in America today?

Better—Do you believe in the concept of sin?

Jargon. Most industries or endeavors have created their own vocabulary, a kind of insider-speak that is known to people intimately involved in such activities. In surveys, it is useful to avoid such jargon. Such unknown language might be misinterpreted or could lead a person to feel out of place or ignorant. Use common terminology.

Poor—Are you a fundamentalist?

Better—Do you believe in both the necessity of accepting Jesus Christ as your personal Savior as the only means of gaining eternal life, and in the literal interpretation of the Bible?

Simple Language. No awards are given for the most profound concepts, nor for the most intellectually-phrased queries. Ask your question in simple language. Remember that more than one-third of our adults cannot read or write at an eighth grade level. Write questions that junior high students could understand and answer without difficulty.

Poor—In considering your own eschatological views, would you categorize yourself as an advocate of the premillennial perspective?

Better—Do you believe that Jesus Christ will return to earth to establish rule over the earth for 1,000 years before bringing all the saints to heaven for eternity?

Examples. Do not use examples in your questions. People forget the question and respond to the examples.

Poor—Do you currently serve as a leader within your church, as an elder, a deacon, or Sunday School teacher?

Better—Do you volunteer your time to serve the church in any type of teaching or leadership role?

Reasonable Recall. People have short memories, especially for things they do not consider of major importance. Do not ask questions that expect people to have accurate recall of long-term activities, or the ability to determine the number of times they did a particular activity over an extended time frame.

Poor—During the past year, how many times did you attend the weekend worship services at your church?

Better—In a typical month, on how many weekends would you attend the worship services at your church?

Double-barreled. Some questions are actually two questions in one. When the person provides an answer, you are not really sure which part of the question they are answering. Use of such a question is acceptable if your purpose is to determine how many people meet both qualifications simultaneously, but otherwise, its wording creates a measurement problem for you.

Poor—Do you believe that Jesus Christ was the Son of God and was resurrected after His death on the Cross?

Better—Do you believe that Jesus Christ was the Son of God? Do you believe that Jesus Christ was resurrected after His death on the Cross? (They should be asked as separate questions.)

Leading the Respondent. The way the question is worded can skew the responses given, leading a respondent to answer in a particular way. This bias is often subtle, and may unwittingly cause a respondent without a real opinion on the issue to express an opinion.

Poor—Given the negative publicity surrounding Jimmy Swaggart's ministry, don't you feel that he should leave the full-time ministry?

Better—Do you feel that Jimmy Swaggart should leave full-time ministry or remain involved in ministry on a full-time basis?

Loaded Questions. These questions are worded to make it difficult to answer any way other than that which is supported by the question designer.

Poor—Do you support passage of a federal law which would protect human rights by placing a ban on the killing of unborn children?

Better—Would you favor or oppose a law that banned abortions?

Inappropriate. Not every question should be asked of each respondent. In cases where a respondent has already indicated lack of a particular qualification or experience, it is insulting to then continue with questions that ask for greater detail about that quality or experience. Use skip patterns to direct the interviewer to the next appropriate question to be asked of such respondents. A skip pattern is an instruction that leads to the next appropriate question to ask, depending upon a person's answers. A typical skip pattern might look like this:

Question 3: Did you attend a church worship service within the last seven days?

> 1. yes ....GO TO QUESTION 4
> 2. no........................GO TO QUESTION 6
> 3. don't know ....GO TO QUESTION 6

Because questions 4 and 5 ask about the person's experience at a church service, people who said they had not attended such a service, or whom we could not safely assume had done so (i.e. said they didn't know if they had attended such a service) would be skipped to the next section of questions, which begin with question 6.

A well-designed questionnaire also provides smooth flow from one question to the next. One way of ensuring such continuity is to include transitional sentences whenever a shift in topics occurs. Such phrases include, "Changing topics now"; "I'd like to switch our focus now and talk about..."; "Turning now to a different topic" and "Let's move to a new topic." These bridges both alert the respondent to a shift in gears and make it easier for them to remain confident in their ability to follow the thread of the conversation.

See appendix 4 for some samples of survey questionnaires.

Opening Lines

In a telephone or face-to-face interview, the opening moments of the conversation are critical. Research has demonstrated that if you can get a respondent to answer the first few questions of the survey, more than 9 out of 10 of those people will stick with the questionnaire (for up to 15 minutes). Your opening should be carefully constructed to get the person involved.

One helpful technique is to avoid providing the respondent a chance to drop out of the survey. As soon as the introduction has been read, the interviewer should immediately ask the first question, assuming the respondent will answer and move on to the subsequent questions. Do not pause to give the respondent a chance to beg off before the initial question is asked. By taking the polite route and asking the respondent if it would be okay to continue you will substantially increase the number of refusals received. This would therefore decrease the confidence you can have in the data. If people do not want to participate, they will let you know; you need not make that process easier for them.

The introduction does not need any magic words. Indeed, little time is available for eloquence or verbosity; the introduction should last just 10 to 15 seconds, then move the person right into the survey. However, some concepts you might wish to include in the opening typically enhance the prospects of people participating in the survey. These concepts include the following:

- *The name of the interviewer.* You are trying to make this a personal conversation. To elicit their candor, you must at least be willing to divulge your name to personalize the experience as a show of good faith.
- *The name of the organization you represent.* Be cautious about this. You do not want to identify your church as the sponsor organization if that knowledge will bias people's answers. However, do not lie to the respondent, either. If another organization would be willing to act as the sponsor of the study, you might be able to use their name at this point.
- *The topics that will be discussed in the interview.* This ought to be very general in nature. Telling them the details of the entire study would likely cause some people to drop out of the process, thus biasing the data you gather. Descriptions such as "current issues and matters of public interest" or "the media, life-styles and plans for the future" are sufficiently appealing that they may attract respondents, but vague enough to not turn off people.
- *There are no right or wrong answers.* One of the reasons

people refuse to participate in surveys is out of fear that they won't know the required information. Put them at ease right away by dispelling the notion that you are testing them to see if they are doing their homework.

- *Their answers will remain anonymous and confidential.* People are skeptical (for good reason) of people they don't know who call on the telephone and start asking personal questions. Do your best to ensure them that they can be at ease: you will neither ask for their name nor any other identifying characteristics, and their answers will be combined with those of a number of other respondents, protecting their identity and their reactions.

- *You are not selling anything.* Telemarketing has given survey research a bad name. Let the person know you are seeking information, not selling something, and you will not call them back or give information to others who will call them back to market products as a result of the person's answers to the survey.

- *The survey will be brief.* You can only use this statement, of course, if the survey will be just four or five minutes (or less). People's time is precious; if you can acknowledge that and use it wisely, they are usually generous.

Applying Final Touches

After you have completed the design of the entire questionnaire, go back through it one more time. This time, study it to see if it meets these criteria.

1. Does the survey answer all of your research objectives? Examine your original list of objectives and go through the survey, question by question, determining which objective a question addresses. If there are questions that do not relate to objectives, remove them. If there are objectives that are not adequately addressed, design the questions required to provide the insights needed for better decision-making and ministry perspective. As a general rule, it is important to design

the questionnaire with an eye to specific insights you must provide through the analysis of the data for the research to truly be a valuable and useful resource.

2. How will knowing the answer to a given question make a difference in how you market your ministry? Pretend you received a specific answer to a question and think through how that knowledge would influence your ministry. If the answer would have no effect, whether the hypothetical response percentage is assumed to be high, split or low, then the question serves little purpose. Strongly consider excising it from the questionnaire.

3. Is there a way to determine the accuracy or significance of the data by internal (i.e. use of multiple indicators within the questionnaire) or external (i.e. comparisons with similar surveys) means? Context is vitally important in questionnaire design and data analysis. When the answers come back on a question, will you know if the response levels are high or low? You need to have some type of context—a comparative benchmark—to know if the data are within the realm of reasonability, and to determine the relative meaning of the finding. All information must be placed in context, because life is a series of related events and activities.

Pretesting the Instrument

After you have designed a questionnaire, it is wise to test it (known as a pretest). To conduct a pretest, interview a random sample of 10 to 20 qualified respondents. Mark their answers on questionnaires as if this were the real thing. Here is what to listen for in this process.

- Respondents hesitating before answering a question; this may be a tip-off that they aren't sure what the question is really asking.
- Inquiries from the respondents as to what the question means.
- Almost everyone giving the same answer to a question. This

may suggest that the question is not measuring anything of significance.
- People selecting one of the response options provided to them, but parenthetically making remarks that conflict with the answer they chose.
- Requests for the question to be repeated. If this happens on several occasions for the same question, the wording may be fuzzy or the combination of words may make comprehension difficult.
- The length of the questionnaire may be excessive.
- Skip patterns may be missing or erroneous, causing people to answer questions they should not be asked, or not posed with questions they should be asked.

After the pretest has been completed, make the necessary corrections to the survey and pretest it again. The pretest process is a great learning device because it allows you to identify problems before the rollout among the aggregate sample. Once you start the actual interviewing, you cannot change the wording of the questions. Thus, capturing and correcting as many flaws as possible during the test phase is critical.

Choosing the Right Data Collection Method

When it comes to deciding what information gathering methods to use, you have several choices. Some means of collecting the data are not likely to be used by churches: voice pitch analysis, eye movement tracking, electronic media measurements, on-site conjoint analysis. The methods you will probably choose from are telephone surveys, self-administered surveys and mail surveys. In-home personal interviews are a viable option, but they tend to be too expensive and too difficult to administer to justify examination here.

The advantages and disadvantages of each of these feasible data collection methods are described in chart 9.

Generally speaking, the method most difficult to use successful-

CHART 9

A Comparison of the Advantages and Disadvantages Of Three Data Collection Strategies

Advantages

Telephone surveys

- high quality control
- fast turnaround
- easy to pretest
- moderate cost
- high response rate
- respondent anonymity
- can design a more complex survey
- gives more data
- superior sampling
- can prove open-ended responses for clarity

Mail surveys

- low cost
- completed at respondent's convenience

Self-administered, in-group surveys

- low cost
- high response rate
- immediate turnaround
- easy to administer

Disadvantages

Telephone surveys

- need skilled interviewers
- need phone bank
- respondent inconvenience
- technical failures

Mail surveys

- limited quantity of data
- limited quality of data
- low response rate
- mail not delivered
- cannot probe on open-ended questions
- incomplete data
- hard to pretest
- assumes literacy
- no complex design
- slow turnaround

Self-administered, in-group surveys

- limited quantity of data
- limited quality of data
- sample may not be representative
- cannot probe on open-ended question
- incomplete data
- hard to pretest
- assumes literacy
- no complex design

ly is the mail survey, largely because of the low response rate. Remember, a low response rate means that the information collected is not representative of the target population, and thus negates much of the reason for conducting the study in the first place.

Door-to-door surveys, where interviewers approach a person's front door and conduct the interview while standing on the front doorstep or upon being invited into the respondent's home, were the initial means by which surveys were conducted. These days, though, this method is rarely used, for several reasons.

1. The difficulty of finding a representative group of people at home, due to fragmented schedules.
2. The high proportion of people who live in security buildings and are therefore inaccessible.
3. The challenge of generating a truly random sample of adults based on geographic locations.
4. The threat to the personal safety of the interviewers posed by such interviewing.
5. The cost of having face-to-face interviews conducted.
6. The loss of quality control (i.e. there can be only minimal supervision of the process).
7. The protracted time it often takes to complete such a research project.

Further, if the survey requires frank answers to sensitive topics—which might include what electronic equipment people own (VCRs, personal computers), the nature of their personal relationships, or even their views about God—the sense of anonymity and confidentiality that is important to honest answers may be lost.

Self-administered surveys may be appropriate when a large gathering of people can be induced to simultaneously complete the questionnaire, thus achieving a high response rate. A great example is having the entire congregation complete a questionnaire at a congregational meeting or during the weekend worship services.

Should your church conduct the research process from start to finish? That depends on the level of skill and expertise resident within your congregation and staff. You may wish to handle all aspects of mail or self-administered surveys in-house, perhaps paying a small fee to a qualified consultant to provide feedback on your questionnaire and your data analysis.

Think carefully about conducting a telephone survey. The process is very labor intensive and difficult to manage properly. For several years my company offered churches the option of hiring us to do their telephone interviewing and tabulation, or to do those tasks in-house. We have since ceased to offer the option of having churches do their own field work (i.e. interviewing) because the results were invariably disastrous. Even when the expected number of interviews was completed, it was with a higher-than-expected cost: volunteer burnout, incomplete data, unreliable data, extended time lines and the like.

If you choose to do the fieldwork through the efforts of church members, have an experienced person manage the process for you. This might be a member who works in marketing research for a living, a professor at a nearby college who has experience in survey research, or a denominational resource person who can lend the necessary expertise.

Regardless of the method you select, if the process seems overwhelming, marketing research firms can always be hired to assist with the project. This help comes at a cost but their expertise and facilities may make the task significantly more palatable for the church. Matters such as recruiting and training telephone interviewers, monitoring their on-line performance, and editing their interviews can be a stressful task for a church.

One final caution regarding the use of surveys. Please realize that a survey is not a means of leading into an evangelistic pitch. Many ministries have utilized this approach, starting out with a series of questions that lead up to a presentation of the gospel or an invitation to a church or some related event, but this is an unethical method. People who agree to answer questions for survey purposes should not be "sold" a religious belief system after they have agreed to give information to an interviewer. This is a bait-and-switch tactic that leaves a negative residue behind for both the church and the research industry. Such tactics not only leave a black mark on the reputation of the church, but also contribute to the increasing skepticism of our population.

If you want to go from door to door and tell people about Jesus, do so. But do not mislead people by coyly gaining their confidence by doing a survey, then transitioning into a gospel pitch. The ends do not justify the means if it requires compromising basic biblical principles.

EIGHT
MAKING SURVEY RESULTS WORK FOR YOU

RETURNING to the dramatic scene of Israel's return to Jerusalem, the priestly scribe Ezra was faced with another task. After neglecting God for so long, the people needed to relearn His law. But it was not enough just to tell them the facts of the law—they needed to get *inside* the law, in order to get God's will inside them. So Ezra and other leaders gathered the people together, and "read from the book, from the law of God, translating to give the sense so that they understood the reading" (Neh. 8:8, *NASB*).

A similar situation exists with the data from modern surveys. Once the information has been collected, you need to make sense of it. Collecting data without adequately interpreting it is as mistaken as reciting laws while having no idea about their "sense" and meaning. Once the data have been collected, you need to make sense of that information.

The most efficient means of doing this is to have all of the data coded and entered into a computer for tabulation. This process can be expedited by precoding the response options on the questionnaire. For example, when interviewers read questions to respondents, they read the possible answers for the person to decide between, and upon receiving an answer, they circle the number of that answer. In this way, when all of the surveys have been completed the data can be quickly and efficiently entered into a computer data file so that the arduous task of tabulating the data is done by the computer.

Example of a precoded survey question.

> *Question 8*: How likely is it that you will attend a church worship service during the next six months, other than for a special occasion such as a wedding, a funeral or a special holiday service? Will you definitely attend, probably attend, possibly attend under the right circumstances, probably not attend, or definitely not attend a worship service in the next six months?
>
> 1. definitely attend
>
> 2. probably attend
>
> 3. possibly attend
>
> 4. probably not attend
>
> 5. definitely not attend
>
> 6. don't know

Your survey might include open-ended questions. These are queries in which people are asked to describe their reactions to a specific question without being given any response options to choose from. The task of the interviewer (or questionnaire, if it is a mail or self-administered study) is to capture the verbatim response of the respondent. (Note that your survey should include as few open-ended questions as possible since they take longer for people to answer, are more psychologically taxing, and more difficult to analyze quantitatively.)

The answers to open-ended questions cannot be precoded (in most cases), but for tabulation purposes, they must be coded after the research has been completed. The best approach is to follow these simple steps:

1. Go through all the questionnaires and list all of the answers provided to the open-ended question.

2. Examine the list of answers and determine how you might order them so that like answers are close to like answers.
3. Create a comprehensive listing of the responses given, assigning a response code number to each answer, listing them on your sheet in ascending order.
4. Go back through each questionnaire and write the appropriate code number next to the person's answer.

When the survey data are entered into the computer, these codes will be entered in the same way as the precoded data, and can then be tabulated for ease of analysis.

The actual data entry and tabulation of the data can be done with the use of a simple spreadsheet program, or by a more sophisticated data tabulation software program specially developed for marketing research studies. (You can identify the names of such programs either by examining the product advertising in industry journals such as *Marketing News, Quirk's Marketing Research Review, American Demographics,* or by consulting knowledgeable sources such as market researchers or marketing professors.)

Tabulation software packages, such as SPSS and SAS, are available and are used on college campuses but are neither user friendly (i.e. easy to understand and use) nor produce data in an easy-to-use format. If those appear to be your only options, you have not looked deeply enough into the marketplace to discern what is available.

Alternatively, you can avoid the entire process of data entry, computer programming, software acquisition and producing the desired data output by hiring a company that specializes in research or data tabulation. In many cases, especially if your primary research endeavors are few and far between, or if the interest and expertise levels of the people working with you is minimal, using a supplier to provide this service is the easiest, quickest, most accurate way of getting the job done.

One of the major reasons you use a computer for tabulating the results is so that you can access more than simple head counts in response to each question. Using a personal computer and a good data tabulation software package will enable you to get printouts with cross-tabulations of the data.

Chart 10 is a sample page of a research printout in a format considered standard in the research industry. Across the top of the page is the survey question asked and the answers are provided on the rest of the page. Along the left-hand column are the response options that respondents had to choose from ("agree," "disagree," "don't know"). Stretching across the top few rows of the page, beneath the question, are 21 separate columns, each 4 spaces wide, known as "banner points."

The first of these columns, headed "total," tells how many survey respondents who answered the question gave which of the possible response options (i.e. the answers from the total sample of respondents posed with that question). The other 20 columns, each headed with an abbreviated description telling who is contained in that banner point, represent different variables or combinations of variables, drawn from this or other questions asked in this survey. Each banner point is based on the answers people gave to one or more survey questions, providing a cross-tabulation of people's answers to the question shown on this page and to the questions in the survey on which the banner point is based.

If you go to the area underneath a banner point and across from a row representing a response option for the question, at that point of intersection you will encounter two numbers. This intersection area is called a data cell. Within the data cell, the first figure, which has no decimal point in it, tells the total number of people who met both the condition described by the banner point and gave the response noted for that question.

On the sample page, under the column headed "total," the statistics tell us that 159 people of the 212 total respondents said they agree with the statement, "there are no specific actions you, personally, can take to help reduce hunger in other parts of the world." Forty-two respondents said they disagree with that statement; 11 people stated that they did not know.

Move to the right two columns, under the banner point "Boomer," which is one of the age-related banner points. You can see that among the respondents who were baby boomers (i.e. ages 27 to 45) 75 of the 87 boomers interviewed agreed with the statement, 11

CHART 10

SOCIAL CONCERN IN AMERICA

DO YOU AGREE OR DISAGREE WITH THE FOLLOWING STATEMENT? "THERE ARE NO SPECIFIC ACTIONS YOU, PERSONALLY, CAN TAKE TO HELP REDUCE HUNGER IN OTHER PARTS OF THE WORLD."

	TOTAL	AGE			BORN AGAIN		EDUCATION			HOUSEHOLD INCOME			CHRISTIAN VIEW ON						SOCIALLY ACTIVE	
		BUS-TER	BOOM-ER	OLD-ER	YES	NO	H.S. OR LESS	SOME COL-LEGE	COL-LEGE GRAD	UNDR $20K	$20K TO $60K	$60K PLUS	ENV-IRON-MENT	PE-ACE	HUN-GER	PRE-JUD-ICE	POV-ERTY	ABOR-TION	YES	NO
WEIGHTED BASE	212	29	87	96	79	134	102	63	43	45	101	27	160	181	159	116	161	134	93	120
AGREE	159 75.0	15 51.3	75 85.6	70 72.6	63 80.1	96 72.0	73 71.3	48 76.2	36 83.9	31 69.7	87 79.5	22 81.6	129 84.0	136 75.2	159 100	91 77.8	131 81.5	99 73.6	88 94.8	71 59.7
DISAGREE	42 19.9	13 45.1	11 12.4	18 19.1	13 16.8	29 21.7	26 25.8	10 16.4	4 8.5	13 30.3	17 15.1	5 16.7	26 16.0	37 20.7	0 0.0	18 15.4	21 13.2	30 22.0	3 3.6	39 32.5
	11 5.1	1 3.6	2 2.1	8 8.3	2 3.1	8 6.3	3 2.9	5 7.4	3 7.6	0 0.0	6 5.5	0 1.6	5 3.0	7 4.0	0 0.0	8 6.8	9 5.3	6 4.4	1 1.5	9 7.9

CONDUCTED BY THE BARNA RESEARCH GROUP, GLENDALE, CA   JULY 1991 of the 87 disagreed, and 2 did not know. These numbers are called the cell counts or frequencies or marginals.

The other number in the data cell, located beneath the frequency, is a percentage. This is called the column percentage because it is based upon the number of people included in the column. The data in the "total" column tell us that 75.0 percent of the 212 respondents said they agreed with the statement, 19.9 percent disagreed, and the remaining 5.1 percent said they did not know.

> **"Most people use research like a drunk uses a lamp post: more for support than illumination."**
>
> David Ogilvy, founder of advertising agency Ogilvy & Mather. From a speech by David Ogilvy

It is also possible to have the computer provide you with a row percentage, in which each data cell contains a percentage of respondents in each cell base on the respondents who gave the response option shown in that row. However, because the banner points are usually comprised of independent variables (that is, respondent answers to that question are independent of the influence of other variables—i.e. your gender is independent of your answers to questions about age or attitudes toward churches), the column percentages are the appropriate percentages to analyze.

The beauty of using cross-tabulations is that they allow you to explore relationships between the pieces of information you have collected. This process permits a more insightful analysis of the data. For instance, it is more useful to know that 95 percent of those who are social activists agreed with the statement shown in the data table and only 60 percent of the nonactivists agreed, than to simply know that 75 percent of the survey respondents agreed with the statement. Strategically, you are now better positioned to create an effective response reflecting the knowledge that social activists are nearly unified in this belief, whereas there was a much greater division among the nonactivists on the matter of hunger resolution.

Perhaps you noticed that in the description above, the explanation stated that 95 percent and 60 percent of the subgroups discussed agreed. The data in the appropriate data cells, though, showed 94.8 percent and 59.7 percent. It is quite common to round off your percentages to the nearest whole number when composing your analysis. The rounding of the percentages makes for easier reading and better recall of the findings, without undermining the accuracy of the information.

Remember the importance of having enough people answering a question, or qualifying for a banner point, to justify statistical analysis. The smaller the subgroup size, the less confidence you can have in the accuracy of the information. The minimum subgroup size for analysis is 40 people. If you have a banner point with fewer people than that, you cannot trust the information. As the numbers of people in a subgroup increase, so does your confidence in the data. As a rule of thumb, you might expect subgroups of 100 people to be accurate to within ±14 percentage points at the 95 percent confidence interval; subgroups of 200 people to be at ±8 points; 300 people, ±7 points; 400 people, ±6 points; 600 people, ±5 points.

Example. The banner point on the sample data table labeled "Buster" has 29 people. Because this subgroup size is less than 40, we have no statistical justification for reporting the findings. If you made claims about the 51 percent of the busters who agreed, you would be misrepresenting the data, since you do not have a large enough base to warrant such conclusions.

On the other hand, notice the figures under the banner point labeled "Boomer." The data in that column suggest that 86 percent agreed, 12 percent disagreed, 2 percent did not know. At the 95 percent confidence level, a subgroup of 87 boomers might be deemed accurate to within plus or minus 14 percentage points, due to sampling error. In other words, if we had taken a census instead of a survey among just 87 boomers, we would have found that among the entire boomer group, somewhere between 72 percent and 100 percent would have said "agree," 87 percent being the most likely response. The 72 percent figure represents 14 points less than the survey response, and the 100 percent figure is 14 points higher than the given response.

Making Sense of the Numbers

In a typical survey we conduct, the data tables produced from a church study contain close to 1 million numbers! Part of the trick of making the information useful is to know what results are really significant strategically; where to look for insightful statistics without spending hundreds of hours in the process; and how to interpret the figures objectively.

One exercise that has helped many of our clients who are new to the research process is to have them take a copy of the questionnaire and for each question fill in the percentages of respondents they believe will choose each possible response option. They are also asked to make notes in the margins of subgroups they expect to have radically disparate responses for the question. This document can then be compared to the actual responses after the data have been tabulated to determine how accurate they were in their expectations. This is one of the keys in research: *comparing reality to expectations, and responding intelligently to factual input, rather than relying upon instinct and assumptions.*

In general, you are looking for the following types of insights from your research, which should ultimately wind up in written form for distribution and for a permanent record of the research outcome:

1. Develop a reality portrait by studying and understanding the frequencies. The goal is to grasp the big picture. Before you dig beneath the surface, be sure you understand the broader landscape.
2. Confirm what you expected would be the case. Research is useful even when it gives you an empirical base upon which to make solid judgments and decisions. Rather than exclaim in frustration, "I already knew that," realize that you did not *know* this to be fact, but *felt* it was reality. Armed with the data, you can now proceed confidently.
3. Uncover some surprises. Rare is the survey that does not reveal unexpected conditions. Do not gloss over these perceptual conflicts; they represent some of the most powerful insights to be gained through research, acting as a correction factor on how you understand your ministry context, experiences and opportunities.
4. Carefully examine the cross-tabulations to arrive at a more

detailed picture of the different people segments you serve or wish to serve. This enhanced detail should be used to foster creative ideas and to develop a more personalized and strategic ministry.

5. Identify changes in attitude and behavior over the course of time. Some of these changes might be identifiable as trends, others as temporary or unexplainable departures from the normal. If comparable historical data are available, a comparison of past and present data can be extremely useful. This could be helpful in generating a bold strategic response to circumstances. It could possibly predict what the future is likely to bring and how you can prepare now to respond more effectively as that expected reality unfolds.

Ultimately, as you analyze the data you are searching for relationships between the numbers. Your task is not unlike that of a good detective: (1) search for clues among the data, (2) try to piece together a logical story based on the available facts, (3) respond to the story with strategic wisdom.

As the data is analyzed, be sure the descriptive understanding and the marketing suggestions emerging from the research are recorded on paper. You may wish to develop a summary of the findings, a comprehensive analysis, possibly a separate paper that outlines the recommendations for future ministry and marketing by the church resulting from the data. Recording these insights is necessary to efficiently communicate the research results. It also preserves for future reconsideration what was learned through the research.

Analysis and Interpretation

In the research field, many experts make a clear distinction between analysis and interpretation. When you *analyze* the numbers, you are telling what the study found: 52 percent agreed with the statement, 16 percent believe a specified perspective, 83 percent fit a given demographic category and so forth. *Interpretation*, though, goes beyond the statement of the figures to tell why those figures are meaningful, or how they might be tied together to create a new vision of what you are studying.

For example, your research *analysis* might cause you to write that 59 percent of the adults in your community are unchurched, and that 20 percent of these people are born-again Christians. Among the 59 percent, the demographic profile is a group dominated by men (67 percent); adults under the age of 40 (58 percent); well-educated people (43 percent have a college degree); upper-income households (median household income of $36,400); and white (87 percent). Marital status and home ownership had no connection to the likelihood of being unchurched.

The *interpretation* of these figures might be that the 59 percent mark is extremely significant because the local incidence of unchurched adults is double the national proportion. The community is clearly a haven for unchurched people, and requires ministries dedicated to identifying, understanding and influencing these people for the cause of Christ. One-fifth of these people ought to be relatively easy to interest in an effective, meaningful church ministry since they already believe in Christ as their Savior. The issue with these people may have to do with negative past experiences with churches. As church marketers, then, you must identify the negative historical baggage and propose a fulfilling church experience that will avoid the pitfalls these people previously had.

As you write out your report on the research, do your best to separate the analysis and the interpretation. Analysis is objective: you are simply telling what the numbers say. The interpretation is subjective: it represents your integration of the information with a real-world, nuts-and-bolts, let's-use-the-data-for-impact perspective. Those who read your report should be able to disentangle, without any difficulty, the objective and subjective statements.

What *Is* a Community Survey?

Community surveys are research studies that provide a perspective on the community you wish to serve. You may focus on specific segments (e.g. the unchurched, baby boomers, people living within three miles of your church campus) or on the aggregate adult population.

As a data collection strategy, your best bet is telephone surveys. A mail survey will probably garner a very low response rate, unless it is very short and relatively unfocused. In-home, face-to-face interviews are time consuming, put your people at physical risk, minimize quality control and may lose the benefit of anonymity. Telephone surveys are the most efficient approach for this purpose.

The types of information you might profitably derive from community surveys include the following:

- Awareness of your church and others in the area;
- The image people have of your church;
- Church attendance patterns, proportion of unchurched;
- What people look for in a church;
- Personal, felt needs a church could address;
- Reactions to potential community events;
- Religious beliefs;
- Key life-style traits and underlying values;
- Worries and anxieties about the future;
- Past experiences with churches;
- Types of church programs that are most appealing;
- Perceptions of the meaning and purpose of life;
- Sources of fulfillment and frustration in life;
- Likely response to various marketing approaches;
- Feelings about potential names for the church;
- Demographic characteristics of the population.

What *Is* a Congregational Survey?

Sometimes you will need to conduct a reality check with your congregation. Often, church leaders become so immersed in the day-to-day reality of making the ministry happen that they actually lose touch with the congregation. A survey can help bring things back into focus, or to confirm that things are already in focus.

Methodologically, you could use mail, telephone and self-administered surveys to glean information from your congregation. Our experience has shown that the most effective and efficient approach is to utilize in-service, self-administered surveys. You can carve 10 minutes out of your worship service on a weekend. (I know, maybe you think you can't carve out so much time, but believe me, if the information is valued enough, you can.) People can complete a survey that is handed out at that time (or, possibly, as they enter the auditorium). It should be no more than 4 pages in length; you should provide writing utensils; do not have people mark their names anywhere on the survey, and collect it at the end of the 10-minute period.

What about the people who just happen to be missing that day? Generally, such a census provides an accurate evaluation of the congregation. The absence of a few regulars and the presence of a few irregulars will not seriously influence the findings (especially if people's attendance record is measured in the survey and then used as a banner point to provide a reference point).

You can, however, upgrade the quality of the census information by following a couple of simple steps. If possible, you may wish to invite people who attend Christian education classes at the church that weekend to fill out the survey there if they will not be attending the service. Also, encourage people at the worship services the following weekend to ask an usher for a copy of the survey if they were absent the previous week, to complete the survey, and to give it back to an usher after the service is completed.

By the way, avoid conducting your study on weekends when a known, unusual event may affect attendance (e.g. Super Bowl Sunday, Easter, Christmas, Friends' Day) or during times of the year when attendance is not truly representative (e.g. prime vacation weeks during the summer or winter). These steps will help increase the completeness of the data base.

Why interrupt the worship service for this task? Because the people attending the service represent the core of the Body. Worship services are generally the most attended event held by a church. Having conducted such studies with a large number of churches, we have discovered that few people are offended by the process; many appreciate being asked for their input, and for elevating the collection of their thoughts to such an esteemed undertaking.

Note that collecting your data through a self-administered survey during the service is more like a census than a sample. As such, you can have greater confidence in the data, and the larger number of completed surveys may enable you to do a more in-depth analysis of subgroups.

What can you discover from a congregational survey?

- Feelings about the ministry of your church;
- The image your own people have of your church;
- Levels of involvement in the church's ministry;
- Why people are not more involved in the church;
- Desires for the future of the church;
- Personal, felt needs your church could address;
- Reactions to potential community events;
- Reactions to potential congregational events;
- Religious beliefs;
- Evaluation of the various elements of the ministry: the preaching, music, worship, teaching, children's programs, stewardship, facilities, adult ministries, community outreach, evangelism and so on;
- Key life-style traits and underlying values;
- Worries and anxieties about the future;
- Means by which the church could better support people in their personal ministries;
- Comprehension of the church's vision for ministry;
- Types of church programs that are most appealing;
- Perceptions of the meaning and purpose of life;
- Sources of fulfillment and frustration in life;
- Likely involvement in new ministry opportunities;
- Feelings about a capital campaign;
- Demographic attributes of the congregation.

NINE

THE POWER OF VISION

THE preceding chapters talked about the value of information as you develop your ministry. Information is imperative in ministry marketing because it provides the necessary context for understanding what God is calling you to do. Granted, it is possible to forge ahead with ministry in the absence of a well-conceived understanding of your ministry environment (i.e. people's background, needs, perceptions, beliefs and openness to ministry). However, lurching forward without such insight and foresight places you at a distinct disadvantage. Without such awareness, you will engage in seat-of-the-pants ministry. You will always be guessing and hoping that God will bail you out if you do something unwise. You will assume that trial and error will enable you to eventually discover the best means to impact people's lives for Christ.

The value of an accurate information base is that you can do ministry more efficiently: you don't waste time, money or people's efforts. And most importantly, you minimize the chances that you will blow the opportunities to minister meaningfully to those who otherwise might not be open to such ministry.

Information is also critical in the process of grasping God's vision for your ministry. In fact, my work with churches has led me to the conclusion that the single most important element in having an effective and life-changing ministry is to capture God's vision for your ministry. Until you have taken this crucial step, you are simply making a half-baked effort at being a true steward of all that God has entrusted to you and all that He desires to do through you.

Vision is the *starting point* for true ministry. For a Christian leader vision is *not* to be regarded as an option. A person is chosen by God to move His people forward by (1) sharing God's will for that people, (2) shaping them into a true community and (3) participating in the work of the gospel. Vision is part of the heartbeat of a leader; it is the insight that motivates his actions, shapes his thinking, defines his leadership and dictates his view of successful ministry.

If, for whatever reason, you are attempting to lead God's people without His vision for your ministry, you are playing a dangerous game. It is a game that is neither glorifying to God nor satisfying to man.

In every case of visionary leadership I have studied, the vision for ministry entrusted to the leader was not simply a situation in which God required the leader to employ his innate abilities to do what came naturally or easily to him. Vision frequently stretches a person well beyond his existing limits. *Grasping God's vision for your ministry will require you to invest in the vision*—both in attaining the vision itself as well as in implementing the vision.

Do not be put off by the mystical sound of "having God's vision." Neither should you be misled to think that because it is *God's* vision for ministry that He will do all the work, while you stand around and take credit because you have served as His willing conduit. Vision is a proactive process in which you team with God—relying upon your willingness to serve and His wisdom and power—to accomplish a wonderful outcome that represents the fulfillment of His purposes.[1]

What *Is* Vision for Ministry?

When all is said and done, *vision is ultimately a matter of humility and obedience to God.* Visionary ministers are those who have surrendered so completely to Christ that they have committed their day-to-day activities to His plan. Rather than pursuing personal greatness or even greatness for their church, they instead allow God to dictate what they will do, as a matter of personal service and love for Him.

Vision is responding to an encounter with God by saying, "Here am I. Send me!" (see Isa. 6:1-8).

In pragmatic terms, vision might be thought of in these ways:

- Foresight with insight based on hindsight;
- Seeing the invisible and making it visible;
- An informed bridge from the present to the future;
- Sanctified dreams;
- Applied, pragmatic imagination.

To get a better grip on the concept, though, perhaps this more formal definition will help:

Vision for ministry is a clear mental image of a preferable future, imparted by God to His chosen servants, based upon an accurate understanding of God, self and circumstances.

Vision for ministry is personal, future-oriented, God-given, a clarification of a better reality, and stems from a valid perspective of the world and its Creator. It is the tangible plan and intention of God's servant to actively bring about a new and improved world, through His power and prompting, for the good of His people and the glorification of His name.

Vision Is All Around You

Educators tell us that one of the most powerful learning tools is a working model. Fortunately, vision is not like fusion energy—an inspiring and desirable concept that has never been seen in practice. Your life is influenced every day by thousands of visionary leaders' products, services, policies and thinking.

By observing these visionaries you can learn important principles about vision by understanding their attitudes, behavior and experiences. For instance, some business leaders whose lives have been interesting examples of vision in action are John Sculley, president of Apple Computers; Jan Carlson, airline president; Tom Watson, Sr., founder of IBM; and Michael Eisner, CEO of the Walt Disney Company. The social and political arenas have provided many visionaries, too: John F. Kennedy, Ralph Nader, Robert Moses, a seminal city planner in New York City, even Adolf Hitler.

But these people differ from you in a major respect: They relied upon their own vision for the future, rather than God's vision of what He wanted the future to be. There is a huge difference between man's vision for the future and God's vision for the future.

To the worldly leader, vision helps him imagine a better future and foresee the means to create that superior reality. Given a good grasp of existing conditions in the marketplace and the leader's native talent for seizing untapped opportunities, a concise statement of that perspective can be crafted to communicate an alluring view of a better tomorrow. With that vision in mind, plans can be developed and put into practice to bring about the desired outcome.

So far, so good: nothing inherently contradictory to what you stand for, or how you should act in God's service. But for worldly leaders charged with the responsibility of creating, casting and implementing the vision, the key resource in that process is the leader. It is the leader who evaluates the world around him and dictates the opportunities worthy of pursuit. It is the leader who develops the image of the better future and doggedly conveys it in winsome language to those who must be enlisted in the effort to make that vision real. It is the leader who sets the goals and determines the means of satisfying those goals. Without question, the key player in the game is the leader. Unless he or she determines and describes the vision for the future, the supporting team will pursue routine activity with a sense of resignation and aimlessness.

Perhaps no person past or present exemplifies the power of vision better than Adolf Hitler. Millions were moved to pursue his vision of a master race that would change the course of history and make the world a better place to live. Driven by Der Führer's colorful language and by the emotional seduction of the new society promised, good people committed unspeakable atrocities in pursuit of that vision. Without a doubt, no one person's application of visionary leadership principles provides a more commanding understanding of how man's vision for the future, absent of God's direction and definition of that new reality, can so easily go astray.

Christians with Vision

A leader whose first priority is to know and serve God must recognize that because of the sinful nature of man, and the limited capacities we have, a vision for the future created by man is also hindered by those same human frailties. Short of total reliance upon God, our decisions always fall short of their potential. Man's vision for the future ultimately glorifies the Man who gave birth to that perspective.

A Christian leader is one whose decisions reflect not just the will to properly and fully serve God, but also the behavior that confirms his personal commitment to abandon self for the purpose of pleasing Him. The vision pursued by this person is one that glorifies its source, too. It is a vision by, about, and for man.

God's vision for us, on the other hand, is by Him, for us, and about how He can work in tandem with us to create a better world. It is a perfect representation of what the future should be like and should inspire us to aggressively strive for the completion of the vision.

By God's grace we are not left to our own imaginations to concoct an understanding of vision in a Christian context. We have many examples of people who have dedicated their lives to pursue God's vision for the future. By studying their lives and experiences, we can learn much about how God works through committed servants to accomplish His ends.

The Bible contains several visionary leaders. I have found it instructive to dissect the thinking and behavior of Paul, Nehemiah, Joshua and David. Jesus, of course, is the purest example of the enactment of God's vision on earth.

Some of our contemporaries provide additional, practical insight into the role of vision in ministry. Study the lives of Bill Hybels, pastor of Willow Creek Community Church in Illinois; Martin Luther King, Jr.; Donald McGavran, the late professor at Fuller Seminary who founded the Church Growth school of thinking; Pat Robertson, president of CBN; Donald Wildmon, United Methodist minister who has taken to watchdogging the media and what they allow to be broadcast; Beverly LaHaye, founder of Concerned Women for America; Henrietta Mears, seminal Christian educator; James Dobson, founder of Focus on the Family; Tony Campolo, sociologist, Christian author and activist; Mother Teresa, Catholic nun who has created a network of missionary posts committed to serving the poor and Jerry Falwell, pastor who founded the Moral Majority in the 1980s. Many others could be mentioned, many of whom are not public figures, but whose lives and ministries reflect the burning passion of God's vision.

> "God's vision for your ministry is like a fingerprint: there is no other one exactly like it."
>
> George Barna

Undoubtedly, you may not agree with everything these leaders have taught or stood for, or even the tactics they have used in pursuit of the vision. Capturing His vision and devoting all of your resources to it does not mean you are engaged in a popularity contest. Each of these visionaries, in his or her own way, used the talents and resources provided by God in a unique and very personalized manner to have a life-changing ministry. Their commitment to God, their understanding of His vision for their ministry, and their unmitigated perseverance in living the vision has enabled them to mobilize many people to a life-changing ministry.

My caution to you, though, is to avoid trying to be somebody else, or to attempt to copy the ministry of another leader. When you are attempting to capture God's vision for your ministry you cannot do so by imitating the vision of other great leaders.

God wants you to know the vision He has for you. But, just as you are a unique individual, serving in a set of circumstances not found anywhere else in the world, so is His vision for you completely customized to who you are, where you are, and what He wants from you and your situation. Mimicking the vision of other leaders would be wholly inappropriate. Those who have tried to do so have often met with disastrous consequences. Why? Because ultimately they were not being faithful to God; they were following their own desires of the heart, seeking the outcome they cherished.

How Do You Capture God's Vision?

You need four major elements to capture God's vision for your ministry. Mastering any one or two of these areas is insufficient.

First, you must *know yourself.*
Second, *know the ministry environment* in which you have
been called to operate.
Third, *know God* intimately.
Fourth, *get wise counsel* about what you believe to be God's
vision.

I hope this sounds simple—because it is. God has no reason to
make His desires for your ministry complex or mysterious. But He
does have reason to want us intimately connected with and reliant
upon Him for the vision, power and ability to make the vision a
reality.

If you have not clarified *His* vision for your ministry, stop everything you are doing in life. You are just passing time if your waking
moments are not geared to translating His vision for you from
notion to reality. Commit yourself to gain this gift of insight from
Him. Start by working through the four elements to gain His vision.

Know Yourself

These days there is so much focus upon self that we have become a
selfish nation. Please do not turn your back on this process just
because it starts out with a focus on knowing the real you. This is
not "new age" tactics, nor is it simplistic pop psychology.

The thrust of self-knowledge in the context of vision is not to
promote your own desires or pleasures, but to have a clear understanding of who you are and how God has gifted you for service.
Even as you concentrate on knowing who you are, remember that
the reason is to eventually know Him more fully and serve Him
more completely.

To get to the point where He can entrust His gift of vision to
you, start by identifying your deepest motives for being involved in
full-time ministry. This is between you and Him, so there is no hiding anything here. Taking this step can be scary because you are laying yourself unprotected before God. This is not something that is
encouraged much in America or in our churches. Read the Psalms
and Proverbs, though, and you get a clear notion of how important
this transparency is to God.

From this initial examination-point, critically examine the values, attitudes, assumptions and experiences that are the foundation of your ministry. Examine your perception of your strengths and weaknesses. Toward this self-exploration process, you might grapple with these questions.

- What turns you on in life?
- What turns you off emotionally?
- During what situations do you feel most alive or exuberant?
- Which Bible figures capture your imagination? Why?
- What makes life worth living?
- Who are the three most important people in your life? Why?
- Who are the three people you most respect? Why?
- What is your personality type? How does that influence your ministry?
- What are your spiritual gifts?
- What goals have you set and reached during the past five years?
- What goals have you set and failed to achieve during that period?
- What goals are you afraid to set because you do not feel capable of reaching them? Why not?
- In what ways did God make you special or different from others?
- How would you define a "successful" church?
- How would you define a "successful" pastor?
- How would you define a godly Christian leader?
- What differentiates a Christian leader from a non-Christian leader?
- Are you smart enough to do what it takes to please God?
- Are you smart enough to discern His vision for your ministry?
- What makes you cry? Why?
- If you could accomplish only one task in life, what would it be?
- If your friends and family remembered only one thing about you after you died, what would you want them to remember?

THE POWER OF VISION ■ 127

- For what opportunities or outcomes would you be willing to endure physical persecution? Nonphysical persecution?
- Which passages of the Bible speak most loudly and consistently to you?
- What sins do you commit most often?
- How deep is your relationship with God right now? What has the growth curve of the relationship been over the past year?
- What activities do you get totally caught up in—those you are unlikely to grow out of?
- What are the five values of human character to which you feel you must at all times, at all costs, be true?
- What characteristics are you committed to perfecting in your life?
- Who are the five spiritual leaders you have known personally whom you would most like to imitate? Why?
- Who have been the five most influential spiritual leaders in your life, other than Jesus? Why?
- Who has influenced your life the most, other than Jesus Christ? How did they influence you? What gave them that entrée?
- How do you differ from other ministers you know?
- What are the characteristics of an ideal Christian leader? Which of those do you possess? Not possess?

When you are comfortable that you know yourself well enough to understand how God might use you, some of the obstacles you might encounter, weaknesses you must compensate for in your ministry and other key perspectives, move on to the next area for investigation.

Know Your Ministry Context

History shows that all good decisions are made within a realistic understanding of the decision-making environment. If you want to understand His vision for your church, get a grip on the details of your ministry environment. Four dominant elements are related to comprehend that environment: (1) the community, (2) your ministry colleagues, (3) the congregation and (4) your competition.

Community. In earlier chapters of this book, I described procedures to gain insight into the people who live in your ministry area. Some helpful facts to consider are the demographic attributes of the people:

1. Key attitudes they possess;
2. Values that determine their thoughts and life-styles;
3. Beliefs that shape their characters;
4. Life-styles that describe their daily activities;
5. Their felt needs.

Why is this information useful? Because until you know people, you can't expect God to effectively move you to feel for them and to know how best to minister to them.

Colleagues. Never make the mistake of thinking you are in competition with other churches in the area. God has enabled those churches to exist because they are meant to fill a different niche from yours. Because you are not competitors and colleagues tilling different fields, develop a good working relationship with other ministers of the gospel. Understand why God has allowed each of these churches to exist in your area. Determine how your vision differs from theirs.

Why take account of other churches? Because "there is one body" (Eph. 4:4). Because if we are truly God's family; if He is not a redundant, confused God; and if He is going to take care of all of His people; then we must understand the mosaic we represent to Him. To avoid the usual church growth tactic—i.e. stealing sheep from the flocks of other shepherds—command His perspective on how all of His chosen leaders can blend together to form a unified, cohesive team that lets nobody's soul slip through the cracks.

The Congregation. Like it or not, you are saddled with the reality of your congregation. They may not be all that you would like, but they are all that you need to get the job done. To make the most of this entourage, and to lead them effectively, discover the history of the congregation, and gain an accurate sense of the thinking and emotions of the people.

This task is people-intensive. Talk with your people to gain their pulse:

1. Frustrations with the church;
2. Concerns about the church's role in the community;
3. Joys regarding the collective ministry happening there;
4. Hopes and dreams for the days ahead.

If you are the one to whom God will entrust His vision, why bother seeking input from the people you are meant to lead? These people cannot dictate the vision for you, but they can help you know how the vision will affect the church, whether the vision seems truly appropriate for the church (or whether perhaps you have misread God's leading), and how you might best articulate the vision for those who must own and live it.

The Competition. You cannot win a battle until you know the enemy. For your church, who are your competitors? They are all around, and some are not even tangible: television, sales at the mall, religious cults, sports leagues or athletic opportunities, fatigue, family time, hobbies. The list is virtually endless. It is important to identify *who* the competitors are, and also *how committed* people are to each of these competitors.

God has promised that His Kingdom will prevail, that His Church will be victorious. Do you really need to know the competition? Only if you wish to have a deep and lasting influence on your world. Strategic ministry is life-changing ministry; creating a strategic ministry requires you to understand people's alternatives to whatever you will offer to them.

Know God

After all you have been through in life and ministry, this factor may seem simplistic or even insulting. However, it is included in this process for two reasons. Most importantly, whether you are already doing this or not, it is an indispensable factor in grasping God's vision for your ministry. Further, you might be surprised (as I have been) at the substantial number of church leaders who devote little or no time to building their relationship with, and understanding of, God.

It boils down to this: You cannot know His vision for your ministry unless you first know Him. That knowledge must go far beyond acknowledging Christ as Lord and Savior, or affirming a few of His unique attributes. Your relationship with Him must be deep, personal and ongoing.

> **"A zealous sense of mission is only possible where there is opposition to it."**
>
> D.W. Ewing

You might profitably engage in each of the following efforts toward truly knowing Him and building an enduring, personal relationship with Him.

First, study the Bible. Get beyond reading it for the sake of "being in the Word." Allow the richness of the text to unfold His core nature to you. It is a book that unlocks the mysteries of His character, the fullness of His dreams and the wisdom of His methods. If fear of the Lord is the beginning of knowledge and wisdom (Prov. 1:7), get to know Him so well that you reach a balance between respect for a consuming Deity and intimacy with a loving and forgiving Creator.

Read about the visionary Christians who walked the earth hundreds of years before you. Do some mental role-playing, playing the "what if" game toward knowing how He responds to His people. Imagine various scenarios and how they might unfold. Each time a scenario reaches a roadblock or an undesirable conclusion, take a step back, mentally, and see if you can reach a more desirable end by pursuing a different approach. Continue to pursue such strategic avenues until you reach the most desirable outcome by the pursuit of reasonable action steps.

Second, pray to Him. In vision development, prayer is critical because it is a time to let God speak to you. He may do so by conveying impressions you must then pursue in more tangible terms. He may do so by speaking in words that seem audible to you. Be silent, be focused, be subservient. Realize that God seems to speak most clearly to Christian leaders when they make a conscious effort to allow Him to lead the conversation and impart wisdom in His own way, in His own timing. He is in control. Pray for His vision and for your ability and willingness to fulfill it.

Third, consider fasting. Although this is a discipline clearly out of sync with contemporary life-styles, the examples given in the Bible show fasting as a popular means of getting closer to God. If you can fast as a means to better focus on communication, do so.

Why go to all this effort to get a vision that God ultimately wants us to have, anyway? *Because He is just as interested in the process we are willing to engage in as He is in the fact that we may eventually prove to be effective stewards of the vision.* His goal is to have a significant relationship with you. If you take the time and make the effort to really get to know Him, even if it means substantial sacrifice on your part, the motives and effort will not go unnoticed.

Seek Objective Wisdom

We tend to surround ourselves with the people who love us, who make us feel good, who appreciate our ministry. Visionaries have the same types of emotional needs, but they instead surround themselves with people whose counsel ensures that other people will appreciate the ministry they lead.

What an unusual blessing it is to have people who will speak honestly and openly regarding your efforts to serve God, and to provide objective reactions to your perceptions of God's vision for your ministry. The wisdom of reliable counselors may offset your tendency to filter God's vision through your own lenses, and therefore bring you back to a more complete understanding of God's desires for you.

One of the most difficult circumstances in your vision development journey will be when a trusted adviser tells you that your journey does not seem finished or entirely reasonable. Do not see such advice as a sign of failure on your part, but rather as an indication that the process was prematurely interrupted. You and your church will be better off because you persevered and sought to clarify and expand the vision.

If these people are not capable of getting the vision from God, is it really feasible that they can provide reliable cautions about your own understanding of the vision? Absolutely! Throughout the Bible, God uses the counsel of wise people to steer key servants in the right direction.

Common Pitfalls You Can Avoid

Briefly, here are six common barriers that hinder people from grasping God's vision for their ministry. Do whatever you must to avoid these obstacles.

• *Vision by consensus.* God does not really care if everybody likes His vision for your ministry. Vision is not determined by a vote. It is imparted directly.

• *Vision by committee.* Because He gives His vision to a chosen leader, the head of His church, committees play a secondary role in the vision process. Once the vision has been discovered by the leader and communicated for the Body, the committees may be responsible for creating related strategies and for carrying out the vision. But they are never charged with the role of providing vision.

• *Vision by default.* You do not simply continue doing what you have been doing and assume that if it was not what God wanted, He would let you know. You cannot shortcut the process by relying upon history and circumstances as a gauge for the future.

• *Vision by mimicry.* Every church has a unique vision to fulfill. When you copy what another church is doing, you are asking for trouble since they are operating with a different set of resources, circumstances, opportunities and a disparate vision. You can imitate the *process* a leader goes through to get God's vision, but you cannot successfully imitate the vision itself.

• *Vision by repetition.* If you decide your vision can be determined by distilling what you have been doing that seems to work, and continue to do more of the same, you are not pursuing God's vision.

• *Vision by dictate.* If your denomination or other ruling body provides you with the vision for your church, run for cover. No external entity can insinuate itself in the place of the head of the local body and dictate what the vision must be. The denomination may have a vision of its own, which its member churches are expected to be a part of, but that body cannot reasonably determine what God is calling a local unit to accomplish.

Vision Is Definitely Not a Quick Fix

We live in a fast-paced, quick-fix society. Vision may promise to bring about a more efficient and effective ministry but it also takes time. There is no way to predict how long it will take for you to capture God's vision for your ministry. We know it won't be done in an intensive afternoon session behind closed doors. And we know that God enjoys the process as much as the product. But how long—we can't tell.

Going by the experience of other visionaries is of little help here. Some leaders claim they caught the vision after a few days of intensive struggle, prayer, reflection, solitude and total commitment to the process. Others admitted that it took months. All of these leaders were well-intentioned, highly trained, qualified pastors. When God is ready to transfer the vision, He will do so. Not a minute before. Do not give up the process: enjoy it as a means of deepening your bond with Him, and see this as one more building block in your relationship.

Vision Is Different from Mission

Most of the churches I have worked with make a fatal mistake: They believe that mission and vision are the same thing. Please, recognize that vision is *not* a synonym for mission. Every church must have a clear mission and a clear vision. What is the difference?

Mission is the overriding ministry calling of the church. It is a definition of the church's reason for existence. The explanation we call mission provides a broad-based, philosophical statement about what the church is called to do. It distinguishes the work of the church from the driving aims of a business, government, family or any other type of organization.

Vision sharpens the focus of mission. It offers a detailed understanding of what makes the church distinctive, by establishing what it will concentrate upon accomplishing within the broad boundaries of its mission. Mission gives the broad parameters; vision provides a narrower understanding of how to respond to the ministry environment. Because your church cannot effectively be all things to all people, your vision will specify the direction your church will take to have a deeper influence on a targeted segment of the potential ministry universe.

Perhaps your mission involves a focus upon evangelism. Your vision portrays some key characteristics of how your evangelistic focus will be uniquely enacted. Your mission may allude to edification. Your vision underscores how that process would work in your church, and why it might look different in your ministry context from others. Perhaps worship is highlighted in your mission statement. If worship is a central factor in your vision, the vision statement would distill what makes your style or approach to worship unique or compelling.

> "You are unique, and if that is not fulfilled, then something has been lost."
>
> Choreographer Martha Graham

In your community, every Christian church probably has the same mission. They should. Churches exist to share the gospel, to provide a relational base for spiritual growth, to teach the Word in all its meaning and intricacies, to build a deeper relationship with God through prayer and other disciplines, to reach out to those around us with compassion and so forth.

But why would God call churches to all do the same thing for the same group of people in the same manner at the same time? He doesn't. And that is why vision is so important. It distinguishes one part of the Body of Christ from another, and enables you to focus on what you have uniquely been called to accomplish.

In the end, then, you should have two separate, related statements that describe your ministry: your vision statement and your mission statement. Some examples are provided in charts 11 and 12.

Communicating What God Gives You

After you have spent the required time to grasp His vision, you must get it into circulation. Here are four important factors to consider.

First, distill the vision to its bare essentials. Provide people with a brief, user-friendly statement—no more than one paragraph (two or three sentences maximum). Use powerful words that communicate pictures of what the preferable future will be like. Avoid theological mumbo-jumbo; only a few can penetrate that terminology

CHART 11
Examples of Church Mission Statements

- To know Him and make Him known.
- To reach the lost at any cost.
- To worship, reach, build and pray.
- To save the unsaved and support the saved.
- Exalt, edify, equip and evangelize.
- To send the laborers into the fields for the harvest, armed with the tools needed to reap, replenish and grow.
- To love God by loving His people; we will accomplish His plan, in His timing, through His strength, for His glory.
- Preach the gospel, teach the Bible, create community among the saints, show compassion to the needy.
- Restore all of mankind to a right relationship with God the Father, God the Son and God the Holy Spirit.
- Establish God's Kingdom on earth, through people.
- Use every resource at our disposal to transform people's lives through authentic Christian ministry.
- Carry out the Great Commission, live out the Great Commandment, pursue the Great Commander.
- Know, love and serve God in all walks of life, at all times, using every resource available.

and get inspired by it. Your vision statement is your expression of what He has set aflame in your heart; your description of that calling must grab people's minds and hearts and get them excited about where your church is going. It is what they must remember as they pray about the church's outreach, as they participate in the planning and decision-making of the congregation, and as they minister on behalf of the body of believers. It is the handle people grab to understand how your church is different from the others in the area, and what makes yours a viable alternative.

Second, make a concerted effort to personally champion the vision by getting it in front of people. Preach about it. Bring it into

CHART 12
Examples of Church
Vision Statements

• To provide the greater metropolitan area with a church geared to the needs of baby boomers who are nominal Christians, offering a ministry that is sensitive in personality and characterized by a loving, forgiving, accepting environment.

• To equip professionals in New York City to impact their web of relationships, focusing on reaching non-Christians through cell groups and marketplace ministries that address urban needs.

• To be a growing community, passionately modeling the life of Christ through significant relationships with seekers (as well as believers). We will demonstrate the relevance of Christianity through contemporary and creative expressions of our faith.

• To identify, train and support believers as leaders who carry the ministry of the local church into the world. We will provide them with a place to encounter God in worship and encouragement.

• To reach out to the greater metropolitan area toward raising up four new churches by 2000; to demonstrate God's love, creativity and power by caring for people and working in cooperation with other ministries to reach the region for Christ.

• To provide a forum for significant relationships for residents in the southern portion of the county. We will assist people in building relationships that respond to people's needs, hurts and interests, in the context of a culturally relevant experience with Christ.

• To present Christ in a contemporary, creative, credible and caring way to all people, in an environment where people from the community can grow to their full potential in Christ.

• To offer older adults a secure environment that provides personal care, with outlets for community service.

• To be a center for Christian education, unsurpassed in quality; giving people alternative routes to discover the totality of the Christian faith.

focus in the midst of theological discussions or strategic debates. Have special meetings in which you talk to people about the vision and what it means in relation to their involvement in the church. Include it in your letters to the congregation. Print it on your stationery. Write articles about the application of the vision in your monthly newsletter. Drive the vision home every chance you get.

Third, make the vision the basis of all ministry plans, strategies and tactics. No important decision in the church should be made without considering the relationship of that opportunity to the vision. If the vision is what defines who you are and where you are going, you ought to constantly base your decisions upon that statement. It is your filter for all of your thinking and activity.

Fourth, as the pastor, you may wish to develop a more extensive statement or document describing the vision. This paper might never be seen by others. Its purpose is to solidify in your own mind the importance, nature and applications of the vision to your ministry. Expand your understanding of the theological, programming, personal and community implications of the vision. Think through what it means in how you apply your ministry resources to ministry activity. Write it in a format and language that expresses who you are, regardless of whether or not others would relate to it. This one is for you: it is an exercise geared to enable you to totally absorb the vision into your being.

Ownership of the Vision

If the vision is going to take hold and make a difference in the church's ministry and ultimately in people's lives, you must dedicate yourself to making sure that as many people as possible understand it, embrace it and live it.

Easier said than done? Yes. Impossible? No.

Some steps you may engage in to spread ownership of the vision include the following.

- Meet personally and regularly with key decision-makers, leaders and respected people to share the vision with them. Ask for their input on how to implement the vision in their sphere of influence and activity. Offer to help them in the process—and follow up on that promise.
- Live the vision personally. You cannot justifiably ask people to make sacrifices, change their habits and live in a given manner if you, the architect of the vision, won't do the same. Modeling a vision-based life-style is important for others to fully comprehend what it looks like in practice. Otherwise, vision remains an empty concept.

- Regularly share examples of the vision in action where it has had a life-changing impact. People are drawn to worthwhile behavior. They must be frequently informed of what difference the vision makes.
- Give other people in the congregation opportunities to champion the vision. If this direction and purpose is perceived to be the brainchild and province of the pastor alone it will lose its glamour. If, however, everyone can see that the vision has been accepted by others and is making a real difference in their lives and ministry, it becomes more appealing and desirable.
- Encourage all teaching in the church to be related in some tangible way to the vision. This, of course, should also be modeled by the pastor in all messages, teaching and other speaking.

Capturing God's vision is hard work. Putting it into practice is an even tougher assignment. But the fruits justify that effort. And remember the alternative: "Where there is no vision, the people perish" (Prov. 29:18, *KJV*).

Note
1. For a more extensive discussion of vision, see *The Power of Vision*, George Barna (Ventura, CA: Regal Books, 1992). This book is dedicated to define the concept, dispel the myths, explain the process and explore the application of vision for church ministry.

Ten
Strategy in Ministry

TO maximize your marketing effectiveness you need a plan. But your plan must be more than the combination of a series of actions or ideas. A great plan is based on great strategy. If you want to reach your full potential in marketing your ministry, think strategically.

Strategic marketing refers to a state of mind more than to a set of procedures. The strategically minded marketer is one who engages in marketing for a higher, well-conceived purpose.

Thinking strategically enables you to create the most favorable circumstances for your church by carefully using resources to respond intelligently to your existing (or future) opportunities. You could have a variety of responses to a given marketplace condition. A few of these responses are strategically advisable; most of them are not. Your challenge is to lead your church to respond in one or more ways that result in significant forward movement toward your ministry goals.

Great strategy gives you a competitive advantage. Remember, like it or not, you are in a competitive marketplace. If you do not create effective ways of reaching people and meeting their needs, someone else will. Generally speaking, your competition is not other churches; your competition is secular organizations. You are up against ABC, NBC, CBS, K mart, Sears, Nordstrom, Denny's, Sizzler, McDonald's, Pizza Hut and so forth. You are also taking on a variety of life-style options (e.g. reading, sleeping, visiting friends, family time, traveling, swimming, hiking, team sports). Know that your approach to reaching and touching people must be able to compete successfully with the audience appeal strategies of these marketing-savvy organizations. You are engaged in a battle for the minds and hearts of people. Play the game well or prepare to lose.

> ## "Neither a wise man nor a brave man lies down on the tracks of history to wait for the train of the future to run over him."
>
> Former president Dwight Eisenhower

Strategy is not a technical skill that emerges from a vacuum. A great strategist utilizes a combination of rational analysis and the creative allocation of resources to arrive at a unique, but vision-driven response.

Some objections to "marketing ministry" seem to be based on the misconception that to do strategic planning and purposeful marketing is to take matters out of God's hands and place them in our own...to rely on human wisdom instead of God's. Nothing could be further from the truth. Marketing strategy in ministry seeks *God's* strategy. It must be like that employed by King Jehoshaphat in the unusual battle described in 2 Chronicles 20. Facing certain defeat by human standards, the king relied on divine strategy. The people fasted and prayed. They assembled to seek help from the Lord. They worshiped. And strangest of all, they sent the singers to the front lines instead of the bowmen! As they began to sing and praise, God Himself defeated the enemy (see vv. 22-30).

Here was a battle that was truly "not yours, but God's" (v. 15). *But that did not mean that the king was to do nothing.* His planning and strategy were as purposeful as that at any corporate marketing meeting. He simply tied his strategy to God's vision.

Great strategy always relates closely to the vision. Is it possible to conceive a great strategy that does not further your drive toward fulfillment of your vision? No! Such a strategy may be clever or unique or intriguing, but if it fails to satisfy its true purpose (i.e. achieving the vision), then it is not a great strategy for your organization.

Do Churches Compete with Each Other?

Competitively speaking, you may think of opportunities provided by other than churches as those over which you wish to have a competitive advantage. Your competition for people's minds, hearts, time and other resources is legion. As alluded to earlier, there are countless options for spending one's time: participating in religious activities is not only one of many alternatives, but many people see such opportunities as the least attractive of the many choices available.

Think realistically about the decisions people make about religious participation. When a person is deciding whether or not to give money to your church, they weigh that option against the other thousands of ways they could spend that money. As they consider whether or not to attend a church service, they compare the perceived benefits such an experience will provide with those offered by some of the competing activities. It is relatively rare that a person's dilemma is to make a choice between the options offered by two churches in the community. More commonly, the choice reflects a preference between what a church offers and what a nonchurch institution offers—and that is assuming that the church-based option makes it to the point of serious consideration.

Yet, under certain circumstances, people might be faced with a choice of competing alternatives from different churches. Doesn't this mean churches are then competing with each other?

Yes, but not in a negative manner. It is not biblically improper or indefensible to have many churches in the same community. It is entirely possible that the reason God allows His people to be separated among so many different congregations is because He realizes each group, strategically speaking, will reach a relatively small proportion of the total population. Each congregation, then, represents another resource available for penetrating a given sector of the population.

If every church truly operated from a base of God's vision, we would likely see a community in which a mosaic of purposes and target audiences resided among those churches. As each church responded obediently to God's vision for ministry, they would reach their market. One church might effectively penetrate the white baby buster market with a traditional style; another might reach the same people group, but with a contemporary style; still a third church might appeal to nonwhite busters. One church might be best equipped to attract single baby boomers, another better poised to reach boomers who are married and have young children.

Should these churches consciously exclude people who are outside their target group? Absolutely not. However, because different population segments respond to different ministry opportunities, marketing stimuli and the like, focusing marketing efforts on a target group allows for a more efficient attraction of that market. Strategically, targeting your limited resources to reach a specific population segment will enable your ministry to be more effective than if you attempt to reach every people group in your community, meet the needs of every person in the area, and remain a spiritually viable ministry.

When different churches in the community seek to grow in numbers, by capturing the unchurched population, they will take steps that place them in direct competition for those unchurched people. But here is the difference: when competing against nonchurch entities, churches should strive for a *competitive advantage.* Nothing is wrong with seeking to attract people away from movie theaters, shopping malls, extended hours of sleep, or reading if the alternative is to provide them with the spiritual direction, nourishment and challenge they need to live more successfully in God's eyes.

When competing against other churches, the objective should be to develop a *comparative difference.* Thus, rather than attack another congregation, or take actions that might ultimately harm another ministry through aggressive tactics, the thrust should be to make it clear to the audience how your church differs from other churches, and let them make the decision as to which church best suits their needs.

Once again, there may be the temptation to worry that people, in evaluating the alternatives, might make the wrong choice. Realistically, we cannot control that situation. If you have done your best at communicating what your church is about, the rest is in the hands of the Holy Spirit. Your obligation is simply to promote your church in such a way as to let people know you exist, why you exist, how you differ from other alternatives and to deliver on the

STRATEGY IN MINISTRY ■ 143

promises you made in any outreach efforts. We can confidently leave the rest to God.

Yes, you are in a competitive environment that includes other churches. Yes, your messages compete against each other to reach the audience. No, in the truest sense of the competitive spirit, you are not seeking to grow your church at the expense of another.

A Strategic Attitude

Given that your church will benefit significantly by having a strategy behind its ministry efforts, someone must assume the rule of chief strategist. Knowing something about strategists is useful.

If you study people who exemplify great strategy in their marketing efforts, you will find a number of common characteristics. Evaluate your own tendencies and determine if you think like a strategist.

Insightful. Strategists tend to rely upon a blend of instinct, inspiration and information. They recognize the importance of numbers to help frame a situation or identify obstacles and opportunities, but they realize that strict empirical analysis may be misleading or limiting. Too much emphasis upon statistics can squelch the creative spirit—and strategy requires that the individual employ the imagination toward concocting new strategies. The ability to balance input—instinct, experience, imagination and accurate data—makes the strategist effective.

Well-informed. Although balance of input is a distinguishing characteristic of great strategists, so is their insistence upon having current, accurate and comprehensive information. Such input does not form the only basis upon which they make decisions, but it forms a critical base on which they rely for guidance.

Creative. As you consider your options in a given situation, you can either adapt to your circumstances or seek to innovate and thereby change them. A great strategist opts for the latter approach. Adapting is a characteristic of people who allow their environment to shape them. Such people focus upon process rather than potential and outcome. Innovation, on the other hand, frees a person from the constraints of systems and history. These people would rather die than copy the strategic thrust developed by someone else. It resides in the minds and hearts of individuals who redesign the world for their own purposes. Allowing your creative energy and talents to emerge through your thinking can result in winning strategy.

Risk-takers. Great strategy is often unpredictable. Why? Because most people set limits on their thinking, limits defined by the low level of risk they are willing to assume. A great strategist, though, realizes that vision requires change; change requires risk; and risk is minimized when it results in a competitive advantage. The element of surprise can be a great benefit to a marketer. Great strategic decisions often stem from the willingness of the marketer to stretch the boundaries of common thinking and practice to create a new paradigm.

Consistent. When the vision is in mind, the focus of strategists is set. But their decisions, too, are a natural outgrowth of their input, their vision and their determination to arrive at the optimal choice to maximize past, present and future realities. Great strategists may arrive at unpredictable solutions because they slice and dice the world differently within their minds; but the fact that they will arrive at such a unique perspective and call to action is itself predictable.

If you do not think in this way, you are probably not destined to be a great strategist. That is certainly nothing to be ashamed of, but for the health of your church, it is something to be acknowledged. Some people are born with this gift, others develop it. Importantly, though, people who do not think strategically should not be invested with the responsibility of determining the strategic view for a church. If the burden of strategic thinking has somehow fallen on your shoulders but you do not have the ability to perceive the world in this way, be willing to move aside so someone who does think strategically can provide this critical element.

Ways of Establishing a Strategic Advantage

Four generally recognized slants to maintain or win a strategic advantage for your church are listed below. Consider how these might work in your situation.

Reallocate existing resources. Each competitive organization operates with a limited pool of resources. However, if all of the organizations competing for people's resources allocate their own resources in the same way they have been doing—the status quo "business as usual" scenario—there will be no significant change in the ability of any of those organizations to attract people.

In such a static environment, it would be prudent to evaluate how your church is deploying its resources, and to shift the ways the existing resource base is spent. By employing a different formula you may seize upon a tact that might break through the predictable patterns and realize a greater return. The strategic challenge in this case is to determine a new means of ministering without compromising your beliefs or increasing your resource base. Consider a more productive, more creative or more customer-satisfying ministry offering.

For example, perhaps the businesses and churches in your area (your church included) spend most of their marketing resources on direct mail and newspaper advertising. Without changing your marketing budget you might totally shift your emphasis to radio and events, and reap greater results. Maybe your church would find that spending more money on the children's ministry than on teenage ministry leads to a more dramatic impact on kids and their parents. In another case, concentrating people's attention on participation in small group studies rather than continuing to promote a midweek service for supplemental Bible education might result in a renewed enthusiasm about the church's ministry, and a broader reach within the community.

Resource shifting works best when a church is in a state of decline or has plateaued, when performance is lagging behind expectations and when a church wants to grow but is in a competitive environment and has a small budget.

Exploit a competitive advantage. This is essentially an expansionist strategy, to be used when your church is meeting or exceeding its goals, or when you notice your competitors are floundering. The major thrust is to intensify efforts to do what you have done well en route to reaching your current position of leadership, or to pinpoint the reasons underlying your competitors' weaknesses and move to fill the needs that their frailty has left unmet.

For instance, your area may lack a strong English as a second language (ESL) program in the public schools, despite a constant influx of non-English speaking people into the community. The church services you have conducted in Spanish for Hispanics have attracted a large following. Strategically, you might expand your foothold into the Hispanic community by introducing an after school ESL program, or an adult ESL program during evenings. As another example, suppose your church has a moderately well-attended high school program. In studying your community, you discover that no other local Christian church is doing much with this segment. You could expand your potential by pouring more resources and emphasis into the high school ministry.

Change the rules. On occasion, the best way to win a strategic advantage is to reexamine the nature of your environment and redefine the process itself. This requires the ability to assess objectively all the factors and procedures that comprise the existing arena of competition. It also demands a willingness to accept risk as a necessary evil in the development of a new set of rules by which you might define the environment.

The key ingredient in this process is a constant desire to know why that which now exists must continue to exist in the same form. Asking "why?" and responding in a unique manner is the crux of this approach.

Changing the rules is a good strategy when your church has a good product to offer but is essentially unknown, or when yours is a small congregation that wants to grow but resides in a relatively stable church environment.

Churches change the rules of the game when they (1) hold their worship services some time other than Sunday morning, (2) alter the components that comprise the worship service itself, (3) recast themselves as a community service organization and design their operational efforts accordingly, (4) alter the leadership structure to reflect a novel balance of authority and responsibility between the laity and professional staff.

Introduce product innovation. Sometimes you can bring about positive change in your ministry by creating something that has not been created before. The sheer novelty of the new method may be appealing to people, or may exact a deeper loyalty or commitment from existing supporters, especially if the innovation responds to an unmet need of theirs.

Your church might find this strategy most useful if (1) you have a substantial resource base, but the resources themselves (e.g. people, facilities) are different from those used by competitors; (2) the church marketplace itself is predictable and stagnant or totally new (e.g. a new subdivision), (3) your target audience segments are particularly attracted to novelty and creativity.

Would using a combination of video, live drama and a 10-minute sermon be a new way to communicate the truth to people attending your worship service? Suppose your Christian education program was built on the concept of one-on-one discipling that took place after the Sunday service, in restaurants and other establishments around town, instead of the traditional Sunday School approach? If your church used Christian rap and hip-hop music as the dominant style in its services, would that be viewed as innovative, and give your church a competitive edge in reaching certain market segments?

Loser Strategies

Two strategies, in particular, rarely (if ever) work for an organization that is interested in anything more than hanging on for dear life.

The first of these loser strategies is the *me-too strategy.* In this circumstance, someone else has already entered the marketplace and co-opted the target market you had hoped to reach by beating you to the punch. By merely imitating what the market leader does you operate from a position of weakness. Strategy is about differentiating yourself in the mind of the consumer so that you arrive at a competitive advantage (or differential). Telling people that your strongest benefit is being able to do the same thing that someone else has already made a name at doing is not at all compelling.

What do you do if another church has carved a niche in your market by doing exactly what you planned to do? You have several choices. First, you may throw caution to the wind, do what is easiest, and decide to follow the me-too strategy regardless. Prepare to minister in a constant state of struggle. Second, you may decide to move to a different location so that you are not directly imitating the strategy and ministry of another church. Third, you could adopt one of the four strategies mentioned earlier, surrendering the primary positioning you had hoped to claim in favor of another suitable strategy.

The other loser strategy is the *status quo* strategy. This approach pursues stability—the "don't rock the boat, keep everything just as it has always been" philosophy. This type of maintenance strategy is almost always a signal that the church is in a death spiral or has already died and just does not know it. Because the objective of strategy is to place the church in more favorable circumstances, seeking to keep things unchanged is tantamount to losing ground. You can be pretty well assured that if you adopt a status quo approach, you will lose whatever territory you now occupy on the strategic terrain because more aggressive, forward-thinking, risk-taking, self-confident organizations will leave you in the dust.

Thinking like a great strategist means you will determine where your church fits into the broader context of opportunities for people in your target market, and how the church itself compares to what other churches in the area have to offer. There is no "perfect" strategy, so do not waste precious time fretting over whether or not you have developed an unassailable approach. Great strategists realize that a competitive world requires urgency in response, flexibility in thinking, willingness to try new things and to see obstacles as challenges, not as limitations. They also recognize that timing is a crucial element in a successful strategy: Implementing a strategy too soon or too late can cause an otherwise brilliant strategy to fail miserably.

ELEVEN

POSITIONING: WHO IN THE WORLD DO PEOPLE THINK YOU ARE?

IN 2 Kings 7, the Bible describes a desperate situation. Israel's enemies, the Arameans, were encamped against them in fearsome numbers. There seemed to be no way for the outnumbered Israelites to survive the impending battle.

Then suddenly God made the enemy to hear a mighty noise like the rumbling of chariots and the thundering of horses' hooves. Supposing that hordes of Egyptians and Hittites had joined the Israelites to do battle against them, the Arameans fled in a panic.

What had happened? God had *positioned* the Israelites in their true light. After all, the mighty God was on their side! So the terror-stricken Arameans' perception that Israel was a powerful nation was in fact true.

"Positioning" your church is equally important, since it determines that bundle of insights people have about who you are, what you do, what you offer and what you stand for.

Positioning Your Church

When people become aware of an organization, such as your church, they catalog the known information regarding that entity in some way that helps them make sense of the organization. The ways we categorize such information enable us to order our reality. By placing the information into such a context, we are more capable of responding rationally to the world around us.

The way we categorize organizations might be thought of as a perceptual map. In our minds we maintain a three-dimensional model of the organizations with which we interact. That model contains a multitude of indexes upon which we can compare and contrast organizations.

Every organization is positioned somewhere on the map. The challenge to you, as a strategist or marketer for the church, is to define how you want your church to be positioned in people's minds, and to take the steps required to facilitate such a positioning.

Positioning is not creating something entirely new in people's minds. It is the art of helping people shape or reorganize existing knowledge in a way that fosters an impression about the organization that corresponds with known reality.

Do not confuse position with image. Your church's image reflects its reputation. Your positioning reflects people's perceptions of your strengths and weaknesses in relation to your competitors. You can have a great image (e.g. the church that concentrates on helping the poor, the church that recognizes the value of women, the church that loves all people) but be poorly positioned (e.g. relatively boring services, comparatively weak teaching, the most snobby congregation in the city).

One of the keys to positioning is to be the first to get to the desired position within people's perceptual maps. Why? Because in our information-saturated, overstimulated, laden-with-choices society, people remember and accept the first entity that satisfactorily fills a mental void for them.

Think and Act Strategically

In positioning your church, think and act strategically. Start by defining the attributes people consider important, and by examining the attributes people ascribe to your church and to your competitors. Armed with such insight, determine what places on people's perceptual maps are not already occupied by a strong competitor. Chances of dislodging them are quite small. Given the alternatives, carve out a meaningful place on the perceptual map of your target audience by communicating something entirely compelling, credible and distinctive about your church.

Here are some of the positioning statements some churches we have worked with have adopted. Churches have a tendency to call these their themes or slogans. In essence, they are the positions they want people to grasp regarding the ministry.

- Where people care about other people.
- Where children are our most precious resource.
- Demonstrating God's love through compassionate action.
- Where biblical truth is taught without compromise.
- We treat your time with respect.
- Church like you have never experienced it before.
- Serving the needs of the African-American community.
- Serious about God.

Notice that each of these expressions is simple and memorable. When the "average" community resident is asked to describe a given church, if that congregation has effectively positioned itself, it is this type of statement that would be described.

Be Credible

You will encounter problems, though, if you choose to position your church in a way that is of no interest to your target audience or that has no credibility because it conflicts with the prevailing image of your church. Positioning is not a means of manipulating people's thoughts to correspond with what you want them to think about your church. Positioning is a technique to aid people's recall of your church in a positive, believable and helpful light. Attempts to make people perceive you in a way that conflicts with their prevailing notions will result in perceptual dissonance, which in turn generally ends up in a church being rejected as self-deceived, deceitful or a chameleon.

For example, one church used the phrase "bringing forgiveness into people's lives" as their positioning statement. The problem was that the church was widely regarded by people in the local area to be "fundamentalist," "judgmental" and "joyless." One woman outside of the congregation described the church as a place that would "tighten your face muscles." Most of the people this church passionately wanted to reach dismissed the concept of the church being a place of forgiveness as a dream more than a reality. Their image torpedoed their desired position in people's minds.

Formulate Your Position

But how do you decide what position you wish to occupy in people's minds? Here are a few clues.

First, of course, be sure all options you consider are biblical. Paul was willing to become "all things to all men" (1 Cor. 9:22). But this flexibility was within the boundaries of his mandate to be faithful first to his Lord.

Second, consider what characteristics of a church or congregation really matter to your target audience. Nothing is gained by positioning your church in a manner that is irrelevant to your market. How do you know what your target market might consider as important traits? This is an area where the analysis of current, accurate and reliable information is indispensable. Use your data gathering and analysis capabilities to clearly identify what people are looking for in a church and what kind of felt needs they have that a church might address.

From experience, I know how difficult it can be for some churches to put their own preferences on hold in favor of being able to reach the intended audience. Recently I worked with a Lutheran church on their marketing efforts. They listened politely and attentively to the insights about positioning and ultimately went against counsel by choosing to position themselves as the church that upheld the time-honored traditions of that denomination in the face of a changing society. To the leaders of the church, this was a position worth staking out and fighting to protect. Unfortunately, to most adults in that city—even to those who had been raised Lutheran—it was not a position that held any appeal.

Were the traditions practiced so fervently by that church bad, absurd or dishonorable? No. But they should not have been the

CHART 13

Image Attributes Chosen by a Church as Desirable Characteristics to Possess and Promote

- friendly people
- Bible-centered
- makes ministry enjoyable
- achieves excellence in all its efforts
- example of faith in practice

- credible teaching
- interesting, informative teaching
- changing people's lives
- contemporary approach
- strong leadership
- the church of the future

heart of the church's strategic positioning, given their target audience (young adults). The traditions they sought to preserve and bring to life could probably have remained, untouched. However, in giving people a positive point of recollection about the church, i.e. a position that would encourage them to consider that church as a competitor for their attendance, a different focus was necessary. No matter how open-minded that target audience might be, the core attribute the church chose to highlight in its positioning effort was perceived to be of little value or, in some cases, repulsive. This caused the church to be positioned as "irrelevant" to most of the target audience.

Over the next few years, that church proved incapable of achieving numerical growth, despite some aggressive marketing efforts. It remained small because the turf it had claimed as sacred was meaningless to most of the people the church had hoped to reach. Consequently, when people thought about what to do with their Sunday mornings this particular church was not on the list of options.

Third, determine what image you would like your church to have. The list in chart 13 represents one church's attempt at doing so. Come up with your list of key qualities. Realize that you cannot have everything in your profile. When thinking through your desired image, limit your imagination to the 10 most important characteristics. It is unrealistic to expect people to remember an image of your church that is more detailed than this.

Fourth, consider the data that are on the perceptual maps of the people you wish to reach. If you are going to avoid making bad decisions regarding your positioning, you must know where you and other organizations stand regarding image.

Perhaps a simple way of tracking the image you and other churches in the community have is to complete a comparison chart, such as chart 14. By completing this chart as you think people in your target audience would, based on your marketing data, you can better understand the competitive landscape. Use the following key to interpret the meaning of the numbers assigned to each church:

1 = very effective/strong ministry
2 = effective/strong ministry
3 = average ministry
4 = not too effective/strong ministry
5 = weak ministry

Chart 14 was completed with the needs of Garfield Community Church (GCC) in mind. I have taken the liberty of using fictitious church names for comparison on the chart. (GPC could mean Grace Presbyterian Church; LCPC could mean La Cresta Presbyterian Church, etc.) Given the assumed image that people have of that church, its strongest characteristics are mission and vision, friendliness, Bible emphasis, music, home groups, opportunities for involvement, and is viewed as contemporary. If this congregation wishes to carve out a niche for itself, those not currently occupied by any of the other seven churches known to the target segment, would be the congregation's friendliness. Alternatively, it could be positioned as the contemporary church with great music that is not charismatic or Pentecostal.

Simultaneously, the ways the other churches might be positioned in the minds of GCC's target audience would be as follows:

GPC: the multiethnic church,
LCPC: strong on the Bible and missions,
Vineyard: contemporary and Spirit-led.

CHART 14
Relative Images of Churches in the Community, From Perspective of Our Target Population

Attribute	GPC	GCC	LCPC	Vineyard	Calvary	UMC	St.Mark's
emphasize Bible	2	2	1	3	2	3	4
local missions	1	4	1	2	5	4	2
overseas missions	2	4	1	3	5	3	3
family support	3	3	3	3	4	3	3
preaching	3	3	2	3	4	4	4
music	3	2	4	2	4	4	4
evangelism	3	3	3	2	4	5	5
contemporary	3	2	4	1	5	4	5
Christian education	3	4	3	3	4	3	4
home groups	4	2	3	3	5	4	5
multiethnic	2	5	3	3	5	4	4
clear mission	2	1	1	2	4	3	4
clear vision	4	1	2	2	4	4	5
leadership	3	3	2	2	4	4	4
broad participation	2	2	3	3	3	3	3
facilities	1	4	3	3	1	1	3
part of community	3	4	3	3	4	3	4
friendly congregation	3	1	4	2	4	3	3
Spirit-led	3	3	3	1	1	5	4
liturgical	3	5	3	5	5	2	1
youth ministry	3	4	2	2	5	4	4

Notice that a few of the churches (Calvary, UMC, St. Mark's) currently do not have sufficient unique strengths to gain a distinctive position within the market. Strategically, they need to determine how their ministries will be differentiated from those of the other churches—if, and only if, the target audience being pursued by GCC is the same target audience they, too, are seeking. If the targets are

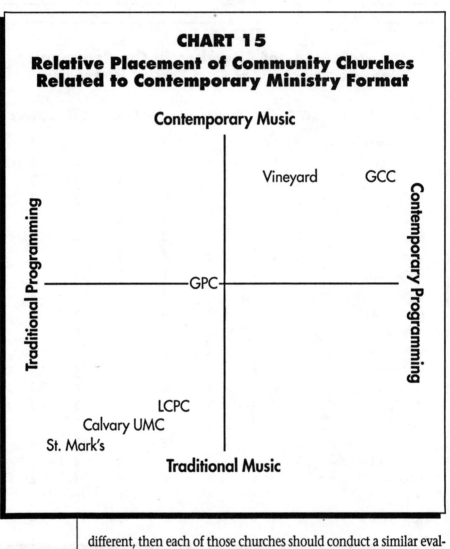

CHART 15
Relative Placement of Community Churches Related to Contemporary Ministry Format

different, then each of those churches should conduct a similar evaluation among their own target groups and discern their existing image, and ultimately select a novel positioning point.

Another useful tool is to graph the placement of your church and the others in your community on a double-axis chart, such as that shown in chart 15. The purpose of this exercise is to take a variable for which your church might wish to stake its position, and see where on this grid each of the competitive churches might be placed. In the example shown, for instance, GCC emerged as the church most likely viewed as having creative programming and contemporary music. The only church in the same quadrant was Vineyard. Positioning GCC as contemporary, without getting its positioning confused with that of the charismatic-oriented Vineyard should not pose a problem for GCC.

Parenthetically, notice that four of the seven churches charted would experience disastrous consequences by positioning themselves as contemporary. The target audience would not view that positioning as consistent with the image they have of those churches, and would likely reject those bodies outright.

Using such simple tools as the charts shown in these pages, and reliable information on which to base judgments for strategy, defensible decisions can be made. A good marketer will (1) understand what is important to the target audience; (2) create an ideal profile for the church's image, an image that may not currently exist but which is readily achievable; (3) accurately determine how the church is currently perceived. That marketer will conceive a strategy for positioning and marketing the church accordingly.

(Note: How you communicate your position to your target audience is not a matter of strategy but a matter of including your position in your overall marketing plan.)

Segmenting the Potential Audience

All of the preceding discussion requires that you engage in target marketing. The terminology used to describe target marketing gets confusing. When you hear about target marketing, audience segmentation, segmented marketing, niching, micro-marketing, it is all the same thing. This is the process of dividing the aggregate population you could serve into discrete, definable portions, and identifying one or a few portions on which you will focus your efforts. Almost all successful marketers these days engage in target marketing.

In America in the '90s, mass marketing is, for the most part, a corporate artifact. When television and other media came into play, providing marketers the opportunity to cost-effectively and quickly reach millions of people at once, they seized the opportunity. The population, for the first time viewing itself as one massive consumer unit, accepted mass marketing as a new era in product dissemination. People were willing to be grouped into the mass population for marketing purposes. A different attitude about self, nation, community and possessions resided in the hearts of people from 1950 to 1985.

Over the past 5 to 10 years, some dramatic shifts have occurred in the marketplace. Demographically, the population is less homogeneous than it used to be. Three decades ago we had two primary racial groups (whites and blacks), two primary marital segments (singles and marrieds), three basic generational divisions to contend with and a population that did not move much. Today, the population is fragmented into too many segments for any demographic variable we evaluate. Race? We now must address the needs of whites, blacks, Hispanics (and the various segments within that market), Asians (and the several groups of Asians). Marital configurations have blossomed from the two basic groups to encompass the never-been-married, first-time married, divorced-and-remarried, single parents, widows and so forth.

At the same time other changes happened. New technologies became available for personalizing communications whether the medium was telephone, mail, television, radio, on-line computer capabilities, facsimile machines and other higher-end methods. Computers and laser printers reshaped our thinking and capabilities regarding output, while data base management has become a necessity for marketing efficiently. Even the way people think about themselves—more as isolated, unique individuals who require customized service—has changed substantially.

To cope with these major shifts in almost every dimension of life-style and business endeavor, marketers have had to adapt by adopting a responsive methodology. That approach is niche marketing—identifying a specific, relatively limited portion of a market you seek to satisfy with targeted services. The key to making this approach work for you is to select a portion of the market that you know intimately, that you can readily reach and satisfy, and that will satisfy your own needs as you market to them.

Your church cannot be all things to all people. As some say, these days you must niche or be niched. Organizations are focusing on ever-smaller units of the universe, and in so doing, are providing better and better services, making the competition for even a small segment of the population more intense.

So how can your church respond? Offer people a restricted product base (i.e. services people need), one that fits your vision for ministry and that you can provide with excellence. Focus upon meeting the needs of a targeted portion of the aggregate area. Once you have established your ability to understand and satisfy a given segment of your area you may choose to expand to another segment.

Which Segments Should You Choose?

Entering this brave new world of marketing, in which the largest audience is viewed as anathema and the smaller group is seen as most desirable, how would you actually select a market segment as your target audience? In the absence of a magic formula for niching success, employ these five guidelines in your selection process.

1. *Know them well.* Because niche strategies depend upon access to a substantial amount of reliable and detailed information, do not select a segment about which little is, or will be, known. You need consistent updates of data on the size of a market segment, how they live and think, and what their needs are. Unless you have this information, other marketers (who probably do have it available) will entice that niche away from you by offering a ministry (or other product or service) that fills a more significant void in their lives than you do.

2. *Be sure they are reachable.* Some segments are attractive, but finding them is next to impossible. One church wanted to minister to women who had experienced abortions or the loss of a child. How do you find these women? Another congregation was hoping to locate and attract community resi-

dents who were substance abusers. Once again, not a readily available market.

Niche marketing requires communication efforts and providing services geared to the special needs and interests of a relatively narrowly defined group of people. In other words, if you miss the desired audience with your marketing appeals a residual market will not likely compensate for the oversight. Niche marketing leaves less tolerance for error than does mass marketing. Be sure you know how to get to your designated segment.

3. *Ask whether your capabilities suit their needs.* Do not make the mistake so many churches make: Go for the largest segment. In many cases, a church of older adults does not have the ability to attract baby boomers even though boomers may be a segment that is numerically appealing. Carefully analyze your corporate culture and the types of segments to which you could potentially minister effectively. If a target group that would otherwise be appealing is not one with which your church is likely to relate, do not target that segment.

4. *What is their size?* The market you select as your target should be large enough to enable you to survive. If you select a segment that is too tiny you will spend an enormous amount of resources attempting to reach and minister to a group that cannot provide the necessary economies of scale to justify being targeted.

At the same time, the segment you select should be small enough so as to facilitate a narrowed, differentiated focus. For instance, targeting "families" is far too broad. The needs, backgrounds, experiences and interests of families differ widely. You have single-parent families, traditional families, multigenerational families (i.e. grandparents, parents, children under the same roof), empty nest families, families with infants, families with teens or young adults and so on.

5. *Is there a reasonable prospect for success?* If your church will live or die on the balance of bringing homeless people into the congregation, you may want to reevaluate that segment as being your dominant market. Some segments simply

do not hold enough promise of success to justify putting all of your eggs into that basket. Toward that end you ought to have a sense of what has been done by other organizations seeking to capture the loyalty of a given segment before you identify them as your target group.

Likewise, learning about your environment will help you know of other organizations who have already tapped out a specific niche. Baby boomers, for instance, represent a broad but highly sought after market among churches. Focusing on boomers with kids in your community may be a market that has already been exhausted. Look for segments that remain relatively fertile.

TWELVE

CREATING A MINISTRY-DRIVEN MARKETING PLAN

WOULD you allow a building contractor to construct your church buildings without having a plan completed and approved before starting construction?

Would you encourage your son or daughter to take a random series of courses at college, without selecting a major, or determining the courses needed to graduate, or mapping out a plan for which courses to take each semester?

If you elected to drive cross-country for your two-week vacation, what are the odds that you would wake up on your first vacation day, jump in the car and drive on whatever open roads you encountered? It is more likely that you would first take the time to identify your ultimate destination and the special stops en route. Then you would develop a travel schedule, select the highways and other roads you would take, and accumulate the resources needed to successfully complete the trip.

Would you consistently preach sermons without the benefit of thinking through the issues of interest to your congregation, the passages of Scripture that could be applied to those issues, and the life applications that would make the message come alive for the audience? Although some speakers may take this "wing it" approach, the preachers of greatest renown always approach their public opportunities with a plan in mind: study notes, an outline, preconceived illustrations, the closing "clincher."

When it comes to marketing your church's ministry, you need to take the same careful approach to chart your direction and steps for the future. The failure to use the resources at your disposal to create a workable plan is tantamount to accepting inefficiency, frustration and unrealized potential.

The saying, "Those who fail to plan, plan to fail" may sound trite, but it is consistently proven true.

One of the trademarks of great war heroes is that they carefully work their way through a process of planning for battle. Recall how carefully Joshua planned the invasion of Canaan. He began gathering facts about the enemy when he went on the spying mission with 11 others. After Moses' death, Joshua sent two more spies into the city of Jericho. When God was ready to deliver the city into Israel's hands, Joshua was ready, too.

Other great military leaders also gather military intelligence, assess opportunities in light of their understanding of mission, evaluate their resource base and create a plan for attack. Although the battle garb and weaponry has changed over the centuries, the basic approach has varied little. Joshua, David, Napoleon, Adolf Hitler and Norman Schwartzkopf have more in common than you might believe. The core of that commonality, though, is their reliance upon a carefully crafted and meticulously implemented plan that led to their battlefield victories.

The experience of business leaders in our own century is no different. Whether you examine the practice of brilliant upstart companies, such as Steven Jobs's Apple Computers and Bill Gates at Microsoft, or the outstanding performance of mature companies such as Walt Disney Company in the 1980s under the leadership of Michael Eisner, the result is the same. Each of these companies got to where they are today by patiently and carefully surveying the landscape, recognizing unique opportunities, understanding their customers and competitors, and following an intelligent plan to get where they thought they could be.

In the same manner, your church must understand its circumstances and potentials and arrive at a plan for the most effective ministry possible. To strive for anything less lofty would be to disobey God's command that we do all as if we are doing it for Him directly. All of our efforts in life are to be geared to bringing Him glory.

What Is a Marketing Plan?

A marketing plan is a document that describes the goals, objectives, strategies and tactics to be used by your organization within a prescribed time period. It is the master outline that gives you a basis for moving forward in enabling your organization to reach its greatest potential.

From a church's context, the marketing plan prepares the ministry to more effectively reach new people and to support the existing church family by outlining the action steps the church should embrace for a life-changing ministry.

The plan is more than just a series of laudable ideas or concepts, though. It serves as a blueprint or map to get you from where you are today to where you want your church to be within that predetermined time frame. For each objective, strategy and tactic included in the plan, related references to funding needs, timing and the other resources are required (e.g. personnel, licenses, congregational approval) to help enact that marketing action.

Do Your Homework First

The preceding chapters in this book have addressed much of the preplan work that needs to be completed so that a reasonable plan can be developed. That work is done in preparation for the composition of your plan. Do not try to write your plan until you have completed the following preliminary work:

1. Collected sufficient information to understand the community in which you wish to minister: the demographic characteristics of the people, their felt needs, the key attitudes and

behaviors that define their values and life-styles, their religious experiences and backgrounds.

2. Collected sufficient information to understand your existing congregation: their demographics, life-styles, values, spiritual gifts, reasons for being part of your church, personal ministry goals.

3. Collected sufficient information to intelligently analyze your ministry context: the status, experience and goals of other churches in the community, the identity of your chief nonchurch competitors, the proportion of unchurched adults, the target group of each church and other competitors.

4. Clearly articulated your mission and vision for ministry with the ability to communicate both in an effective way to your congregation.

5. Determined the resource base you have to draw from as you begin to reach out to the congregation and community in ministry.

6. Reflected on the strategic positioning and image of your church, the opportunities and obstacles that such image and positioning present, the pertinent strategic options facing your church, the specific niches filled and not yet filled by your and other churches, your target market.

Assumptions

In preparation for developing your marketing plan, it is useful to identify the assumptions on which your plan will be based. Articulating your assumptions enables you to backtrack and revise your plans more quickly and competently should the ministry environment change. As you implement your plan and observe its impact, you may determine that changes are in order. Before making changes in your carefully conceived plan, though, it is important to determine why such changes are necessary. Was it a bad strategy? An improper analysis? Did the environment shift in unpredicted ways? One or more of your basic assumptions about the community, about your church, about ministry implementation or about other elements may be wrong or is now outdated. Identifying the erroneous assumption can help you foresee other changes required in your plans before you make serious mistakes.

Similarly, when you see your assumptions in print as you are developing your plan, they sometimes appear unreasonable and deserving of change. When you notice the unwarranted assumptions that must be true for the plan to work, don't move forward with plans that originally sounded logical. You can save yourself a lot of time, trouble and wasted resources by righting the wrong assumption and creating a more viable plan from the start.

Here are a few examples of assumptions. Some may be accurate, some not. The key is to identify the working assumptions.

- The expected 5 percent population growth over the next three years will be demographically identical to the existing population base.
- The congregation will sustain a ministry funded at the $650,000 level during the next 12 months.
- The music ministry can utilize the talents of members of the church, without having to pay for external assistance.
- The congregation has heard, understands and embraces the vision for ministry; spending large amounts of resources on communicating it and gaining initial ownership is not necessary. The vision-casting efforts should be geared to reminding people of the vision and strengthening their comprehension and ownership of it.
- The marketing plans developed will be publicly accepted and embraced by the pastor, and championed by the board of elders.
- Although the information gathering process generated insights into people's awareness of the community's churches, and how each is positioned, that information could be inaccurate since it is based on assumptions about people's perceptions and feelings based upon observation and a limited number of in-depth conversations with people about other churches.

Doing all of the preplan work takes time and energy. Think ahead! You cannot wait until the last minute, call a committee meeting, and throw together a viable plan in an afternoon or evening of intense labor. It will take literally months of consistent effort to pull all the information, creative ideas and reasoned thought together so that a wise plan can be tailored to your church's needs, opportunities and capabilities.

Pieces in the Puzzle

Your plan will contain four primary elements that relate to the actual marketing efforts of the church. These elements are your (1) *goals* for ministry, (2) marketing *objectives*, (3) the *strategies* related to a specific objective and (4) the *tactics* recommended for a given strategy. The four elements are inextricably tied together to form a guide to marketing action for the benefit of the church.

There is some dissension within the marketing community about the difference between goals and objectives. Some marketers say they are separate though related, others claim they are the same thing. Do not worry about it: The real answer is not one of the keys to gaining eternal salvation! It seems that the safest route to pursue is one in which the four elements noted above are clearly differentiated. On matters like this, your best strategy is to err on the side of detail, rather than generality. In reality, I rarely find that churches become confounded or paralyzed by having to distinguish marketing goals from marketing objectives.

Goals

Goals are the overall outcomes you wish to achieve in ministry. They provide the big picture, without getting bogged down in the details of measurement, style, approach or anything else. Your goals must directly relate to both your mission statement and your vision for ministry. In the most general sense, goals provide you with a sense of direction. They suggest if you are going east, north, south or west, without pinpointing the highways you will take, the rest stops you will make, or the schedule for travel.

An example might help clarify this definition. Perhaps your church's mission is to help people in your community to know, love and serve God. Your vision might refer to a desire to reach baby busters through a ministry based on service to the surrounding communities. Your goals might therefore include some of these:

- Expose young adults to the gospel;
- Provide people with opportunities to put the love of Christ into action;
- Encourage people in their service and sacrifice for the cause of Christ;
- Offer significant opportunities for young people to learn about Christ in culturally meaningful ways.

The goals themselves should be general enough to leave you plenty of latitude for developing a more specific approach. The specifics will be made obvious through the other three elements (i.e. objectives, strategies, tactics).

Objectives

Objectives are intimately tied to your goals, and make them more concrete and achievable. An objective is a clear statement of exactly what outcome you wish to reach. One way objectives do so is by being stated in a way that makes them measurable. Unless you have a means of figuring out if the objective has been satisfied, it is very difficult to market with continued vigor and enthusiasm. You keep trying, but gain no real sense of accomplishment. With such clarity, the shape of the ministry starts to come into focus.

A good marketing objective meets the following criteria:

- It is clearly and concisely stated—usually a sentence or two of very compact information.
- It is obviously tied to one of the ministry goals.
- It provides specific information against which your actual marketing efforts can be measured; thus, it includes detail regarding timing, budget and actual results.
- It is consistent with the overall purposes of the ministry and

with all of the other activities undertaken on behalf of the ministry.

- It is challenging but reasonable; if it is too simple to achieve, it fails to push you to your potential; if it is too much of a stretch, it leaves you frustrated.

Objectives typically relate to several different areas of ministry. The key dimensions are: drawing new people to the church, satisfying the spiritual needs of people, providing opportunities for personal ministry, addressing the felt needs of people, and attending to the responsibility of the church, as an institution, to the community at large.

For each goal you identify, you may have several objectives. It will often take a variety of smaller outcomes to arrive at the big picture goal you have set.

Following through on the mission, vision and goals used above as an example, you might have the following objectives for that church. Note that each of the objectives is clearly related to one (or more) of the goals.

- Lead 50 baby busters to Christ this year, for under $5,000 in program expenditures.
- Increase by 10 percent the number of adults in the church who read the Bible daily—by September—having line item costs of $1,000.
- Facilitate getting five homeless people in the community into paying jobs and permanent housing before November 15, spending up to $7,500.
- Sponsor at least three needy children, as a church, through an overseas missions agency—before Christmas—at $25 or less a month.
- Get at least 15 adults involved in on-site, short-term, international missions this year, at no cost to the church.
- Conduct an educational forum each quarter, attended by at least 30 people (most of whom are *not* church members), related to a current social problem and how the Bible provides a realistic perspective on the solution.

Strategies

In the preceding chapter the notion of thinking strategically was discussed. This is one of several places within the marketing plan itself to demonstrate the quality of your strategic thinking. Initially, of course, your goals and objectives should reflect a strategic mindset. Your actual ministry and marketing strategies, though, provide a more transparent mechanism for you to use your strategic capabilities to move your ministry forward.

The strategies you include within your marketing plan refer to the courses of action you will pursue to satisfy your objectives. The strategies are tied directly to specific objectives, just as the objectives were tied to the goals.

Strategies are dynamic in nature. Realize, too, that for any given objective, you may have a choice of many different strategies. A good strategist will identify the various options, evaluate the potential of each, then choose those that harbor the greatest promise for success.

Whereas goals give the broadest perspective on the church's direction, objectives make that view more focused and concrete. Strategy takes the objectives and describes ways you can take practical steps to realize the objectives. They do *not*, however, spell out the exact and detailed steps you will take to make the strategy happen. That is the purpose of tactics.

Sticking with the themes generated earlier, here are some of the strategies that might have been assumed for the church.

- Sponsor a Christian concert hosted by the church, with a short, nonthreatening, soft-sell introduction to the church, geared to expose young non-Christians to the gospel in a relevant context.
- Equip young adults within the church for evangelistic outreach.
- Place heavy emphasis upon promoting the Bible as a valued life-assistance tool.
- Work cooperatively with a nearby homeless agency toward assisting five specified homeless adults.

- Challenge Sunday School classes to join together to adopt needy children as part of the church's missions campaign.
- Establish an ongoing, hands-on relationship with the Baja Mission.
- Sponsor a debate on the "politically correct" movement and its implications for life from a Christian perspective.

Tactics

Tactics are the street-level marketing activity. These are the detailed, specific, hands-on activities that take place to put the strategy into action. If your strategies have been properly developed, it should be a relatively simple matter for your people to identify the types of tactics that must unfold to make a strategy come to life.

> "I began the revolution with 82 men. If I had to do it again, I'd do it with 10 or 15 men and absolute faith. It does not matter how small you are if you have faith and a plan of action."
>
> Fidel Castro, President of Cuba

As you are developing your objectives, you will discover that it is impossible to determine elements such as timing and funding unless you have a clear sense of the strategies to be pursued and, especially, the tactics that will be put in place. The tactics employed ultimately determine the success or failure of your marketing. That is, the clearest objectives and most brilliant strategies in the world are of little value if the implementation ideas are inadequate. It is critical to carefully conceive, evaluate and implement your tactics.

Again, you will face a multitude of tactical possibilities for any given strategy. If your strategy calls for a Christian concert, think about the myriad of tactical decisions you face.

- What band should you hire for the event?
- Should you hire one band or more than one?
- Should it be a local band of good repute or a nationally known band?
- Should you charge an admission fee, or make it a free concert? If you charge, how much?

- Should you advertise the concert on radio? If so, which stations? What times of day? How much of an advertising budget? What ad copy should you run?
- Who will be the master of ceremonies at the concert? What is the underlying purpose of that function given the objective of the concert?
- Where should the concert be held: on the church grounds or in a "neutral" venue?

The list could go on for quite a while—and should! It is important to exhaust the possible questions, answer them, and make sure that your tactical plan for each strategy is complete. All of the tactics proposed to implement a given strategy should be consistent with the aggregate philosophy of ministry and other ministry tactics that will be undertaken by the church in its various ministry efforts.

The information shown in chart 16 offers a cursory look at the goals, objectives, strategies and tactics that have been alluded to in the preceding examples.

Developing a Plan Around Your Resources

Part of the aggregate planning process should be to determine what resources you will have available for implementing the plan. This requires a sensitivity to faith and reality. On the one hand, you know that God wants you to reach the world for His glory, and that He will bless your efforts toward that end. On the other hand, He does not give you a blank check and ask you to assume He will provide every resource you want, when you want it, even if the purpose is to conduct a highly effective ministry. You will have limited resources and must create a plan that works as efficiently as possible within the boundaries of such a limitation.

Yet another tension point is planning around what you expect you will have to get the job done, and refusing to limit your sights by what is known and tangible. There is no easy solution to getting a realistic perspective on this matter. However, recognize that the

CHART 16
Hypothetical Outline for a Partial
Marketing Plan for a Church

GOAL 1: Expose young people to the gospel.

Objectives:
- See 50 baby busters accept Christ as their Savior within 1 year, at a total cost of $5,000.
- Generate a 10 percent increase in the number of young adults in the church who read the Bible daily; budget—$1,000.

Strategies:
- Sponsor a Christian rock concert to give gospel exposure among young adults.
- Train young adults in the congregation in evangelism.
- Heavily promote the Bible as a practical, life-assistance tool.

Tactics:
- Make *NKJV* Bibles available to people at cost.
- Conduct a quarterly evangelism workshop, led by an associate pastor on 3 consecutive Thursday evenings, for 90 minutes each session.
- Prayer team to include these goals and objectives in their prayer foci.
- Do a sermon series on the credibility of the Bible.

GOAL 2: Provide opportunities to put Christian love into action.

Objectives:
- Help 5 homeless people get jobs and housing within the year; allocate $7,500 for this outreach.
- Sponsor 3 needy, overseas children by the end of the year, at a maximum of $25 a month.

Strategies:
- Work cooperatively with a local homeless agency to assist 5 local homeless adults.
- Fund child sponsorship through Sunday School classes.

Tactics:
- Interview relevant homeless agencies and select one to work with.

continued

- Advertise through the church's newsletter and in its worship bulletin to solicit volunteers to help.
- Have outreach committee chairperson address Sunday School classes each month regarding the sponsorship project.

GOAL 3: Encourage service and sacrifice for the cause of Christ.

Objective:
- Have at least 15 people involved in on-site, international, short-term missions work this year; no funds allocated (they must raise their support).

Strategy:
- Establish a working relationship with Baja Missions toward integrating people into their work.

Tactics:
- Appoint a liaison to Baja Missions.
- Identify two 3-day, holiday weekends as time for outreach through Baja Missions.
- Make a series of announcements from the pulpit regarding the opportunity.
- Include information in the monthly pastoral letter about the opportunities.

GOAL 4: Offer significant opportunities for young people to learn about Christ in culturally meaningful ways.

Objectives:
- Conduct an educational forum to be attended by 30 or more people who are under 25 years of age, regarding biblical content.

Strategy:
- Sponsor a public debate on the values and theology underlying the politically correct movement.

Tactics:
- Identify debaters who will represent each side of the issue well.
- Advertise the event through local college radio and newspapers, and through our church's communications vehicles.
- Establish the event date and entry fee.
- Identify the event place and time.
- Tie event in to teaching topics in the college and young adult Sunday School classes.

plan itself ought to be reasonable, but should stretch the church. Setting your sights too low facilitates complacency and self-satisfaction. It enables the church to make some progress but overlook great opportunities.

As you develop your plan, then, seek to have a realistic assessment of your ministry's resource base. Expect to grow, but calculate a reasonable rate of growth. If you find the church growing faster than anticipated, it would be in your best interests to modify the plan in midcourse to reflect that growth and utilize the fruits of the growth toward conducting an expanded ministry.

What resources ought you to evaluate? Most important are the following categories:

1. People (laity): how many, how much time they will give, what skills and talents they offer, their levels of experience and commitment to your ministry.
2. Staff: background, training, experience, capabilities, commitment, growth potential.
3. Finances: how much, when it becomes available, any earmarked funds.
4. Production resources: what buildings and grounds are available for use, equipment, supplier relationships.
5. Tools: past marketing plans, research studies, consultants, communications pieces.

Other resources need to be considered, too—e.g. time and reputation—but do not represent the same priority as those listed above.

Given a well-grounded assessment of the resources you can call upon to bring your plan to life, create the objectives, strategies and tactics that will satisfy your mission, fulfill your vision, and excite your congregation through the effective outworking of targeted ministry.

Plan Procedures

As is true for almost any meaningful activity or concept, *ownership* by the people who will be asked to run with that idea or activity is crucial. This is true for your marketing plan. It may be easier to isolate yourself from the pressures of your daily environment and emerge with a marketing plan that gets handed off to the church leaders as their assignment for the coming year. However, the greatest success is achieved when the people who must make the plan happen, have a stake in its development. This is comparable to a wholesaler "selling *in*" his product to retailers. Without this vital step, there won't be much "selling *out.*" The retailer must accept ownership of the product if the total transaction is to be effective. Ownership, for most people, means playing a part, however minor, in the creation of the plan.

Receiving ownership in the plan can be achieved in various ways. Which of these can you profitably use in your church to sell in the planning process and the plan itself to the broadest range of people, with the deepest level of commitment resulting?

- Have the preliminary data-collection steps (i.e. research and analysis) done by the laity.
- Have the responsibility for identifying the resource base completed by lay people.
- Assign staff members the task of interfacing with the laity toward creating a unified understanding of the challenges and opportunities facing the church.
- Ask the teachers in the church—e.g. adult Sunday School teachers, small group leaders and others—to discuss these matters with their students. Encourage them to incorporate the mission and vision of the church into discussions, toward understanding people's hopes, dreams, fears and expectations regarding the future of this ministry.
- Have committees take the mission and vision statements and work through the strategies and tactics that would emanate from their area of expertise and responsibility.
- Create a planning task force that includes representatives from the various factions of the church to create the plans desired.
- Hold a congregational meeting at which the preliminary version of the plan is outlined for people, with subsequent

opportunities to provide input and to indicate how they wish to be involved.

- Distribute copies of the proposed plan at the time of the annual stewardship campaign. This enables people to see the scope and direction of the ministry and see the potential tangible benefits of the ministry. It helps them recognize why they ought to be supportive of the church and its activities.
- Have the pastor champion the plan from the pulpit and through other pastoral communications to enable the congregation to see its value and potential impact.
- Develop a system for gathering input from people prior to the development of the plan. This helps them feel like their ideas have an outlet and that their input can be factored into the creative process.

One of the keys to encourage ownership for the plan is a high-profile acceptance of it by the senior pastor. If the pastor ignores the plan or the process, the signal sent to the congregation is that the plan is of little or no value. As the leader of the church, the pastor must forcefully support the plan. Recognize the difference between being the primary creator or implementer of the plan and one of its chief proponents. Although the pastor need not be the one who conceives it or who takes every element within the plan from printed page to the streets, he must be the one who supports the plan in its final form and encourages the rest of the congregation to do so, as well.

Another key to conferring ownership is to appoint a champion for the plan—someone other than the pastor who will embrace the marketing process and the resulting marketing plan as the crux of his or her ministry within the church. The role of this person—variously known as the planning director, director of strategic ministries, pastor of ministry development, resource management director or by other titles—is to keep the plan in the forefront of all ministry decision-making engaged in by the church.

Do not make the mistake of thinking this person's task is simply to coordinate the process of developing the plan. That is one possible and very important function. Once the plan has been completed, implementation is critical. Over the course of a year, reminders of the marketing objectives outlined in the plan to those engaged in ministry is a major responsibility. Having a plan in place, no matter how many people were involved or how long the process took, does not guarantee that anyone will follow any of the dictums, recommendations, suggestions or ideas contained within the pages of the plan.

For instance, when church committees or task groups are making decisions in their areas of outreach, the planning director may wish to remind them of the obligations and challenges presented to them within the plan. When the budget is being developed for the coming fiscal year, the planning director may be able to enhance a viable budget development by reminding the budget makers of the needs identified in the plan and the resource such efforts require. As the pastor develops his sermon schedule for the coming year, the planning director might push for topics or applications that reflect the ministry thrust identified by the plan. Without question, the opportunities for the planning director to keep the plan in front of the people are myriad.

Another element of this job is accountability. Most churches, sadly, are very weak at holding people accountable—not just for implementing the plans themselves, but also for the quality of that implementation. Once again, it might be the planning director, or it might be someone else, but the plan must be championed by someone who will not only get the job underway, but see to it that the job is done right.

What Does a Marketing Plan Look Like?

Appendix 6 of this book contains a relatively short marketing plan that was developed by a small, nondenominational church. It is not the perfect plan. But it represents an honest attempt that incorporates all the key elements and it will probably get them pretty far down the road. Undoubtedly, as they learn from their experience, subsequent plans they produce will be more complete, more challenging and more professional. As a model, it is both do-able and reasonable.

Chart 17 shows a sample table of contents from a typical marketing plan. Notice that a marketing plan for a church ministry is essentially the bible for marketing the ministry. It contains all of the pertinent background documentation, as well as the plan (i.e. goals, objectives, strategies, tactics). The value of this arrangement is that you have everything you need in one place. You do not need to refer to each section with equal frequency, but should you need to find some element of the aggregate plan—e.g. the vision statement, or the community research data, or even the annual ministry budget—you know right where to get it. This comprehensiveness helps to make the document more indispensable.

The report does not need to be long—no extra jewels are placed in your heavenly crown due to the number of pages in this document. The key is utility, not quantity. The report ought to contain as many pages and sections as necessary to facilitate the most effective and efficient marketing of your ministry. Some of the marketing plans I have seen from Fortune 500 companies are as thick as the telephone book. On the other hand, Procter & Gamble Co., one of the most innovative and consistently successful marketing organizations in the world, asks their product managers to create a 10-page plan (or less) for their product line.

Revising Your Plan

As the year progresses, and you have had a chance to implement some of your strategies and tactics, you will learn more about your ministry environment. The new insights you gain ought to influence the ways you market your church. Always learn from experiences and incorporate new insights into future efforts. And while you are at it, incorporate those insights into your plans for the future marketing of your church.

As you examine the seven steps in the marketing process (see chart 3, chapter 2), note that feedback is a critical component of the process. Try to be sensitive to the response of your organization and

CHART 17
Table of Contents
Bethany Baptist Ministry Marketing Plan for 1992

Section	Description	Page
1	**Table of Contents**	1
2	**Introduction:** an overview of the planning process and the contents of this document	2
3	**Summary of the Plan:** a synopsis of the highlights of the plan for 1992	6
4	**Ministry Mission:** restatement of our mission	9
5	**Vision for Ministry:** a restatement of our vision for ministry	10
6	**Background Information:** a compilation of the facts that were examined in preparing the plan	11
7	**Ministry Goals:** an explanation of what we desire to see as the influence of our ministry	32
8	**Ministry Resources:** a description of the tangible resources we can use in the implementation of the plan	37
9	**Ministry Marketing Plan:** a description of the objectives, strategies and tactics to be carried out this year	46
10	**Schedule:** the time line on which our ministry plan will unfold	59
11	**Marketing Assignments:** recommendations for the assignment of responsibility for each of the areas of activity defined in the plan	63
12	**Marketing Budget:** the funding required for the plan, times at which the funds are needed, and line item definitions	67
13	**Feedback and Evaluation:** efforts to make toward remaining sensitive to our progress, both successes and difficulties, toward reaching our goals and objectives	72
14	**Closing Remarks and Exhibits:** additional documentation related to the plan, and the pastor's endorsement of this plan	75

your audience to your marketing efforts. As you learn what works and what does not, alter your plans accordingly. At the very least, make notes for yourself that will influence your plans for the coming year.

Just a note of caution, though, about tempering such sensitivity. Learning about your organization's abilities, the unique qualities of your ministry environment, and other useful insights can help you be more effective. Yet, it is possible to be so overresponsive to such input that your plan is being constantly and radically revised. This could throw the entire ministry into turmoil and chaos. A plan is meant to prevent that very condition.

The planning director, then, must also have the ability to discern between those new insights that require immediate reaction and those that ought to be filed away for future inclusion in the decision-making and plan development process.

THIRTEEN

MARKETING COMMUNICATIONS: HITTING YOUR TARGET

ONE of the factors that will determine the ultimate success of your marketing efforts is your ability to effectively communicate information to your target audiences.

You will create and deploy two types of communication as you market your church's ministry. These types are known by their chief end purpose: *acquiring* new numbers and *retaining* those you receive. Within each of these approaches you will develop various messages, utilize different media to convey these messages and rely upon different styles of communicating.

Acquisition Communications

Your church's marketing plan probably calls for some level of numerical growth, to be reached by focusing on reaching a particular segment of the community. Perhaps you are seeking to reach the unchurched. Perhaps your objectives call for an increase in the number of teenagers who get involved in the youth ministry at your church. Maybe your goals and objectives have defined a specific niche within the adult market as the group to whom your growth efforts will be directed. It is to those types of audiences that your acquisition communications are geared.

In most cases, acquisition communications by churches are developed either to persuade people to participate in the life of the church, or to embrace a personal relationship with Jesus Christ as the nucleus of their lives. Such communications are aimed at moving the audience from a point outside the body of believers, either viewed as the local congregation you lead or as the aggregate group of people who have accepted Christ as their Savior, to a commitment to Christ through involvement in His Church.

Acquisition communications may require you to publicize your church's image. Alternatively, it might involve what amounts to a sales pitch: an attempt to get a person to take an action desired by your organization. That action might be attending a worship service, visiting a small group Bible study, reading the Bible, listening to an audiotape you provide, or some other activity they would not have normally engaged in without the persuasive communication to which they were exposed.

Retention Communications

People who are already part of your church, though, would not be much interested in acquisition communications. Yes, they have an interest in your church and they have made a commitment to follow Christ. However, the objective of the acquisition communication is not relevant to their lives at this time—they have already made the commitments sought after by the communication. Consequently, they would not pay attention to the communication, figuring (rightly so) that the message was intended to be received by someone else.

Yet, it is imperative to communicate with the people who already are part of your ministry. They need to be updated on what is happening, encouraged with church news and biblical teaching, exhorted through ministry and life-style challenges and made aware of outreach opportunities and experiences. To influence the thinking and behavior of the committed, then, you engage in a form of communication different from that used to influence the unreached.

This second type of communication is *retention communications*. This effort is directed to those who are already part of the Body of Christ, as demonstrated by their involvement in your church. Your emphasis in these communications is not so much to persuade as to inform. The assumption underlying these messages is that because of their existing commitment to Christ and to ministry as a life-style, the key to make effective ministry easier for these people is to (1) inform them of basic Christian principles (i.e. teaching), (2) alert them to future opportunities, (3) encourage them with insights into past or current circumstances.

> **"Advertising is what you do when you can't go see somebody."**
>
> Fairfax Cone, cofounder of the Foote, Cone and Belding advertising agency

Retention communication can be empirical or persuasive in nature. Empirical efforts are designed to inform people by providing factual information they can process and use in a manner they deem suitable. Persuasive efforts are used to facilitate or cause a given course of action: attending an event, providing resources needed for ministry and so forth. Thus, even though these people are already committed to the church and the ministry, communication is important to give them direction, insight and motivation for active engagement in their faith.

In reality, a neat, clean division between persuasive communication and informative communication does not exist. Most forms of communication blend persuading and informing into a message that accomplishes some degree of both purposes. Effective communicators consciously strive for a well-conceived blend of the two. Be cognizant of the difference, though, so that as you consider what types of communication you send to people, your message reflects a desirable balance between the two.

Your church will need to engage in both types of communication if it is to remain a healthy church. Congregations that focus solely upon retention messages tend to become ingrown and often experience numerical stagnation and limited community influence. Churches that place all of their emphasis upon acquisition communications generally experience frustration due to low commitment to the congregation. These are the churches where the back door phenomenon is in full force. Many of the people make an initial commitment to the church, but then they depart within a relatively short period of time because their developmental needs are not met. Although communications are not the only means of addressing their need to grow spiritually, the lack of emphasis placed on interacting with the people inside the church is symptomatic of a ministry that is so outwardly-focused it neglects the spiritual needs of its members.

The Communication Process

Many textbooks have been written to explain the theory of communication: the process in which a message is developed by the sender, encoded in images and sound, transmitted by a communication medium, decoded and interpreted by the receiver. We will not focus upon the theory underlying effective communication.

Let's take a moment, though, to consider the process of communicating on behalf of your church's ministry. Experience shows that to reach people you must think through a strategy. Random communication results in random response. It is neither predictable nor beneficial for the ministry. Once you have determined the nature of your ministry and the necessity of reaching people with information about your church and their own spirituality, you should create a plan for your communication activity.

Communication Objectives

Your first step might be to identify the communication objectives you need to satisfy, to see your ministry move forward as articulated in your marketing plan. Your communication objectives spell out what needs to be communicated, to whom and for what purpose. Addressing both acquisition and retention goals, here are some types of objectives you might pursue in your communications efforts.

- Creating positive awareness of your church and its ministries.
- Encouraging people to contribute more money to fund the ministry.
- Preparing people for specific courses of action to be taken by the church that might normally result in negative feelings toward the church.
- Informing the congregation of future plans and the reasoning behind those plans.
- Inviting people who have no church affiliation to attend events at your church.
- Recruiting, encouraging or acknowledging the volunteers regarding ministry involvement.
- Laying a foundation for the development of new or deeper relationships between people in the church.
- Expressing gratitude to individuals who have contributed in some tangible way to the ministry.
- Directing the ministry efforts of the paid staff.
- Explaining perspectives on an issue with the intent of influencing upcoming decisions related to the issue.
- Encouraging those presently committed to active ministry through the church to remain so committed.
- Exploiting a competitive advantage.
- Confronting negative information regarding the church, its ministry, its people or its plans for the future by proposing an alternative point of view.
- Reshaping people's perceptions about the relative importance of conditions or responses, the quality and impact of such elements, or the parameters of the potential marketplace.
- Reinforcing people's decisions regarding involvement with the church or its ministry.

Whatever your communication objectives are, they should be directly tied to the marketing objectives of your church. Communicating with an audience consumes resources—time, money, physical resources and the like. It is in the best interests of your church to carefully think through the details of how any given communication process will help your church achieve its ministry goals. There is no value in communicating for the sake of communicating.

Try to avoid the tendency to overcommunicate with people. In America, people are overwhelmed with communication; much of it is unnecessary, meaningless or poorly targeted. The best dictum to follow is one your mother might have said to you when you were younger: If you don't have anything worth saying, just be quiet. You generally communicate more effectively by saying less than by saying more, and by communicating only when necessary, rather than incessantly.

The message you communicate is likely to be shaped in some respect by your perceptions about the audience segment for which the communication is designed. Telling a teenager about the importance of attending a worship service must be done differently from trying to convince a baby boomer of the same necessity. In trying to persuade unchurched people to attend your church, the message you send to an ex-Catholic who wants to attend church but is fearful and ignorant of what Protestant churches are like, takes a different approach from one you would take if your audience were born-again Christians who had turned their backs on church because of past bad experiences in a congregation. Thus, as you determine what types of information must be conveyed by your church, it is important also to underscore the target audience for such communication efforts.

How do you know who the target audience is? If your marketing plan is properly developed, the plan itself will indicate the intended recipients. How do you define your communications objectives? Again, your marketing plan is the key: Your communications are a response to a need outlined in the plan. As you develop your communication devices, the marketing plan will be one of your key tools for determining the nature of your message, methods and monetary needs.

Getting ready to communicate a message also requires you to count the cost and check the calendar. If you are communicating through some type of direct or mass medium—that is, through some means other than word-of-mouth—the costs add up very quickly. The cost of communicating may, in itself, determine the actual medium you will eventually use. For instance, the average commercial run during the Super Bowl costs an advertiser more than $700,000 for a single airing, and many thousands of dollars to create and produce. No church in America can afford such an extravagance, nor would such an airing provide the targeted results that churches typically seek to achieve. However, commercials broadcast on local radio stations cost $20 to $30 an airing, so if a station has a good track record of reaching the type of people who comprise your audience, scheduling a flight of radio spots might be advantageous and effective.

One means of getting a perspective on costs is to determine ahead of time what your communication budget will be. Outline the various pieces of communication scheduled for the year as outlined in your marketing plan. Then get cost estimates for different media strategies. Here is how one church approached this task.

What communications will we send to our audiences this year?
Our marketing plan identifies the following:

- Monthly newsletter to church members;
- Weekly worship service bulletin, with one insert;
- Monthly letter from the pastor to church members;
- Annual report, about 50 pages long, for each church member;
- Yellow Pages ad;
- Brochure prepared for first-time visitors;
- Mailed invitation to community residents to attend:
    1. special Easter sunrise service,
    2. Christmas Eve candlelight service,
    3. membership drive community mailing;
- Annual stewardship campaign letter;
- Annual congregational meeting letter regarding election of officers, policy changes;
- VBS flyer to homes of parents;
- Weekly newspaper advertisement in *Courant-Journal*.

How much will these communications cost?

- Our current newspaper ad runs weekly, is 2 line-inches by 2 columns, with one photo, and costs us $480 a month. To expand the ad to twice the line-inch count would increase the cost to $840 monthly. Decreasing the size to 1 line-inch would drop the cost to $300 monthly.

- A mailing to each household in the community, sent third-class bulk rate, nonprofit mail, costs 11.1 cents a piece in postage; an average of 20 cents a piece if we use a self-mailer; an average of 12 cents each if we send a letter; about 3 cents for each piece handled by the letter shop; about 1 cent a household for the mailing labels of community residents. First-class mailings cost 29 cents for postage; postcards are 19 cents.

- Mailings to the congregation reach about 350 households. The letters from the pastor, sent first-class, average $155 a mailing (2-page letter). The monthly newsletter, in the 11x17 folded format (4-page), sent second-class postage, runs about $105 an issue, delivered. Postcards sent to the congregation by first-class mail typically run about $90, inclusive.

- Radio spots on the classical music station run $15 for 30-seconds during early morning, midday, late night; $27 during morning drive time; $25 during evening drive time. On the soft rock station, spots run $10, $16, $18, during their respective time slots; on the MOR (Middle of the Road) station, the spots cost $9, $13, $13, respectively.

- Television spots (30-second) can be acquired for local sponsors by our cable company. Costs vary by the channel on which the spots run. The best audiences for us may be USA Network and Family Channel. Ads run $75 on USA Network, during prime time, $55 during fringe, $35 during morning. Rates on The Family Channel are $70, $57 and $40, respectively.

- Only 2 outdoor signs (billboards) remain available to us since all others have long-term commitments. The sign at Sherman and Wilson runs $150 a month, minimum 6-month contract. The sign at Broadway and Ninth rents for $400 monthly, and has a 1-year minimum.

- The ad in the Yellow Pages (1 column by 1-inch) runs $95 a month. Switching to other directories drops the price, but also the coverage and the readership. Dropping the display ad and sticking with a line listing in boldface would cost $35 a month.

What has worked—or failed—in the past?

- Television never seems to reach our audience. If they are reached, it may be that our low-budget production has failed to motivate them to respond. TV does not seem to be in our future.
- Radio has had mixed results. It seems better at creating interest in special events than in growing attendance at regular events (such as worship services). The people who generally respond are young adults.
- The Yellow Pages seems responsible for about one new family each quarter. They are generally new to the community and seeking to find a church to replace the one they left when they moved.
- The direct mail campaign to bring adults in during our membership drive has never had much impact. Suggest we either increase the number of mailings sent to homes and target those households to reflect our target demographic, or drop direct mail.
- We have never tried outdoor ads, but First Baptist claims that their experience was negative—one year, no apparent impact.
- The church mailings seem to hit their mark. The newsletter is read by a seemingly high proportion of the church participants. The pastor's letters have a high profile. The reminder postcards seem to hike attendance at events. The annual report, however, does not seem to get much of a read, nor do the stewardship materials.

Armed with this type of information, a church can make more informed decisions about how to communicate in the future. Some of the key decisions, though, require additional consideration: the selection of media, timing of the media use and the nature of the message or messages to be communicated through such advertising or other appeals.

Using the Mass Media

Several forms of media are available to your church to convey a message to an audience. The most common of these are radio and newspapers, although some churches also use television and magazines. The media are usually known as mass media, because they deliver to the mass audience (as opposed to a targeted or segmented portion of the aggregate audience). In considering the potential value of these media, you should know how media analysts evaluate the impact of these media. Using various research, they look at information such as ratings, share, gross rating points, audience demographics, impressions, reach, frequency and CPM. Here is a brief description of these terms, and how you might apply them to your decision of which media to use.

• *Share:* This is the percentage of the total viewing or listening audience who is watching or listening to a given program. The share is expressed as a number: "The Tonight Show" has a 27 share, meaning that the program has 27 percent of all people watching television while that program is on the air. Used for radio and television analysis, the cost of your advertising is set in conjunction with the ratings and share of the audience delivered by a given program. If, for instance, you contact a Christian radio station and ask about their advertising rates, you might find that their highest rated program commands substantially more money for a commercial than do other programs they air.

• *Rating:* Also used by radio and television stations, the rating is the percentage of all people who could potentially listen to or watch a program who were actually doing so. Unless every potential viewer/listener is tuned in, the rating will always be lower than the share, since the denominator on which the rating is calculated (i.e. the total possible audience) is larger than that for the share (i.e. the actual audience during that time slot). Also expressed as a whole number, if you were told that the "Paul Harvey Report" has an 18 rating, that would mean that of all the people with access to a radio in your market, 18 percent of them listen to his program.

• *Gross rating points:* If you add up all the ratings of the programs on which you advertise, the total represents the gross rating points (GRPs). This number gives you a rough idea of the amount of "media weight" or emphasis that has been placed on advertising your product. If you advertise on a program with a 10 rating (meaning 10 percent of the aggregate possible audience was tuned in), twice during a program with an 8 rating, and once during a show with a 6 rating, your GRP total would be 32 (10+8+8+6). Technically, this implies that you have shown your message to the equivalent of 32 percent of the households in the market. Theoretically, the more GRPs you buy, the more times your advertisement has gained exposure.

• *Impressions:* This is the same as GRPs, but is expressed in terms of the total number of people reached, instead of as a percentage. Realize that, like GRPs, the impressions made with your advertising refer to the equivalent number of people who have seen the ad. In reality, though, there is likely to be considerable duplication of people; neither GRPs nor impressions tell you how many unduplicated households or people have been exposed to the ad.

• *Reach:* This represents the number of people or households who have seen your advertising within a prescribed period of time— i.e. your total unduplicated audience. Used in all media research, reach refers to a 4-week period for television or radio; for magazines or newspapers reach reflects the total reading audience for a specific issue or edition. Reach is most useful when attempting to calculate the aggregate impact of a given medium. For instance, if you run an ad on 4 radio stations, you might have purchased 65 GRPs. However, when the same people are counted just once, you might discover that 45 percent of those GRPs represent the same people who were exposed to the ad more than once. Your reach, then, would be 20 percent. Also remember that the ratings systems in place today do not measure actual attention paid to your ad or the percent who recall the ad, but only the proportion who were exposed to the particular medium in which it ran.

• *Frequency:* This describes the average number of times people or households, depending on your unit of measurement, have been exposed to your advertising. Frequency is important because research has shown that the typical consumer must have multiple exposures to a message before grasping the content. Frequency is often used in conjunction with reach to determine a media schedule that will deliver the most cost-efficient, targeted audience for the advertiser. By combining these measures, for example, you could create a series of media scenarios for your advertising and analyze their likely impact. You might learn that a given schedule of radio spots would deliver 40 GRPs a week, resulting in having reached 32 percent of the male audience that is 18 to 34 years old, having an average frequency of 1.7 exposures during a 4-week period. By using media schedules and research, available from a media buying agency or an advertising agency that might handle your media buying, this type of analysis is possible.

• *CPM:* This stands for cost per thousand and serves as a standardized unit of cost. Typically, you would determine the CPM for different media efforts and select the approaches that provide the most efficient audience delivery.

Making sense of your media schedule is no simple task. In fact, if you purchase advertising time or space without the benefit of audience analysis, using measures such as those described above, you are begging for trouble. Making decisions without the pertinent information is unwise under any conditions. Doing so in a media buying context can undermine good ministry intentions and otherwise strong marketing efforts. Bad media decisions can rapidly consume your budget for no apparent gains, adding to your ministry frustration, impairing your ability to be good stewards of funds and causing your congregation to be gun-shy about ever using the media again.

To reduce much of the anxiety and danger related to using the paid media in your marketing efforts, you might consider the possibility of working with a qualified media buying agency or advertising agency. Even though your account will likely be tiny compared to most of the accounts the agency handles, you might find an agency that is sympathetic to your needs, or one that specializes in working with limited-budget nonprofit organizations. Agencies that buy media time or space get a commission (generally 15 percent) from the media whose time/space they purchase. Every time they place an ad in the newspaper for you, the cost will be the same to you, but the agency will receive a commission for bringing the advertiser to that media outlet. Beware, though: In some markets newspapers do not allow commission for religious advertising, since they charge lower rates for such ad space. One of the great values of working with reliable media buyers is that they can provide you with a media plan that suggests the reach and frequency such advertising might generate.

Using Targeted Media

In the past decade the nature of audience communication has changed radically. Although television, radio, newspaper and magazine advertising formerly represented the dominant means of reaching an audience, more and more advertisers are moving away from reliance on these mass media. Instead, they are turning to "targeted media"—communications vehicles that enable them to reach a more narrowly defined, concentrated audience.

As people have become more sophisticated and segmented, so has the media used to reach them. Many organizations spend enormous amounts of money advertising their products, but never rely upon the traditional mass media to convey their message. Why? Because there is so much waste in the delivery of the audience; in other words, of the total audience who might be exposed to the ad, only a small fraction of that audience (e.g. 2 percent) are your target group. Yet, you pay to reach the 98 percent who you know will not be interested in your product in order to reach the 2 percent who fit your target audience profile. That represents a massive amount of wasted money and really limits your chances for success.

You can turn to targeted media to reach the hard-to-find people. What are these media? Direct mail, card decks, specialty publications and telemarketing are the most common. In some ways, you can even treat radio and cable television as forms of targeted media since many of them now reach such specialized populations.

The fundamental concept of targeted communications is that by

CHART 18
A Comparison of the Cost of a
Mass Mailing and a Targeted Mailing

Cost component	Cost per Thousand	Community-wide Mailing (50K HH)	Targeted-household Mailing (10K HH)
Brochure	$200 at 50k $250 at 10k	$10,000	$2,500
Mailing list	$40 for all $65 for segments	$2,000	$650
Handling	$5	$250	$50
Postage	$111	$5,550	$1,110
Total cost		$17,800	$4,310
Cost per household		$0.356	$0.431

sending your message only to those individuals who are likely to have an interest in the message, you have achieved greater efficiency in your communications. Rather than earning a certain level of awareness among people who are likely to have no interest in your product or service, you can normally achieve a higher level of awareness among your target audience for the same, or less, money spent on communication.

Direct mail remains a valuable tool for church marketing. Assuming your church has identified a specific segment of the community it seeks to pursue, in demographic terms, your mailings can be directed to households that contain such people. Although the cost of using a targeted mail campaign usually winds up being higher per household than is true for a mass mail campaign (i.e. mailing to every household in the targeted geographic area), your budget can be stretched much farther and generally reaps greater dividends. The chart above shows a comparison of how a mailing to all 50,000 households in one community would have cost a church $17,800; a mailing to the 10,000 households most likely to have an interest in the church's message sent ran $4,310.

Notice that for the targeted approach, the cost per household was higher. Why? Because the cost of printing the brochures was higher due to the smaller print run and the mailing list was more expensive because it is more selective. Yet, here is what the choice boils down to. This church could spend $17,800 to send a brochure to each household one time. It could spend $4,310 for a single exposure to the households most likely to be interested in the message being communicated. Or it could spend $17,240 (less than the cost of a single community-wide mailing) to reach the target audience *four* times, either with the same message or with different brochures. Given these options, and knowing that multiple exposure to a message increases the likelihood of impact, which option would you choose?

Do not be naive about the use of any type of media, targeted or mass. The proportion of people who respond to such communications tends to be minute. The average response to a direct mail promotion is around 1 percent. Some churches have found that they have garnered up to a 10 percent return through a multi-stage, targeted mail campaign. Be aware that no matter how clever and appealing your mailings may be, a relatively small proportion of the audience will respond in the desired manner.

A variety of formats can be used in direct mail campaigns. The most common are postcards, letters, self-mailers, newsletters. Even though the majority of adults still examine every piece of mail they receive, you must work hard to ensure that your piece stands out from the crowd and quickly communicates that it is a piece worth reading.

Using Free Media

Do not overlook communication opportunities that cost you nothing, or very little. These free media sometimes possess the highest levels of credibility, as is the case of word-of-mouth (WOM) communication. Churches have begun to develop entire communications campaigns founded on a WOM strategy, largely because the research consistently suggests that church attendance is increased largely through the use of WOM. People most frequently visit a church because someone they know and trust talked with them about the church and invited them to attend. Often, those same people who visited with a friend had rejected the call to visit the church that had been promoted through mass or targeted media. It was the credibility of the personal relationship that established the viability of the message.

Some of the better-known types of systematic WOM campaigns include:

1. The Friends Day approach—a church identifies a special day in which everyone is charged to bring a specified number of friends to visit.
2. Community Cleanup Days—a church takes responsibility for combing the streets of the community to pick up garbage, enlisting friends to help in the cause, sponsoring some type of cookout afterward at the church for those who participated.
3. A 10k run/walk for the homeless—people in your church seek outsiders to sponsor them in a 10-kilometer run designed to raise money to feed, clothe and shelter the homeless people of your community.

These are only a few of the person-to-person types of programs churches might undertake to get more people acquainted with and interested in your church.

WOM ought to be recognized as a frontline form of media to be utilized by your church. Do not assume that effective WOM will happen on behalf of your church. People must be encouraged to use their relationships as a means of reaching people. They must be taught what information to convey and how best to convey it.

Other free media are impersonal and do not have nearly the punch of WOM, but can be used for good effect. Signs and posters placed in strategic locations, such as on bulletin boards in high-traffic, public places (public libraries, public schools or universities, shopping mall kiosks) can result in greater awareness of an event or organization. Handbills, the flyers handed out to people on the street or placed in shopping sacks by sympathetic merchants, can also have a positive effect.

Get Help

Knowing how to work your way through the media market is no simple task. New technologies are emerging all the time, using sophisticated measurement systems that provide complex statistics. And with the limited media budget your church probably has for communications, it is important to make the most of every opportunity and every cent available to you. It would be best to assign this area of marketing activity to someone who understands media marketing and who will provide consistent guidance for the church. Poor media marketing can quickly swallow your budget or communicate the wrong image or message. Take the media management process as seriously as you want the recipients of your message to take your church.

FOURTEEN

MARKETING COMMUNICATIONS: WHAT TO SAY, HOW TO SAY IT

WRITE the vision," God said to the prophet Habakkuk, "and make it plain" (Hab. 2:2, *KJV*). Nothing is more important for the success of your ministry than communicating clearly.

Creating the Communication Elements

Apart from decisions regarding what media to use, some key considerations in communications development will motivate the desired response among your target audience. These considerations include your headlines, the body copy, the illustrations and the offer. Other elements, such as the medium, the layout, typefaces and timing (as in seasonality) are also of importance. However, since most of these types of decisions can be made in conjunction with experts such as media buyers, we will concentrate on some of the elements that you will have a more direct influence upon.

The vast majority of advertising prepared for churches relies upon printed media for distribution—newspapers, direct mail, handbills and Yellow Pages. The guidelines that follow are offered with the print media in mind, although most of these principles apply to other media, such as radio and television, as well.

Headlines

Many respected marketers make no bones about their belief that the single, most important element of any persuasive communication effort is the headline. Some experts state that their own experience indicates that headlines are responsible for 50 to 75 percent of the success of their communications. Reams of research has been conducted to explore the impact of headlines. Here are several commonly held conclusions.

- Communications with a weak headline prevent the rest of the vehicle from gaining the desired exposure.
- A strong headline has the ability to cause hard-to-reach people to spend time investigating the information conveyed in the communication piece.
- A few proven rules help to develop strong headlines.

Here are some of the keys to creating a strong headline.

1. Stress *benefits* in your headline. We live in a benefit-driven society. People's time is short, so they cut to the heart of the issue and try to determine immediately if a message holds much promise of providing them with a desired benefit. Sensing no such compelling element, they will move on to the next piece of communication until some personal benefit of interest captures their attention. Make the appeal or offer clear and immediate, and describe how the person will be better off in life as a result of having your product or service. The headline is no place for subtlety.
2. The claim must be believable. Today's consumers have been burned often enough that they no longer take the claims of advertisers at face value. They are skeptical of all claims and only pursue those that appear to be valid. Whatever claim your headline makes must seem reasonable and must have the facts to back it up.

3. The key to grabbing the reader's attention is to appeal to their *self-interest*. Your headline can take several approaches: provide news, arouse curiosity, or appeal to a person's felt needs and personal interests. The best headlines manage to accomplish all three approaches; the most critical element of the three, however, is to underscore points of personal interest or need to the reader.

4. The most effective headlines are those that use *concise and simple language*. People sift through information quickly. An effective headline is one that uses a few well-chosen, direct, easy-to-understand words that grab them and pull them into the message. Ornate wording, excessive verbiage, scholarly language, pedantic prose serve no useful purpose. Create a headline that is direct rather than clever. Clever headlines often require too much energy to figure out, or they may intimate that the message is cute but fluffy. Most people do not take the time for such messages.

5. *Be positive*. People dislike negative advertising. Although a case can be made for its use, the research generally concludes that such approaches raise the prospect of conflict in the mind of the reader, causing the potential audience to steer clear of the situation. Alternatively, the negative slant may position the sender of that negative message to gain an image as being one who is confrontational, defensive or aggressive. These are not the attributes you want to have associated with your church.

How can you write great headlines? Study the ones that have a proven track record—the ones developed by successful direct mail copywriters and that get used over and over again because they work. When you write your headlines, do so with a clear sense of the purpose of the communication—to get people into your church, to make them read the Bible, to motivate people to join a small group Bible study, to get them to come to a community event and so on. Write a number of possible headlines, then select the best of the bunch. Then test it.

Which of these headlines would work better for a small church that wants to increase its Sunday morning attendance?

Discover What the Bible Says About Your Family

Visit Us This Sunday and Have the Greatest Worship Experience of Your Life

Both call for action. However, the second headline is long, is not credible and does not address a desired benefit. Granted, to people who know and love Jesus, the idea of a great worship service is inspiring. But the reason you are advertising is to reach those people for whom the concept of worship may mean little, and who certainly do not find worship services to be motivating enough to get them out of the house on Sunday morning. They need something more captivating.

The first headline would likely draw more people. It gets directly to the point and offers people a benefit of moderate to high perceived value. Most Americans believe the Bible is a good and useful book. However, they generally do not feel they know what it says—especially about something as important to them as their family. The headline promises that they will learn something of interest and something that is credible because it is based on the Bible.

Which of these headlines is most likely to draw better?

Don't Visit Our Church Unless You Want Your Life to Be Changed Forever!

Meet Some Neighbors Who Want to Know You

The first headline starts out negative. People like a challenge, but the challenge itself must be credible and compelling. The assumption underlying the headline is that the target audience does not like life—a bit presumptuous, and not supported by research. Further, the notion that attending a church will change a person's life forever is, from the perspective of the average consumer, a wild and unreasonable claim.

The second headline is shorter and addresses a felt need (loneliness) with a possible solution. It has no implied threat, only an opportunity to build relationships with people who are likely to be open and friendly. This is the type of image you could use most advantageously in developing your church's image.

Body Copy

"Body copy" is the term used to describe the wording used in the communication itself, apart from the headline or the captions under pictures or illustrations. If your headline is successful, people will examine the body copy for more information about the promise made in the headline.

Your opening sentences must be real grabbers. Again, because people are deluged with information they are looking for an excuse to reject your communication. If the headline is strong enough, they try the body copy; but if it does not immediately continue the same level of interest and personal gain, they will move on to their next task.

What makes body copy compelling?

- *Benefits.* Not only should the headline allude to specific benefits to be realized, but the body copy must really drive home the advantages of the product or service about which you are communicating.
- *Continuity with the headline.* Once your headline puts people in a specific frame of mind, or raises particular expectations, they read the body copy because they want further insight into the element to which you alluded. Do not disappoint them.
- *Emotional and intellectual information.* Provide people with a reason why, communicated with a sense of enthusiasm, excitement, passion and commitment.
- *Credible information* that supports the basic contentions made in your communication.
- *No fluff.* Copy that gets to the point, in an interesting but direct manner, captures people's attention and persuades them much more effectively than circuitous, flowery prose.

- *Depth of information.* People won't take the time to read volumes of information, neither are they moved by copy that is so brief and superficial that they only get a few morsels of information. In general, make sure the copy is long enough to communicate effectively the driving sales points, but concise enough to ensure that they will read what you have written.

Some helpful writing hints are: (1) avoid negative copy, (2) do not mention the names of your competitors, (3) write the copy with a specific audience in mind (perhaps you could establish a composite person in your mind whose character and values represent the target audience), (4) urge the reader to take swift and specific action, (5) create the copy when you feel energetic, fresh and excited about the product or service.

Using *subheads* in the body copy is one of the most effective tools available. When beginning a new section in your body copy, or making a key point, the use of a subhead will call attention to that item. Research has shown that many people read the headline, scan the subheads, and look at the illustrations and captions before making a decision to read the body copy itself.

Visuals

I doubt that the person who first said "a picture is worth a thousand words" literally meant one thousand words, but even in our over-communicated, ad-cluttered society, pictures have retained their ability to slice through the clutter and drive home their point. Testing of a wide range of communications formats, styles, copy strategies and visual presentations consistently finds that visuals are among the most effective means of communicating with people.

If at all possible, strive to include some illustrations in your printed communications. This might involve photographs, drawings, charts and graphs, or other types of pictures. Make sure that the illustrations you use are clearly connected to a key sales point you wish to make. And always use captions for your pictures. Some of the research we have conducted for Fortune 500 companies has underscored the importance of captions. The sentence or two that gets printed beneath an illustration invariably gets read by the consumer, making that wording a prime opportunity for emphasizing a significant fact your target audience needs to know.

The types of pictures best suited to advertising or communications meant to persuade are pictures of people, pictures of the product being used or a demonstration of the benefit received from someone who has made use of the product. It seems that the pictures still most capable of arresting people's attention are those of children and animals.

Extensive testing of illustrations reveals that when pictures of men are used, men are the ones most likely to examine the picture and accompanying copy. When pictures of women are used, women are the most likely audience. Why? Apparently, the picture is a signal that the information is geared to people like themselves. The picture helps the person to discern, quickly, whether or not the message is targeted to them.

> **"The great enemy of clear language is insincerity. When there is a gap between one's real and one's declared aims, one turns, as it were, instinctively to long words and exhausted idioms, like a cuttlefish squirming out of ink."**
>
> Author George Orwell

The exception, of course, is when the picture is revealing not a person but a sexual allusion. The beer commercials that feature scantily-clad women parading up and down beaches are fairly good at gaining the attention of men, but seem surprisingly inadequate at closing the sale for the product. If the point of the advertising is to earn product recall and increase sales potential, this approach is probably not advisable. Selling through sex is certainly not an appropriate strategy for a church.

Other Considerations

Many other elements can be studied regarding your advertising. Here are a few to keep in mind.

- *Typeface.* The style of type should be legible. The point size sufficient to allow people from your target audience to read it with ease. Use of bold and emphasized type should be sparce but strategic.
- *Layout.* Strive for a professional, clean, flowing, uncluttered look. The placement of the illustrations, the amount of white

space and the distribution of the copy should be intelligent, built around ease of reading and stand out as attractive.

- *Color.* Color can help or hinder your print communications. Black and white pieces can communicate more effectively than high-cost four-color pieces, if the technique is used properly. Work with a good artist who has a great sense of color and spacing to achieve the desired effect for the lowest budget. Consider combinations that save money and capture attention, such as use of one or two ink colors, achieving a third color by using a tinted paper stock.

- *Seasonality.* At certain times of the year people make decisions about certain products or services. People do not need to hear about VBS programs in the winter, nor is anything achieved by mounting school enrollment programs in the fall. People have already made their decisions and have just begun the new school year. Launching membership drives during the late spring or during the summer months is usually disastrous. No matter how good your materials are, recognize the decision-making calendar on which people operate.

- *List reliability.* If you conduct a direct mail campaign and rent a list (i.e. mailing labels) from a list broker, make sure the list is continually being updated, and that the original source is reliable. Some lists are compiled—pieced together from several other lists. Others are original—developed by the list owner from original research. Sometimes, rented lists are updated by the owner just once a year, which means that up to 20 percent or so may be outdated by the tail end of the year since 15 to 20 percent of the population changes location each year.

Mixing Media

Most communications experts will tell you that your best media strategy is one that relies upon a blend of several media to reach your desired audience. This multi-media strategy enables you to reach people in different contexts, with different messages geared to making the same impact and retards the potential for commercial wearout.

After you have identified what your media budget will be and who your target audience is, use the available research to create a media plan that will provide the most cost-efficient means of reaching your target group as many times as possible. If you can major on targeted media, do so. If you can use mass media to your advantage, without cheating your marketing effort financially, pursue those opportunities. The important thing is not which media you choose, but what outcomes result from your choices.

Testing Your Message and Creative Presentation

One of the central tenets of effective communication is testing. Just as the three core principles of real estate are location, location, location, the central principles around which influential communications are built are testing, testing, testing.

Two methods of testing are informal testing and formal testing. Your best strategy is to employ as many methods of testing your communications as possible. Remember, with many people in your target group you will have just one chance to persuade them to take the action or embrace the perspective that you desire. It is in your best interests to maximize that opportunity by using the strongest possible communications.

Suppose you have written a mail piece or a newspaper advertisement. How might you test that communication vehicle? Try these approaches.

1. After you have written the piece, let it sit for one or two days, then come back to it. Having a fresh perspective, you can more objectively evaluate whether the piece adequately conveys the key points you wish to put before your target audience.
2. Have someone else read your headline and body copy out

loud to you. As you hear the words you can get a perspective different from when you stare at them on the page at your desk. As the reader stumbles through certain sections you can be fairly confident that the difficulty is the wording, not their reading ability. After you have made your own notes ask them for their opinion of the copy.

3. A more formal approach to testing might be to seek the opinions of people who might be part of the target audience. Focus groups are an ideal means of having your target audience respond to the communication. (See chapter 5 for more information on this research technique.)

4. You might attempt a real-world evaluation by conducting an in-market test. If you wish to evaluate your direct mail, for instance, you might divide your mailing list in half, randomly, and send two different versions of a communication, each version to half the list. By including some way of tracking the response, you can determine which approach worked better. In such testing, limit the test variables to a single item so that you know what caused the variation. In other words, if you send out a self-mailer (i.e. brochure) that has the same body copy but different headlines, you can determine which headline was more effective. If you sent out two entirely different brochures—different headlines, illustrations, body copy, paper stock, size, typefaces—you would know which brochure was more effective, but would not have any idea why. Next time you develop a brochure for a direct mail campaign, you would be no wiser than before regarding what elements are most useful when trying to persuade your target audience.

Similarly, you can test your communications that might run in newspapers or magazines by split-run testing (putting one version of an ad in half of the printed editions, the other version in the other half).

Ultimately, your testing should enhance the impact of your communications. In chart 19 are some of the most common mistakes made in communicating with your target audience—mistakes you can avoid in the creative stages of developing your campaign, or that may be detected through your testing of a finished product.

Public Relations

Another media-driven approach to communicating with your target audience is to make use of the media through an editorial focus. This might entail getting news releases published or having feature articles written about the church and its people. These approaches cost little but can reap enormous benefits because the dissemination of the information by the media appears to bear their stamp of approval.

At a minimum, your church should have a special mailing list of all of the mass media outlets that reach your community. This includes all of the newspapers, television stations and radio stations that serve your area. You should be sending them news releases on a regular basis about key news or events related to your ministry. You would be surprised at how often a professionally written, sharp-looking news release will see the light of day in the media (especially local newspapers).

What is newsworthy about your church? The following are some typical items that formed the basis of news releases sent by churches to local media, and were picked up for coverage by these media.

- Creation of a recycling station located in the church parking lot. Anyone with recyclable materials could drop off these materials for collection.
- Hiring of a new pastor or associate pastor including information about his or her background and new responsibilities.
- Plans for expanding or renovating the church buildings and facilities.
- A special event, such as a concert, speech or other presentation, to be delivered by a person of repute.
- Awards or commendations bestowed upon the church, its

CHART 19
20 Common but Avoidable Mistakes Made in Church Communications

1. Promoting the features of your product or service rather than its benefits to the target audience.

2. Advertising benefits that are of little importance to your target audience.

3. Seeking creative development (or approval) from a committee rather than from one or a small number of individuals who are very focused on the task at hand.

4. Operating with unrealistic expectations in mind regarding the ability of your communications to reach the audience and persuade them to act as desired.

5. Promising more than your church is likely to deliver.

6. Attempting to have an impact through communications with a budget that is too small.

7. Not getting the message in front of the target audience often enough; single-exposure communications have limited impact.

8. Trying to be too creative. The communications that win awards are often not the ads that result in effective communication.

9. Imitating the communications efforts of other churches and ministries.

10. Making fun of the audience: Regardless of your intentions, the audience is notoriously thin-skinned.

11. Entertaining instead of selling people on your main idea.

12. Engaging in negative advertising: People often remember the negativity rather than the positive solution you are offering.

13. Failure to gain objective feedback on how the target audience responds to the message and its execution.

14. Using the wrong medium to convey the information to the intended audience.

15. Focusing your copy on the product or service rather than upon your audience.

16. Setting arbitrary limits on the amount of copy rather than using as much copy as it takes to efficiently make your point.

17. Using the wrong appeal: When you don't know the audience intimately, sometimes it's easy to misjudge what they perceive to be the most attractive appeal.

18. Complexity: The most effective communications are those which demonstrate simplicity in form and content.

19. Failure to arouse people's curiosity.

20. Confusing graphics: People will not make the time to disentangle that which appears convolluted.

leaders or its members by some outside organization such as an association, a denomination or a government agency.

- Publication of a new book by the church's pastor, including a synopsis of why the book was written and the central thesis of that book.
- A schedule of Easter or Christmas services, along with announcements regarding related events or services (such as child care).
- A trip to a foreign country, as a short-term missions project, taken by a staff member and members of the church. The release described their experience at the site and the impact it made on their lives. A few pictures, taken by one of the individuals on the trip, made this into a high-profile story.
- A retrospective of the life of the church on its 50th birthday.

The events or circumstances you propose for release through your local media will vary, of course. However, realize that as part of the community, if something is taking place within the life of your church, it may well be deemed newsworthy by your local media. It is in your best interests to find out. Not everything you present to the media will be covered, but the fact that you gain free exposure to a wide audience with the apparent sanction of the media makes the effort well worth your while.

In some cases, the news releases sent to the media were not used immediately, but were held for use in a larger, related story at a later date. In other cases, the news release itself was not used, but the media made a note of the name of the church's pastor as a person who was a local expert and an involved person regarding a local issue of importance. The pastor was contacted regularly for a "Christian viewpoint" on that issue, generating very positive coverage for the church, positioning it as a socially active and concerned body.

Another reason for getting to know the people in the media locally is that they possess much useful information that could benefit the church as it develops programs and marketing concepts. The media leaders are also key gatekeepers in the community. Getting to know them personally not only enhances your chances of gaining exposure through their medium, but also enables you to influence their views on issues. Since the media has such a profound impact on what people believe and the life-styles they embrace, influencing these gatekeepers is, in itself, a viable and powerful ministry, if handled properly.

Writing a News Release

There is no uniform or "right" way to write a news release. However, plenty of gaffes can be avoided by knowing and attending to a few simple rules.

Every day, journalists are flooded with news releases. At a recent seminar of editors and journalists from leading newspapers, radio and television stations, the word came through loud and clear to the nonprofit organizations that comprised the audience: "Don't waste our time with unprofessional, trite, poorly conceived communications." The media rely, in part, on organizations to alert them to newsworthy situations, but they are also sensitive to being used for the organization's purposes. Their task is to provide news and perspective, and they are happy to get help in their job; but they are cautious about relying on information of low credibility.

One study suggested that the average news release receives less than two seconds of time from the journalist who receives it. This means that your release must be a winner from start to finish—in appearance, format, content and audience selection. Here are a few ideas for you to consider as you create news releases.

- Create a special letterhead for news releases sent from your church. Sending your releases on your church stationery may have the effect of either turning off journalists not predisposed to churches, or appearing too much like a letter, rather than a piece of mail designed to make the job of the journalist easier. The large letters at the top of the page (or running vertically along the left margin of the page) should spell out "news release" to clarify the purpose of the correspondence.
- Provide a brief synopsis of the key information in a one or two sentence opening statement preceding the title. This

frames the issue for the journalist and enables him to quickly pick up the direction of the piece.

- Write the release in journalistic style: Begin with the most important information and work your way through to the least important factors.
- Whenever pertinent and possible, provide photographs that would make the story more newsworthy or appealing to the reader. If photos are available but not accompanying the release, indicate that photos are available upon request.
- Limit the length of the release. If the story is hot, the journalist will follow up for more information. The key for the release is to capture the attention of the journalist. Be sure to provide the name and telephone number where a responsible contact person can be reached should the reporter require additional information.
- Include quotes from pertinent individuals if possible and relevant. This personalizes the story and saves the reporter from having to make the necessary calls and conduct an interview.
- If the information has a time element when it can be released, that date should be noted at the very start of the release with a phrase such as FOR RELEASE ON JANUARY 25. Otherwise, it is helpful to use the phrase FOR IMMEDIATE RELEASE at the beginning of the release.
- If the release concerns something of a theological or spiritual nature, cleanse the copy of terminology that only the ecclesiastical crowd will recognize. The media are in business to communicate effectively with the common person. Inserting terms that such people are unlikely to comprehend will earn the release a rapid and unceremonial death.

If you decide to use news releases to communicate with the community, you might request a brief appointment with the news editors of the local newspapers and radio stations. Bring a sample release with you and get the editors' reaction to it. Each person has a preferred style, and learning how to meet the needs of the information gatekeepers can help both parties. During the meeting you should ask questions that will help you work within the media outlet's system more effectively: (1) the slowest news days, (2) the best person to send your releases to, (3) the best way to send your releases, (4) specific elements to include or avoid, and so forth.

News Events

On occasion, your church will engage in some type of event that might be newsworthy. Take advantage of the opportunity for media coverage by calling the local news bureaus and inviting them to the event. It might be a news conference in which a church representative announces some type of action, or some momentous activity takes place:

1. A church boycott of a store;
2. The donation of a large sum of money to a community charity;
3. Announcement that the pastor is running for elected office;
4. An official statement regarding the impact of a local policy;
5. The opening of a new facility;
6. The retirement ceremony for a revered, long-term pastor;
7. A community-wide family event that draws a thousand people.

Because these events consist of important information of interest to the community, the media may send a reporter to cover the event. The free exposure you receive can be invaluable. If you have the ability, and the event warrants the effort, you may prepare a press packet for members of the press who attend. The packet might include the text of any verbal presentation that is made, a pertinent photo for media use, a backgrounder (which is a brief report providing the background details related to the central issue), and other documents or materials that might help reporters get a clear understanding of, and useful angle on the story.

Get Your Message Across

At the start of the marketing process, as you think about the awesome challenge of getting your message across to your target market, that task may seem overwhelming. That is a natural initial reaction. It *is* an awesome task to communicate clearly, just as it is to preach a clear and motivating sermon or to teach a captivating and life-changing Sunday School lesson. But the potential impact of your marketing communications is no less significant—and no more difficult. It will take planning, careful reflection, toying with different strategies, and testing your efforts on small but reliable groups of people before going full speed ahead with a final product.

God has provided your church with the tools, the techniques and the technicians to get the word out to your target audience about your church. Your task is to pull those resources together and provide sufficient guidance to see the process maximize its productivity. Like many of your church colleagues around the country, you will reap the joy of knowing you are getting through to people when you have figured out how the marketing communications process can be another invaluable tool in your ministry toolbox.

APPENDIX 1—NINE BIBLE STUDIES:
A BIBLICAL PERSPECTIVE ON MARKETING YOUR MINISTRY

THE following Bible studies shed light on what Scripture shows about marketing a church's ministries in order to reach its community effectively with the gospel. Each study has been designed for individual or group use during a 40- to 60-minute session. The questions in each study are intended to help you and your group find out for yourselves what the scriptural passage says in its own context, how it relates to key principles of marketing a church's ministries, and how you can apply what you have learned to your church's ministries.

The Bible studies cover four themes that are key elements in helping your church market its ministry and impact its community more effectively with the gospel:

One idea would be to use these studies in a one- or two-day retreat with your leadership team to share God's call to vision.

Other ways to break down barriers to vision in your church:

- Help organize a home Bible study based on the concepts of vision found in this book; include the following Bible studies as a foundation for the study.
- Encourage the formation of a prayer team that intercedes for you as you search for God's vision in your ministry.

BIBLE STUDIES

God and Change in Marketing a Church's Ministry (4 studies)

   I. Our Unchanging God
   II. Serving God Through Change: Making Ministry Relevant to Your Community
   III. Changing Ministry to Meet People at Their Point of Need with the Gospel
   IV. Change in the Way Paul Acts and Communicates the Gospel to Two Different Groups

Vision and Marketing a Church's Ministry (3 studies)

   V. Vision and Visionary Leadership in the Old Testament
   VI. Vision and Visionary Leadership in the New Testament
   VII. Receiving God's Vision for Your Ministry

Planning and Marketing a Church's Ministry (1 study)

   VIII. Strategic Planning for Effective Ministry

Evaluation and Marketing a Church's Ministry (1 study)

   IX. Evaluating the Effectiveness of Ministry

God and Change in Marketing a Church's Ministry

I. Our Unchanging God

Change is difficult, especially when it seems to be out of control. In the midst of life's changes, God's unchanging faithfulness acts as an anchor for our soul (Jas. 1:17; Heb. 13:8). The term "immutability" has been used by theologians to denote God's unchanging and perfect nature. The following passages underscore the fact that our God is unchanging and faithful.

A. Read the following verses and briefly summarize in your own words what the passage says about God's unchanging nature.

Numbers 23:19,20

1 Samuel 15:29

Psalm 110:4

Malachi 3:6

Hebrews 7:12, 21

Hebrews 13:8

James 1:17

B. Can a man remove the blessings of God? Why or why not? Which of the above passages answer this question?

C. What do the above passages say about God's character? How is He different from us? Who is the author of change?

D. Psalm 102:23-28. According to this passage, which things change? What does not change? What kind of person will endure through changes according to Psalm 102:24,28? What does it mean to you to be the Lord's servant (102:24)?

II. Serving God Through Change: Making Ministry Relevant to the Community

Read 1 Corinthians 9:15-23.

A. In 1 Corinthians 9:1-14 Paul tells the Corinthians he and his fellow workers have a right to receive financial and material support from them for his work among them. Why didn't Paul claim the support he deserved for preaching the gospel according to 1 Corinthians 9:16 (see Acts 9:1-16; 26:16-18)?

B. How did Paul change the way he ministered for the sake of those he ministered to (1 Cor. 9:18; Acts 18:3; 1 Cor. 4:11,12; 1 Thess. 2:9)? What barrier was Paul removing from his ministry (1 Cor. 9:15,18)?

C. What barriers can you identify that keep you from implementing the vision for ministry God has given you and your church?

D. What does Paul mean by saying he has become a slave to every-one (1 Cor. 9:19)?

E. First Corinthians 9:22 suggests that Paul made himself and his ministry relevant to the needs and interests of those he preached the gospel to. (Compare Paul's effort to reach a Gentile audience in Acts 17:22-31 and a Jewish audience in Acts 22.) Does this mean that Paul compromised the gospel? If he did not change the message and content of the gospel, what did he change?

F. What purpose does Paul give for changing or adapting his actions and the way he communicates the gospel to one group or another (1 Cor. 9:22)? Why is Paul "all things to all men"?

G. Though Paul says he has "become all things to all men" (1 Cor. 9:22), which specific group of people did God give Paul a vision to reach with the gospel (see Acts 9:15; 22:21; Rom. 11:13; 15:15f.; Gal. 1:16)?

H. Though God wants you to be sensitive to every group of people in your community, which particular group or groups might He be giving you a vision to reach with the gospel?

I. How would you describe Paul's philosophy of ministry in 1 Corinthians 9:15-23? Is he sensitive to culture without compromising the truth?

J. What changes would be involved if you and your church tried, like Paul, to make your ministry relevant to the group of people God has given you a vision to reach for Christ?

III. Changing Ministry to Meet People at Their Point of Need with the Gospel

How much should a church's ministry be adapted to the needs and interests of its community? Is God concerned about how relevant a church's way of doing ministry is to the community? The following passages help answer these questions.

Read Luke 7:29-35.

A. Who is represented by the children who played the flute and who sang a dirge in the marketplace?

B. Was the message of the gospel that God spoke through John the Baptist the same or different from that which He spoke through Jesus? Compare Matthew 3:1 and 4:17.

C. Were the styles of ministry of Jesus and John the Baptist the same or different (Luke 7:33,34)?

D. Which aspect of the gospel did Jesus emphasize (see Matt. 9:13; 12:7; Luke 10:37)? Which did John the Baptist emphasize (see Matt. 3:7-12; Luke 3:7-9)?

E. Did Jesus or John the Baptist compromise the gospel through the different strategies they used to communicate the gospel to their target audiences?

F. How were the target audiences of Jesus and John the Baptist similar or different? What level of faith or background in faith did the crowds have who went out to the Jordan river to listen to John (Luke 3:8,15)? How were those that Jesus spent time with and ministered to different (Luke 7:34)?

G. Which group would correspond to churched people in our society today? Which would correspond to the unchurched?

Read Matthew 4:23-25; 8:14-17; 9:35-38; Mark 1:29-34,38,39.

H. How did Jesus meet men and women at their point of need through preaching and teaching the gospel of the Kingdom of God?

I. How did Jesus' ministry of healing demonstrate to His audience that God's Kingdom is near (Mark 1:15; Matt. 11:2-5; Luke 4:18,19)?

Read Matthew 10:1-8; 28:18-20; Luke 9:1-6; 10:1-16.

J. Is the way that Jesus commanded His disciples to teach and minister the gospel similar or different from the way He Himself taught it and ministered it?

Read Matthew 12:22-28; 14:15-21.

K. How did Jesus illustrate His teaching about the Kingdom of God in Matthew 12:22-28 in such a way that it met the blind and mute man at his point of need?

L. What did Jesus do in Matthew 14:15-21 to meet the hungry crowds at their point of need? Which teaching about the Kingdom was Jesus illustrating (Matt. 6:25,26,33)?

IV. Change in the Way Paul Acts and Communicates the Gospel to Two Different Groups

Read Acts 17:22-31.

A. How did Paul make the gospel relevant to the Athenians? How did Paul use topics they were interested in to introduce the living God and Jesus Christ to them (Acts 17:22-23)?

B. What illustration did Paul use in Acts 17:28 that showed his listeners he was conversant with their culture and their way of thinking?

C. What two activities made Paul familiar with his target audience (Acts 17:23,28)?

D. What are two ways you and your church might familiarize yourself with the target group God has given you a vision to reach with the gospel?

Read Acts 21:17-26; 21:40-22:21.

E. Before Paul witnessed about Jesus to his Jewish countrymen in the Temple in Jerusalem, what did he do (Acts 21:23-26)? How did he become like them?

F. Does the fact that Paul observed purification rites to show respect for the law (his countrymen's traditions) mean that he believed he was under the law (saved by the law)? (See 1 Cor. 9:20; Rom. 6:14; Gal. 5:18.)

G. What activity can you and your church engage in that shows your community or target group that you respect and care for the issues they care about?

H. How did Paul make his message about Jesus relevant to his Jewish countrymen? What cultural handles did he use to make his message relevant to them (Acts 21:40; 22:2,3,12)?

I. What cultural handles can you use to make the living God and Jesus Christ relevant to the group God has given you a vision to reach? What are they interested in? What do they find important? How can you, like Paul, frame the gospel in words and concepts relevant to them?

Vision and Marketing a Church's Ministry

V. Vision and Visionary Leadership in the Old Testament

Read Proverbs 29:18.

The *King James Version* translates Proverbs 29:18, "Where there is no vision, the people perish." The *New International Version* renders the verse, "Where there is no revelation, the people cast off restraint." The Hebrew word *khazon* in Proverbs 29:18 is variously translated "vision" *(KJV, NASB)*, "prophecy" *(RSV)*, and "revelation" *(NIV)*. Each of these translations underscores the fact that true vision comes only from the Lord.

A. Compare the various translations of Proverbs 29:18 *(KJV, NIV, NASB,* etc.) and rewrite the verse in your own words.

B. What does this verse say about why you and your church need God's vision for your ministry?

From the following passages of the Old Testament, what can be learned from these people about how the vision God gave them affected their lives?

C. Abraham in Genesis 12:1-3; 15:1-7; 17:1-15. Why did God state and restate three times the vision He gave Abraham? What circumstances and plans in Abraham's life were affected and changed by God's vision for him on each occasion?

D. Moses in Exodus 3:1-10. How much strategic detail did God add to the vision He gave Moses (Exod. 3:11-22; 4:1-17)?

E. Joshua in Joshua 1:1-5. How much detail is included in God's vision for Joshua about the direction and goals of God's plan to lead Israel into the Promised Land? How is the additional direction from the Lord in Joshua 1:6-9 related to the vision in 1:1-5? How important to the vision was identifying and marshalling resources (Josh. 1:10-15), information gathering (Josh. 2:1, 22-24), and strategic planning (Josh. 3:1-4; 6:1-7)?

F. Nehemiah in Nehemiah 2:12. How did Nehemiah receive a vision from the Lord to rebuild the city of Jerusalem (Neh. 1:3,4; 2:4,5)?

G. David in 1 Samuel 17:34-37,45-48. What attitudes and qualities did David's vision of God's plan for Israel inspire in him (1 Sam. 23:15-18)? What attitudes should the vision for ministry God gives you and your church inspire in you?

H. How did God's vision for each of the following prophets cause the prophet to change the way he lived and ministered?

Isaiah 1:1; 6:1-10

Jeremiah 1:4-19

Ezekiel 1:1-28; 2:1-10; 3:4-9

VI. Vision and Visionary Leadership in the New Testament

From the following passages of the New Testament, what can be learned from these people about how the vision God gave them affected their lives?

A. Jesus' vision for ministry to the early church in Acts 1:4-8. What specific vision had God given His people that began to be fulfilled and implemented on Pentecost in Acts 2:14-22? How was this event related to the vision Jesus gave the Church in Acts 1:4-8?

B. Paul's vision for ministry in Acts 9:15; 26:15-23. How did the vision God gave Paul affect the way he lived and ministered (2 Cor. 11:23-28)?

C. Peter's vision for ministry in Acts 10:9-16; 11:4-18. How did God's vision for Peter to evangelize Gentiles restate and underscore Jesus' vision for the ministry and outreach of the early church in Acts 1:8? How did it change Peter's plans for evangelism?

D. How was Paul's ministry affected by continuing to receive strategic direction from God in Acts 16:9,10 and 18:9? What does this suggest about continuing to consult God as you implement the vision for ministry He has given you and your church (see Prov. 3:6)?

E. What conclusions can be drawn from these New Testament passages about the way God uses vision?

F. Does God give men who are visionary leaders or prophets to the Church today? Read Ephesians 4:11. Has God left us without vision today?

G. What vision for ministry do you feel God may be giving you and your church?

H. What vision for ministry did God give His Church in Matthew 28:18-20; Luke 24:46-49; Acts 1:8? (Compare Matt. 10:1-8 with 28:18-20; also see Luke 9:1-6; 10:1-16; Mark 16:15-20.) How much strategic detail is included in these passages?

VII. Receiving God's Vision for Your Ministry

How did the early church receive its vision for ministry from God? One account recorded in Acts occurred in A.D. 47 in the city of Antioch in Syria.

Read Acts 13:1-3.

A. What is the Church doing as the passage unfolds? Describe in your own words what worship is (Luke 24:52,53; Acts 1:14; 2:42,47; Eph. 5:18-20; Col. 3:16); what fasting is (2 Chron. 20:3,4; Acts 14:23).

B. Who was present? Note names. What do these names tell us? What kinds of people are found within the Church?

C. What is the significance of the Holy Spirit's saying "Set them apart"? (Acts 13:2). What is the significance of the laying on of hands?

D. What are some of the tasks of the Church according to this passage?

E. What vision does God's Spirit give to the church of Antioch with regard to the work to which He called Paul and Barnabas (see Acts 13:2; 19:15; 22:21; 26:16-18)?

F. Has God given you and your church a vision through pointing to a certain person or persons whom He has gifted and given a burden for a particular ministry?

G. Once the Holy Spirit's direction was stated in Acts 13:2, what did the Church do in 13:3?

H. Were the actions in Acts 13:3 seeking confirmation of the message, or do they reflect hesitation on the part of the church?

I. What do you feel is the most significant point today's church should learn from this historical event in Acts 13:1-3?

J. What do James 4:13-15 and Proverbs 3:6 show about implementing and maintaining the vision for ministry God has given you and your church? How does ongoing prayer fit into this process (Phil. 4:4-7; Eph. 5:18)?

Planning and Marketing a Church's Ministry

VIII. Strategic Planning for Effective Ministry

How important is strategic planning to effective ministry? What did Jesus have to say about planning? The following passages offer some insight into these questions.

Read Matthew 25:1-13.

A. How are the virgins in the parable similar? How are they different from one another?

B. What is the main point of the parable?

C. How is the readiness of the wise virgins related to planning in this parable? How did awareness of their surroundings and circumstances contribute to the planning of the wise virgins?

Read Matthew 25:14-30.

D. What response did the master make to his servants? Compare his response to each of the three servants. Why is it similar or different? Who failed and why?

E. How many of their talents were the faithful servants willing to risk and invest to get a return? Why was the servant with the one talent afraid to risk investing his talent? What does this show about God's desire for us to risk with Him in ministry?

F. How is risk related to strategic planning in the parable? How much are you willing to risk to implement the vision for ministry God has given you and your church?

G. How are faith in God and risk related (Matt. 14:27-31)?

H. What feeling or attitude can undercut strategic planning and risk-taking faith in God (Matt. 14:26)?

Read Luke 14:27-33.

I. What does Jesus say will be said about the person who starts something and does not complete it due to the lack of planning?

J. What does discipleship have in common with the concept of planning?

K. How is evaluating available resources and the surrounding circumstances related to effective planning in the parable? How can identifying the resources and giftedness available to your church and evaluating your church's community help you plan for effective ministry to your community?

Evaluation and Marketing a Church's Ministry

IX. Evaluating the Effectiveness of Ministry

Scripture shows that judgment is good when we allow it to give direction and guidance to our lives. In 1 Corinthians 11, Paul tells us to examine or judge ourselves and our attitudes before we partake of the Lord's Supper. What place is judgment or evaluation to have in our lives and in the life of a church? The following passages shed light on this question.

Read Proverbs 27:23-27.

A. Paraphrase Proverbs 27:23-27 using your own words to express what you feel the meaning of the passage is.

B. How do the statements of 27:24-27 explain the benefits of knowing "the condition of your flocks" and giving "careful attention to your herds"?

C. What benefits would come from knowing the condition of your church's programs and from giving attention to the effectiveness of its ministries?

Read Mark 6:7-13,30.

D. How specific was the vision and direction Jesus gave the Twelve before sending them out? How was this related to the effectiveness of their ministry?

E. After their mission, what did the Twelve do? Why is it important that they reported back to Jesus?

F. What two things did they report about to Jesus? How was what they did related to what they taught?

Read Acts 14:27,28.

G. What did Paul and Barnabas do? What did they report back? Why did they do this?

H. What do Mark 6:7-13,30 and Acts 14:27,28 show about the importance of evaluating ministry?

I. What can be gleaned from the following passages about the importance of evaluation and about the principles of evaluation?

Philippians 1:27

Colossians 4:7,8

3 John 1:4

1 Thessalonians 3:6

APPENDIX 2

SOURCES OF SECONDARY INFORMATION

Sources of Secondary Data and Cultural Trends

There are many sources of secondary data. Those listed below are among the most reliable sources for national data.

Magazines

American Demographics, 108 N. Cayuga St., Ithaca, NY 14850.

The Futurist, World Future Society, 4916 St. Elmo Avenue, Bethesda, MD 20814.

Advertising Age, Crain Communications, 740 Rush St., Chicago, IL 60611.

Marketing Week, A/S/M Communications, 49 E. 21st St., New York, NY 10010.

The Public Perspective, The Roper Center, P.O. Box 440, Storrs, CT 06268-0440.

Newsletters

Ministry Currents, Barna Research Group, P.O. Box 4152, Glendale, CA 91222-0152.

Emerging Trends, Princeton Religious Research Center, P.O. Box 389, Princeton, NJ 08542.

National and International Religion Report, Wike & Associates, P.O. Box 5139, Springfield, VA 22150.

research alert, Alert Publishing, 37-06 30th Avenue, Long Island City, NY 11103.

Source, Search Institute, 122 W. Franklin, Suite 525, Minneapolis, MN 55404.

State Data Centers

Every state has a center that contains census data and state-collected information pertaining to the population and commerce of that state. Each data center operates differently and provides a variety of services to qualified users. To determine what the data center in your state has to offer, an address is provided for you to contact.

AL: Univ. of Alabama, P.O. Box AK, Tuscaloosa, AL 35487.

AK: Dept. of Labor, P.O. Box 25504, Juneau, AK 99802.

AZ: Dept. of Economic Security, Population Statistics Unit 1, 300 W. Washington, 1st floor, P.O. Box 6123, Site Code 045Z, Phoenix, AZ 85005.

AR: Univ. of Arkansas, 2801 South University, Little Rock, AR 72204.

CA: Population Research Unit, Dept. of Finance, 1025 P Street, Sacramento, CA 95814.

CO: Div. of Local Government, Dept. of Local Affairs, 1313 Sherman Street, Room 520, Denver, CO 80203.

CT: Comprehensive Planning Div., Office of Policy and Management, 80 Washington Street, Hartford, CT 06106.

DE: Delaware Development Office, 99 Kings Highway, P.O. Box 1401, Dover, DE 19903.

FL: Office of Planning and Budget, The Capitol, Tallahassee, FL 32301.

GA: Office of Planning and Budget, 270 Washington Street SW, Room 608, Atlanta, GA 30334.

HI: EDP Division, Dept. of Budget and Finance, 1151 Punchbowl Street, Honolulu, HI 96813.

ID: Dept. of Commerce, 700 W. State Street, Boise, ID 83720.

IL: State Data Center, Bureau of the Budget, Stratton Bldg., Room 605, Springfield, IL 62706.

IN: State Library, State Data Center, 140 North Senate Avenue, Indianapolis, IN 46204.

IA: Census Services, Iowa State Univ., 318 East Hall, Ames, IA 50011.

KS: State Library, State Capitol Bldg., Room 343, Topeka, KS 66612.

KY: State Data Center, Urban Studies Center, University of Louisville, Louisville, KY 40292.

LA: State Planning Office, P.O. Box 44426, Baton Rouge, LA 70804.

ME: Div. of Economic Analysis and Research, Dept. of Labor, 20 Union Street, Augusta, ME 04330.

MD: Dept. of State Planning, 301 W. Preston Street, Baltimore, MD 21201.

MA: Center for Massachusetts Data, Div. of Community Services, Executive Office of Communities and Development, 100 Cambridge Street, Boston, MA 02202.

MI: Michigan Information Center, Michigan Dept. of Management and Budget, Office of Revenue and Tax Analysis, P.O. Box 30026, Lansing, MI 48909.

MN: Minn. Analysis and Planning System, Univ. of Minnesota, 475 Coffey Hall, St. Paul, MN 55108.

MS: Center for Population Studies, Univ. of Mississippi, Bondurant Bldg., Room 3W, University, MS 38677.

MO: Missouri State Library, 2002 Missouri Blvd., Jefferson City, MO 65101.

MT: Census and Economic Information Center, Dept. of Commerce, Capital Station, 1424 Ninth Avenue, Helena, MT 59620.

NE: Bureau of Business Research, College of Business Administration, Univ. of Nebraska, Lincoln, NE 68588.

NV: State Library, Capitol Complex, 401 N. Carson, Carson City, NV 89710.

NH: Office of State Planning, 2½ Beacon Street, Concord, NH 03301.

NJ: Office of Demographic and Economic Analysis, Dept. of Labor, CN388, John Fitch Plaza, Trenton, NJ 08625.

NM: Economic Development and Tourism Dept., Bataan Memorial Bldg., Santa Fe, NM 87503.

NY: Dept. of Economic Development, One Commerce Plaza, Room 905, Albany, NY 12245.

NC: Office of State Budget and Management, 116 W. Jones Street, Raleigh, NC 27603.

ND: State Census Data Center, P.O. Box 5636, North Dakota State University, Fargo, ND 58105.

OH: Data Users Center, Dept. of Development, Box 1001, Columbus, OH 43216.

OK: State Data Center, Dept. of Commerce, 6601 Broadway Extension, Oklahoma City, OK 73116.

OR: Center for Population Research and Census, Portland State Univ., P.O. Box 751, Portland, OR 97207.

PA: State Data Center, Institute of State and Regional Affairs, Penn State Univ., The Capital College, Middletown, PA 17057.

RI: Statewide Planning Program, 265 Melrose Street, Room 203, Providence, RI 02907.

SC: Div. of Research and Statistics, State Budget and Control Board, Rembert Dennis Bldg., Room 337, 1000 Assembly Street, Columbia, SC 29201.

SD: Business Research Bureau, School of Business, Patterson Hall, 414 E. Clark, Univ. of South Dakota, Vermillion, SD 57069.

TN: State Planning Office, John Sevier State Bldg., 500 Charlotte Avenue, Suite 309, Nashville, TN 37219.

TX: State Data Center, P.O. Box 12728, Capitol Station, Austin, TX 78711.

UT: Office of Planning and Budget, State Capitol Bldg., Room 116, Salt Lake City, UT 84114.

VT: Policy Research and Coordination Staff, Pavillion Office Bldg., 109 State Street, Montpelier, VT 05602.

VA: Dept. of Planning and Budget, 445 Ninth Street Office Bldg., P.O. Box 1422, Richmond, VA 23211.

WA: Forecasting Division, Office of Financial Management, 300 Insurance Bldg., MS AQ44, Olympia, WA 98504.

WV: Office of Community and Industrial Development, Community Development Div., State Capitol Complex, Bldg. 6, Room 553, Charleston, WV 25305.

WI: Demographic Services Center, Dept. of Administration, 101 South Webster, P.O. Box 7868, Madison, WI 53707.

WY: Institute of Policy Research, Univ. of Wyoming, P.O. Box 3925, University Station, Laramie, WY 82071.

Books

The Almanac of the Christian World, edited by Edythe Draper, Tyndale House, 1990.

The Universal Almanac, edited by John Wright, Andrews & McMeel, annual.

Statistical Abstract, U.S. Bureau of the Census, U.S. Government Printing Office, annual.

Yearbook of American and Canadian Churches, edited by Constant Jacquet, Jr. and Alice Jones, Abingdon Press, annual.

What Americans Believe, George Barna, Regal Books, annual.

The People's Religion, George Gallup, Jr. and Jim Castelli, Macmillan Books, 1989.

Almanac of Consumer Markets, Margaret Ambry, American Demographics Press, 1989.

Research Organizations

Companies whose primary function is to define information needs and collect the appropriate information have proliferated in the last decade. A few information-providing companies whose work might have a particular value to your ministry are listed below.

Alban Institute, 4125 Nebraska Avenue, NW, Washington, D.C. 20016 (Small-scale research on broad ministry topics.)

Barna Research Group, Ltd., P.O. Box 4152, Glendale, CA 91222-0152. (Custom research for churches, parachurch groups, and broader national studies of American culture and religion. Also provides PRIZM and related cluster data for planting and planning church ministries.)

CACI, 1815 N. Fort Meyer Drive, Arlington, VA 22209. (ACORN geodemographic clustering system, which takes a designated geographic area and profiles the population in that area into 44 distinct market segments.)

Claritas, 201 N. Union Street, Alexandria, VA 22314. (PRIZM geodemographic clustering system, as well as other data services such as computer mapping of a population, reprocessed census data, and statistical modeling.)

Donnelly Marketing Information Services, 70 Seaview Avenue, Stamford, CT 06904. (CONQUEST multi-data base system to examine a given population center according to demographic, media, psychographic and life-style data. Also offers the ClusterPlus geodemographic system.)

The Gallup Organization, 100 Palmer Square, Suite 200, Princeton, NJ 08542. (Marketing research studies conducted on a syndicated or custom basis, using various nationwide data pertaining to religious behavior and belief.)

Glenmary Research Center, 750 Piedmont Road, NE, Atlanta, GA 30308. (Providers of a decennial census of churches in America.)

APPENDIX 3

SAMPLES OF FOCUS GROUP MATERIALS

TO get qualified participants to attend a focus group you must develop a screening questionnaire to be used in the telephone calls made to recruit people for your focus groups. Beginning on the next page is a sample of how such a screening survey might be developed.

This screener was designed to get people with the following qualifications: head of the household, unchurched, Protestant, has kids under 13 and is 18 to 54 years of age (with special quotas by age group).

Sample Screening Survey

Hello, this is (NAME). I'm calling from Barna Research in Los Angeles. We're conducting a brief public opinion survey and would like to include your answers. This will only take about four minutes and all of your answers will remain confidential. I am <u>not</u> trying to sell you anything.

1. To start with, are you the (male/female) head of your household?

   1. yes   CONTINUE
   2. no   ASK TO SPEAK WITH A HEAD OF THE HOUSEHOLD; IF NONE AVAILABLE AT THE TIME, SCHEDULE A TIME TO CALL BACK
   3. DK (Don't Know)   THANK AND TERMINATE

2. About how many times in the past three months have you attended a church service, other than for a special occasion such as a wedding or funeral?

   1. one or more times   THANK AND TERMINATE
   2. none   CONTINUE
   3. DK   THANK AND TERMINATE

3. Do you consider yourself to be Protestant, Catholic, Jewish, or of another religious faith?

   1. Protestant   CONTINUE
   2. Catholic   THANK AND TERMINATE
   3. Jewish/other   THANK AND TERMINATE
   4. DK/none   THANK AND TERMINATE

4. Do you currently have any children under the age of 13 living in your household?

   1. yes   CONTINUE
   2. no   THANK AND TERMINATE
   3. DK   THANK AND TERMINATE

5. What is your age?

    1. under 18   THANK AND TERMINATE
    2. 18-34   CONTINUE, IF QUOTA NOT YET FILLED
    3. 35-54   CONTINUE, IF QUOTA NOT YET FILLED
    4. 55 or older   THANK AND TERMINATE
    5. DK   THANK AND TERMINATE

6. Respondent's gender (DO NOT ASK)

    1. male
    2. female

That completes the survey. Thank you for your help.

As a related part of our research, though, we will be conducting a small discussion group at our office in Los Angeles. We are inviting only a small number of people to participate, and would like you to spend about two hours with us discussing the topics we are studying. We will provide a light meal and will pay you $35 for your help in this project. Your answers will remain confidential, and we will at no time try to sell you anything. Would you be willing to help us with this part of our research project?

IF YES, CONTINUE.

The discussion group will be held on (DATE) at (TIME). Are you available at that time to join with us?

IF YES, CONTINUE.

That's great. You do not need to study anything or come prepared in any way. During the discussion there are no right or wrong answers. After the discussion is completed, we will give you $35 cash as our expression of thanks for your help with our research. Just dress casually and be at our office by (TIME) on the (DATE). Our office is located at (ADDRESS). We will send you directions and a reminder within the coming week. To send that to you, could I please get your name and address.

Every time a moderator leads a focus group discussion, he or she works from a predetermined outline of key questions. The outline is known as the discussion guide. Sometimes the exact wording of questions is put in the outline, sometimes only the theme of the question is listed: it depends on the moderator's personal preference or style.

Shown below is a sample of a discussion guide, used in conjunction with the groups for which people were recruited through the previously shown screener. The questions follow the anticipated flow of the discussion and are grouped in modules. Each module has a time frame shown in the parentheses, to help guide the moderator in using the time most effectively, and to be sure that the modules are adequately prioritized. Notice that this outline anticipates a 75-minute discussion.

A. Introduction (5 minutes)

- Name, role, purpose of a focus group
- No right/wrong answers; be honest, open
- No sales or hidden agendas
- Don't all speak at once; okay to disagree, not seeking to reach consensus
- Moderator is independent; say whatever you like, since moderator has no vested interest in any of the products, services or organizations to be discussed
- Begin by going around the table, giving first name and community you live in, and ages of children at home

B. Community Background (10 minutes)

1. How long have you lived in this community?
2. What do you like best about the community? What do you like the least?
3. Which organizations in the community do you feel are most aware of, or sensitive to, the needs of the people who live here? What makes you feel that way?
4. If there was one reality about the community that you could change, what would that be? Why?

C. Churches in the Community (15 minutes)

1. What churches have you visited in the community?
2. Overall, what is your impression of the Protestant churches in this town? Why?
3. What are the strengths of the local churches?
4. What are the weaknesses of the local churches?
5. Do the churches make this a better community to live in or not? Why? What could they do to make this a better place to live in?

D. White Oak Community Church (20 minutes)

1. Have you ever heard of White Oak Community Church (WOCC)? Have you ever visited WOCC?
2. What are your impressions of WOCC? How did you come to that conclusion?
3. If you wanted to attend a church service next weekend, would you attend WOCC? Why/why not?
4. Suppose your best friend invited you to attend WOCC with him or her next weekend. How would you respond? Why?
5. What could WOCC do to make you interested enough that you would be willing to attend their church next weekend?
6. Compared to other churches in this area, is WOCC more appealing to you, or less appealing? Why?
7. What are the main factors you consider when you think about going to a local church?
8. Given the factors you just listed, how would you rate WOCC on each of those factors?

E. WOCC Ministry Activities (15 minutes)

1. Suppose WOCC sponsored a series of Wednesday evening seminars on household financial management. Would you be likely to attend these or not? Why/why not?
2. Suppose WOCC had a concert featuring a singing group that appealed to young families. How likely is it that you might attend that concert? Why/why not?

3. If a member of WOCC whom you had never met called you one night and asked if you would be interested in receiving several brochures about the church, with no further obligation, how would you respond? Why?

4. What types of activities might a church sponsor or offer that you would find interesting or appealing?

F. WOCC Image (10 minutes)

1. When you hear the name WOCC, what comes to mind? Based on what? Is that positive or negative to you?

2. How would you describe the types of people who attend WOCC (demographics, attitudes, values, life-styles)?

3. Overall, do you feel comfortable or at home with the types of people who attend WOCC or not? Why/why not?

4. What would be the ideal church, to you? Have you ever attended such a church? Where? When?

A written analysis of focus group research can be provided in many ways. The sample shown below is a summary analysis, often called a top line analysis. Rather than providing an exhaustive description of what was said in each group or using extensive quotes from the groups, this summary gives a brief understanding of the key points and the prominent conclusions emerging from this research.

Summary Analysis

This report provides a summary of the insights gained from a series of four focus group sessions held by Barna Research Group, Ltd. (Glendale, CA) on behalf of White Oaks Community Church. The sessions occurred in February 1992 and were held at BRG's focus group facility in Glendale. Sessions lasted about 90 minutes each, and were conducted by BRG personnel.

Community Background

Most of the participants had lived in the community for at least five years. Previously, they had lived in nearby towns.

The aspects of the community that people liked best were the public schools ("new facilities," "caring teachers," "good programs"), the lack of crime in the community, the proximity or adequate shopping, the small-town character of the community, and the access to major highways.

The aspects of the community that people liked least were the rapid building of new homes on previously unsettled areas of land, the increasing road congestion accompanying the rapid population growth, and the occasional odor from the waste treatment plant in nearby Paloma, which occasionally blows into the community.

The organizations deemed most sensitive to the needs of the community were:

- **YMCA:** they initiate new programs whenever they become aware of specific needs, especially regarding family matters.
- **Wayne's Grocery Store:** praised for providing food to the homeless, refreshments for community events, and leadership in blocking additional community growth.
- **Hillside Community Church:** great youth program, aggressive family services program, friendly people, extensive social outreach, conservative but not offensive.
- **Police Department:** responsive to calls for assistance, providing free seminars on home and personal safety, hold classy fund-raising events, seem to anticipate how they might do their job better without being pushed to do so.

The aspect of the community that people would change would be the zoning and building ordinances that allow for extensive new construction of residential and commercial construction in the Parker's Woods and Huntington Park areas.

Churches in the Community

Among the 39 people involved in these focus groups, only 12 had actually attended a service at any local churches. The churches mentioned were: Hillside Community, First Baptist, All Saints Episcopal, First United Methodist, White Oak Community and First Presbyterian.

Impressions of the local Protestant churches were minimal. It seems that these people had never heard much positive discussion from friends and neighbors about local churches and thus did not consider them as viable possibilities. The aggregate impression was that, with the possible exception of Hillside Community Church, due to its extensive social outreach, the churches of the community do their thing with their people on Sundays, but have little enduring impact on the area.

People were unable to identify the strengths of any churches other than Hillside. Its strengths were described as "helping poor people," "caring about the quality of life for all people, not just their own members," "providing a safe place for our kids to play and learn," and "a pleasant group of people who don't hit you over the head with their beliefs, even though they seem quite convinced about them." One person did mention that First Presbyterian had attractive and well-maintained facilities and grounds.

The weaknesses of local churches were summed up by two major thoughts: The churches have nothing of relevance to add to the lives of these people, and they do not seem interested in anyone outside of their "dues-paying members." The exception was Hillside, which was thought of as a caring, outward-oriented congregation.

Only Hillside was considered to be truly a *community* asset. The other churches were described as "religious shelters," "hiding places for the weak and anxious," "irrelevant to the struggles I face every day." Other churches were described as "a private convenience" or a "personal benefit for those who get it."

Overall, participants did not see local churches as making the area a better place to live. Suggestions on how they might do so included the following:

- Offer free child care during weekday mornings so mothers could shop or socialize without their kids.
- Preach sermons that help people live life more successfully.
- Provide social events that allow people with families to meet other people with similar families.

- Open up their recreational facilities to the public.
- Lead people in projects that will enhance the local area: road-side litter cleanup, water conservation training, English as a Second Language classes, household financial management seminars.
- Have the area's ministers band together to fight abusive public policies: extensive building on natural parks and forests, fight the acceptance of the local X-rated magazine store, etc.

White Oak Community Church

About two-thirds of the focus group participants had heard of WOCC. Only about one-quarter knew of its location. Just three had visited the church in the past.

People had very few positive impressions of WOCC. They said that they never hear people talk about the church and most of the participants said they did not know anyone who attends that church. The most common perception was that it was primarily a conservative church geared to middle-aged adults. No ideas were offered regarding what made the church different, special, unusual or appealing.

When asked what church they would attend if they decided to go next weekend, the dominant church was Hillside, mostly because people said they believed the people there were friendly and that the church really cared about the community and the lives of the disadvantaged. A handful mentioned First Presbyterian, mostly because they had been raised as Presbyterians. Two people identified the Methodist church because they knew some people who attended there. One person cited First Baptist because they had been married in a Baptist church.

Not one person identified WOCC as the church they would choose. The reason was that people felt they knew nothing about the church and therefore would be taking too big a risk by attending.

If a close friend invited participants to WOCC, most of the people said they would ask a series of questions about the church. The questions raised by people related to what the church believes; how WOCC differs from other churches; why their friend attends there;

what their experience would be like if they did attend; the demographic character of the congregation; the type of sermons preached by the pastor (long or short, exegetical or application-based, stories or condemnation); the type of music in the service; how long the service runs; what types of children's program is available; the availability of parking; anyone else they might know who attends there; and the time of the service.

To increase interest in attending WOCC, people suggested that the church have a higher profile in the life of the community. Hillside was used as an example of a church that takes its community responsibilities seriously, and whose efforts to build up the community make it an appealing church. Nobody had any spiritual reservations about WOCC, mostly because they had no idea what the church is about or what it believes. However, their main interest was not in theology and structure but in how people are treated and what the church does to "be good citizens" and "put their faith into practice."

When specific elements of a church experience were probed, people indicated that certain aspects were important to them, while others were not. Realize that there is a clear distinction, however, between those elements that will get these people in the door and those that will encourage them to return. Factors that were considered important toward giving them a positive experience were the comfort of the seats; the length of the service; the value of the sermon; the friendliness of the people; the style of music; the lighting (they had a dislike of dark sanctuaries); adequate seating near the back; adequate parking close to the front door; convenient times of services; a well-equipped nursery; great teachers for the children's program; and a minimal emphasis upon giving money.

Future Ministry Activities by WOCC

About half of the participants of the focus groups said they might be interested in the financial seminars sponsored by WOCC. They wanted to know more about the credentials and style of the presenters; the admission fee; the dates, times and location; the topics to be covered; how many sessions, and whether the sessions were integrally related or independent; and how much proselytizing would be done by the church. Most people said that a well-designed seminar providing hands-on skills would be worth paying up to $5 for. There was a great fear that the church would use the seminar as a means to recruit people, or that it was a method of allowing financial consultants who attend that church to simply market their own services to potential clients.

People were wary of the family concert concept. Until they know who the performer is, and are familiar with their music, they would not be likely to attend such a performance.

People came out of their seats in protest against the idea of someone calling their home and offering to send information about a church. They complained intensely that they are harassed by telemarketers and want nothing to do with an organization that interrupts their free time in this manner. Of the 39 people involved in the four sessions, only one person indicated any interest in receiving information offered through a telephone call.

Although no additional activities were suggested by people as a means of introducing a church, the repeated reference to Hillside drove home the point that the unchurched adults in the area are more compelled by a demonstration of faith in action than by a clever marketing event.

WOCC Image

The name of the church (WOCC) evoked generally positive, if vague, impressions. Since people barely knew of the existence of the church, they associated the name with little related to ministry. The characteristics that the name conjured, though, included "strong," "enduring," "pretty," "calm and pleasant," and "a small country church that does not make waves."

Although they were simply guessing, the assumption was that the WOCC congregation is comprised mainly of middle-aged and elderly people who are "Bible readers" and have lived in the community for a long time. They were assumed to be upscale, homeowners, mostly working in professional positions in large companies, probably commute to work in a larger nearby city and have children who are grown and living on their own.

Theologically, they assumed the congregation to be conservative ("probably like a Baptist church" someone said) and that they were attuned to tradition, "old-time music and hymns" and were a generally inward-looking group. They had no sense of what the services are like, how ministry happens at the church, or what value membership at the church would bring.

There was some discomfort with the question about whether they would feel at home with the members of WOCC. Part of the discomfort was because they did not have a firm sense of who those people are, or what they are like. Part of the uneasiness, though, seemed to spring from the suspicion that because the church had not developed a profile of community service or real care for other people, the people would be "kind of like a country club, you know, smiley but snobby."

The attributes of the "ideal church" were varied. Here are some of the characteristics that people said they would most like to experience in their own church:

- People who are authentically friendly, not "friendly on Sunday but cold the rest of the week."
- Consistently doing community service activities because they really care about people and quality of life.
- Preaching and music that is relevant and contemporary; not "church for the sake of church, but something that really helps me, personally, with my life."
- Able to wear whatever types of clothing is comfortable, without feeling that they are not meeting the "fashion-show standards" of some churches.
- Opportunities for meeting new people and getting to know they are available.
- Children's programs are high quality, have good teachers, enough space, careful supervision, tight security, ample toys and other materials.
- Pastor and church staff are available to meet with people at the time they have a real need, not "six weeks from now, when the pastor's schedule has time for me."
- The Bible is used as a key reference work, but is not used as "an instrument of guilt."

- People feel comfortable emotionally being there, "like the church is really happy that you want to be part of what the people are about."
- People give money because they feel like they should, not because they are pressured by the pastor and leaders to do so.
- The buildings are modest but well-maintained and the grounds provide ample opportunity to enjoy outdoor activities as a group.
- Services are held at convenient times (though there was some disagreement as to what this meant; Sunday was not always an option for people).
- The church had an air of happiness and joy, rather than sorrow and oppression and guilt. A few people said they want church to be "a happy time, not a time when I feel miserable because I'm such a lousy person." The ideal church was described as one in which celebration is a critical dimension.

SAMPLES OF COMMUNITY TELEPHONE SURVEYS

As noted in the text, we do not recommend that any organization simply copy the survey developed for, and used by, another organization. The questionnaire you use should be tailored to meet your specific needs and to reflect the unique context of your ministry. The primary advantage of using questions developed and administered in another survey is for comparative purposes.

However, to give you a sense of what such questionnaires look like, and how the questions are constructed, the pages that follow provide several examples of surveys that were designed to gauge the character of the communities to which the sponsoring churches wished to minister. These were designed to be administered by telephone.

Take note of several elements in the questionnaires. For questions with a [ ] preceding a statement to be read, the brackets suggest that the order in which the statements are read is rotated to preclude response bias.

Many questions contain skip patterns, which are the instructions telling the interviewer the next question to ask, depending upon the response given to that particular question. In the first questionnaire, for example, there are two ways of showing the skip patterns. After questions *A* and *1* are the two means of showing the instructions.

Words in CAPITAL LETTERS are instructions for the interviewer and are not to be read aloud to the respondent.

For some questions, a response option will show a (VOL) preceding the answer. This indicates that the answer is a volunteered response. The respondent may say this and it should be marked as such, but the interviewer should not read it as a viable option.

The first questionnaire displayed was conducted within an 11 zip code area, the church's target market. It begins with questions designed to screen out people who were *not* part of the target audience. By the time you get to question 2 you are speaking with the church's high potential market: adults 18 to 50 who live within the 11 zip area and do not attend church.

Potential Target Survey

Hi, my name is (NAME). I'm calling from Barna Research in Glendale. We're conducting a survey of people in the area and would like to include your opinions. Your answers will remain anonymous and confidential and I will not try to sell you anything.

To start with, are you between the ages of 18 and 50?

1. yes	CONTINUE
2. no	ASK FOR SOMEONE 18-50; IF NONE AVAILABLE, SCHEDULE A CALLBACK; IF NONE LIVE IN HOUSEHOLD, THANK AND TERMINATE
3. DK (Don't Know)	THANK AND TERMINATE

1. I'm going to read several different types of activities. For each one that I read, please tell me if you, personally, have done that activity during the last month.

    During the past month, did you (READ ACTIVITY):

Activity	Yes	No	DK
[ ] a. attend a worship service at a Christian church?	1	2	3
[ ] b. go shopping at the Glendale Galleria?	1	2	3
[ ] c. attend a sports event?	1	2	3
[ ] d. attend a music or theater event?	1	2	3

IF Q1A=1, GO TO Q11.
IF Q1A=2, CONTINUE.
IF Q1A=3, TERMINATE.

2. I'm going to read a list of different issues. Suppose an organization in your community offered an event at which you could learn more about the issue I'm going to mention. Assuming that there were no sales gimmicks and no financial commitments required, please tell me how interested you, personally, would be in attending an event that provided information on that topic.

How interested would you be in an event on (TOPIC)? Would you be very, somewhat, not too, not at all interested, or don't know?

Issue or Topic	V	SW	NT	NAA	DK
[ ] a. overcoming addictions in life?	1	2	3	4	5
[ ] b. feeling disappointed or rejected by God?	1	2	3	4	5
[ ] c. ethics and integrity?	1	2	3	4	5
[ ] d. developing personal characteristics that other people admire?	1	2	3	4	5
[ ] e. balancing your time and opportunities?	1	2	3	4	5
[ ] f. understanding different religions?	1	2	3	4	5
[ ] g. evaluating success, life-styles, and values in your life?	1	2	3	4	5
[ ] h. gaining satisfaction from your work?	1	2	3	4	5
[ ] i. social trends in America?	1	2	3	4	5
[ ] j. clarifying what you and other people believe about sex, marriage and personal relationships?	1	2	3	4	5
[ ] k. considering the meaning of death and if there is a life after death?	1	2	3	4	5

3. In many communities in this area, there are educational, social, and cultural events that are open to anyone who is interested in attending. I'm going to list a few events and would like to know how interested you would be in attending such events in the Glendale area. Again, please assume that these events would not have any sales gimmicks.

How interested would you be in attending (READ EVENT): Would you be very, somewhat, not too, not at all interested, or don't know?

Event Description	V	SW	NT	NAA	DK
[ ] a. a concert for parents and children under the age of 9?	1	2	3	4	5
[ ] b. a seminar on household finance and budgeting techniques?	1	2	3	4	5
[ ] c. a seminar on the reliability of the Bible and how it can be helpful to people these days?	1	2	3	4	5
[ ] d. a fashion show for working women?	1	2	3	4	5
[ ] e. a tennis clinic?	1	2	3	4	5
[ ] f. a seminar on raising children?	1	2	3	4	5
[ ] g. a political debate between the candidates for the U.S. Senate?	1	2	3	4	5
[ ] h. a play presented by community residents?	1	2	3	4	5
[ ] i. a fair to raise money for local schools?	1	2	3	4	5
[ ] j. a crime prevention presentation by the local police?	1	2	3	4	5
[ ] k. a multimedia presentation marking 1992 as the 500th anniversary of Columbus landing in America?	1	2	3	4	5

4. How likely is it that you will attend a worship service at a Christian church during the next six months? Will you (READ):

1. definitely attend services?	GO TO Q5
2. probably attend?	GO TO Q5
3. probably not attend?	GO TO Q6
4. or definitely not attend services?	GO TO Q9
5. (VOL) DK	GO TO Q6

5. Do you know which church you would be most likely to attend, or would you decide when you get closer to the time when you decide to attend a church service?

1. know which church
2. would decide at time
3. DK

5A. Would you probably attend a Protestant church, a Catholic church, or some other type?

1. Protestant
2. Catholic
3. other type
4. DK

6. If you had a choice of attending church services on a Friday evening, Saturday evening, Sunday morning, or Sunday evening, which would you prefer?

1. Friday evening	GO TO Q8
2. Saturday evening	GO TO Q8
3. Sunday morning	GO TO Q7
4. Sunday evening	GO TO Q8
5. DK	GO TO Q8

7. What time on Sunday morning would be most appealing to you? (READ OPTIONS)

1. 8:30
2. 9:00
3. 9:30
4. 10:00
5. or 11:00
6. (VOL) doesn't matter
7. (VOL) no preference/won't attend
8. (VOL) DK

8. Suppose there were several churches that you might choose from when you decide to visit a church. Here are a few different qualities that a church might have. For each one, please tell me how appealing that quality would be for a church to have. How appealing would it be to you if the church (READ OPTION): very, somewhat, not too, not at all appealing, or don't know?

Quality	V	SW	NT	NAA	DK
[ ] a. had fewer than 200 people attending?	1	2	3	4	5
[ ] b. used contemporary music instead of the traditional church hymns, and the music was played by a band with keyboards, guitars and drums?	1	2	3	4	5
[ ] c. was informal—that is, the people dressed casually and stayed around afterward to talk to others and have refreshments?	1	2	3	4	5
[ ] d. had special classes and activities for children at the same time as the adult service?	1	2	3	4	5
[ ] e. included a short play or skit in each service, to help illustrate the main point of the pastor's sermon?	1	2	3	4	5
[ ] f. did not take an offering or ask for money during the service?	1	2	3	4	5
[ ] g. emphasized current events in our society and how the Bible relates to those events?	1	2	3	4	5
[ ] h. was friendly but was not overly aggressive?	1	2	3	4	5
[ ] i. did not have a choir?	1	2	3	4	5
[ ] j. did not expect you to participate much in the service?	1	2	3	4	5
[ ] k. was mostly people under 40 years of age?	1	2	3	4	5

9. Think about the churches in this area. Which of the following churches in the Glendale area are you familiar with? Are you familiar with (READ NAMES):

Church Names	Yes	No	DK
[ ] a. Glendale Presbyterian Church?	1	2	3
[ ] b. Glendale Community Church?	1	2	3
[ ] c. La Canada Presbyterian Church?	1	2	3
[ ] d. La Crescenta Baptist Church?	1	2	3
[ ] e. First Methodist of Glendale?	1	2	3
[ ] f. St. James Episcopal Church?	1	2	3
[ ] g. St. Matthew's Lutheran Church?	1	2	3
[ ] h. Immaculate Conception Catholic Church?	1	2	3

10. Suppose a church that you heard about was meeting in a building that was used for other purposes during the week, such as a YMCA or a school. Would that make you more likely to attend the church, less likely, or wouldn't it make any difference to you? (IF MORE OR LESS LIKELY, ASK: Would it make you: much [more/less] or a little [more/less] likely?)

    1. much more likely?
    2. a little more likely?
    3. makes no difference?
    4. a little less likely?
    5. much less likely?
    6. (VOL) DK

11. I have a few final questions for classification purposes. What is your age?

    _____

12. What is the zip code in which you live?

    1. 91201
    2. 91202
    3. 91203
    4. 91204
    5. 91205
    6. 91206
    7. 91207
    8. 91208
    9. 91214
    10. 91040
    11. other: _____
    12. DK

13. Are you (READ OPTIONS):

    1. white?
    2. black?
    3. Hispanic?
    4. Armenian?
    5. Asian?
    6. or of another ethnic background: _____?
    7. (VOL) DK

14. Are you currently married?

    1. yes   2. no

15. Are there any children under the age of 12 living in your household?

    1. yes   2. no

16. When you were growing up, what type of church did you attend most often?

    _____

That completes the survey. Thank you for your help. Have a nice day/evening. INTERVIEWER: BE SURE TO COMPLETE THE FOLLOWING INFORMATION CONCERNING YOUR COMPLETED INTERVIEW.

17. Gender: 1. male   2. female

18. Telephone number called: _____

AA. Date _____

BB. Interviewer: _____

CC. Date of interview: _____

Church Planting Survey

The following survey was conducted within a specified zip code area for a church that was about to be planted. The planters of the church wanted to test a number of concepts before plunging into their new work.

INSERT ZIP CODE FROM LIST—CHECK QUOTA

1. 77089
2. 77504
3. 77546
4. 77581

Hello, I'm _____ from Barna Research in Los Angeles. We're conducting a public opinion survey with people in your area, and would like to include your opinions. This will only take a few minutes. All of your answers will remain confidential, and I am not trying to sell you anything.

1. First of all, are you at least 18 years old?

    1. yes   CONTINUE
    2. no   ASK TO SPEAK WITH AN ADULT IN THE
              HOUSEHOLD
    3. DK   TERMINATE

2. About how many years have you been living in your community? (READ LIST ONLY IF NECESSARY.)

    1. less than 6 months
    2. 6 months to less than 1 year
    3. 1 to less than 2 years
    4. 2 to less than 3 years
    5. 3 to less than 5 years
    6. 5 to less than 10 years
    7. 10 to less than 20 years
    8. 20 years or more
    9. (VOL) DK

3. I'm going to read a couple of statements to you. Please listen to each one and tell me whether you agree strongly, agree somewhat, disagree somewhat, or disagree strongly with the statement. The (first/next) statement is: (READ STATEMENT.) Do you agree strongly, agree somewhat, disagree somewhat, or disagree strongly with that statement?

Statement	–Agree–		–Disagree–		
	Strg	Some	Some	Strg	DK
[ ] a. The Christian faith is relevant to the way you live today.	1	2	3	4	5
[ ] b. The Christian churches in your area are relevant to the way you live today.	1	2	3	4	5
[ ] c. There are not enough opportunities in your community to meet and get to know people.	1	2	3	4	5
[ ] d. There are not enough opportunities in your community to learn about subjects that interest you.	1	2	3	4	5

4. In a typical month, how often, if ever, do you attend a church worship service, other than a special service such as a wedding, funeral or a holiday service?

   1. four or more times (every week)   GO TO Q5
   2. two or three times   GO TO Q5
   3. once   GO TO Q5
   4. less than once a month   GO TO Q7
   5. never/do not attend church   GO TO Q7
   6. DK/refused   GO TO Q7

5. How likely is it that during the next 12 months you will change from the church you currently attend most often to a different church? Is it (READ LIST):

    1. very likely?
    2. somewhat likely?
    3. not too likely?
    4. or not at all likely?
    5. (VOL) DK

6. What is the denomination of the church you attend most often? (IF RESPONDENT DOES NOT ATTEND ONE PARTICULAR CHURCH REGULARLY, ENTER 20.)

1. Assembly of God	11. Methodist
2. Baptist	12. Mormon
3. Brethren	13. Nazarene
4. Catholic	14. non-denom'l/community
5. Church of Christ/Congregational	15. Pentec./4-Sqr/charis.
6. Church of God	16. Presbyterian
7. Episcopal	17. Reformed
8. Evangelical Free	18. Seventh-Day Adventist
9. Lutheran	19. other:_____
10. Mennonite	20. DK/no particular

GO TO Q9

7. I'm going to read a number of different reasons some people might not attend church. Please tell me how important each reason was in your decision not to attend church regularly. The (first/next) possible reason is (READ REASON). Was that very, somewhat, not too, or not at all important in your decision not to attend church regularly?

Reason	V	S	NT	NAA	DK
[ ] a. You don't believe in a Christian God, or are not sure whether God exists.	1	2	3	4	5
[ ] b. You feel you can worship God without going to a church.	1	2	3	4	5
[ ] c. You don't have the time, or are too busy to attend.	1	2	3	4	5
[ ] d. Churches are for people who are weak or struggling; you do not have such a need in your life right now.	1	2	3	4	5
[ ] e. You simply aren't interested in being part of a church.	1	2	3	4	5
[ ] f. You do not know of any good churches in your area which would be worth visiting.	1	2	3	4	5

8. In the next six months, how likely is it that you will attend a service at a Christian church, other than a special holiday service, a wedding or a funeral? Will you (READ LIST):

   1. definitely attend?
   2. probably attend?
   3. maybe attend, under the right circumstances?
   4. probably not attend?
   5. or definitely not attend?
   6. (VOL) DK

   IF Q8 = 5, GO TO Q15

9. I'd like to try something a little different now. I'm going to read a couple of possible names for a new church in your area. For each name, please tell me if that name gives you a very favorable impression of that church, a somewhat favorable impression, a somewhat unfavorable impression, or a very unfavorable impression of that church. The (first/next) name is (READ NAME). Does that give you a very favorable, somewhat favorable, somewhat unfavorable, very unfavorable impression, or don't know?

	(VOL)					
	-Favorable-		-No-	-Unfavorable-		
Names	Very	Some	Opin.	Some	Very	DK
[ ] a. Princeton Presbyterian Church	1	2	3	4	5	6
[ ] b. Tri-Cities Presbyterian Church	1	2	3	4	5	6
[ ] c. Princeton Covenant Church	1	2	3	4	5	6
[ ] d. Tri-Cities Community Church	1	2	3	4	5	6
[ ] e. Tri-Cities Covenant Church	1	2	3	4	5	6
[ ] f. Presbyterian Church of the Covenant	1	2	3	4	5	6

10. Now I'm going to read the list again. Please tell me which one of those churches you would be most likely to visit, if you were looking for a church in your area to visit or attend, and knew nothing about these churches other than their name. (READ LIST.) Which one of these churches would you be most likely to visit? (IF THEY MENTION MORE THAN ONE, ASK, "If you had to choose just one, which one of these would you be more likely to visit?" IF THEY IDENTIFY THEIR CHOICE WITH A NUMBER, REREAD THE NAME TO CONFIRM.)

1. Princeton Covenant Church
2. Princeton Presbyterian Church
3. Presbyterian Church of the Covenant
4. Princeton Community Church
5. Tri-Cities Covenant Church
6. or Tri-Cities Presbyterian Church
7. (VOL) DK

11. What are the main reasons you would be most likely to visit that church, instead of selecting one of the other churches I just named? (PROBE FOR CLARITY WITH "Can you explain what you mean by that?" PROBE FOR MULTIPLE RESPONSES WITH "Why else would you be most likely to visit that particular church?")

_____

_____

_____

_____

IF QA=1, DO NOT ASK Q12b.
IF QA=2, DO NOT ASK Q12a.
IF QA=3, DO NOT ASK Q12c.
IF QA=4, DO NOT ASK Q12d.

12. For a moment, let's continue to say you were looking for a church to visit or join. Remember, I'm not trying to sell you anything, or get you to do anything. How likely would you be to travel to (READ LOCATION) from where you live, if there was a church there you thought you might be interested in? Would you be very, somewhat, not too, or not at all likely to travel to (READ LOCATION):

Location	V	S	NT	NAA	DK
[ ] a. the center of Princeton?	1	2	3	4	5
[ ] b. the northern tip of Princeton, at border of Williamstown?	1	2	3	4	5
[ ] c. Ridgewood?	1	2	3	4	5
[ ] d. the Pleasant Valley Mall?	1	2	3	4	5
[ ] e. Alton?	1	2	3	4	5

13. There are a number of different styles of worship services in Christian churches today. Some are formal and traditional, while others are informal and more contemporary. I'm going to read a number of choices you might have in the type of church you attend. For each choice, please tell me which one you would prefer. The (first/next) choice is (READ CHOICE). Which of those would you prefer? (OBTAIN RESPONSE, THEN ASK) Would you prefer that strongly or somewhat?

Choices	-1st- Option Strg.	Some	(VOL) No Dif.	-2nd- Option Strg.	Some	DK
[ ] a. Either traditional hymns, or more contemporary, modern music in the worship service.	1	2	3	4	5	6
[ ] b. Either a lot of singing and music in the service, or just a little singing and music.	1	2	3	4	5	6
[ ] c. Either the congregation participates a lot in the service, or the congregation does not participate much but observes as the leaders conduct the service.	1	2	3	4	5	6
[ ] d. Either they use a drama skit or dramatic presentation in the service to emphasize what is being taught, or the service would not use drama or dramatic presentations.	1	2	3	4	5	6

14. Some churches offer different types of activities in which people might get involved. If a church in your area had religious beliefs that you felt were acceptable, and (READ ACTIVITY)? Would you be very likely, somewhat likely, not too likely, or not at all likely?

Activity	V	S	NT	NAA	DK
[ ] a. a trusted friend invited you to attend a Sunday morning worship service; how likely would you be to attend that service with them?	1	2	3	4	5
[ ] b. you received interesting information about the church through the mail; how likely would you be to visit that church?	1	2	3	4	5
[ ] c. the church offered a class or seminar on a nonreligious topic that was of interest to you; how likely would you be to attend that class or seminar?	1	2	3	4	5
[ ] d. the church sponsored a social activity for people from the area to meet others living in the area; how likely would you be to attend that activity?	1	2	3	4	5
[ ] e. the church sponsored a volunteer effort to help needy people in your community; how likely would you be to help out in that volunteer effort?	1	2	3	4	5

15. On another subject, have you ever made a personal commitment to Jesus Christ that is still important in your life today?

　　1. yes　　GO TO Q16
　　2. no　　GO TO Q17
　　3. DK　　GO TO Q17

16. I'm going to read six statements about life after death. Please tell me which one of these statements comes closest to describing your own belief about life after death. The (first/second/third...) statement is: (READ STATEMENT). Which one of these comes closest to describing your beliefs? (IF THE RESPONDENT GIVES THE NUMBER OF THE STATEMENT, REREAD THE STATEMENT TO BE SURE IT IS THE RESPONSE THEY MEANT.)

1. When you die you will go to heaven because you have tried to obey the Ten Commandments.
2. When you die you will go to heaven because you are basically a good person.
3. When you die you will go to heaven because you have confessed your sins and accepted Jesus Christ as your Savior.
4. When you die you will go to heaven because God loves all people and will not let them perish.
5. When you die you will not go to heaven.
6. You do not know what will happen after you die.
7. (VOL) DK

17. Now I have just a few more questions for classification purposes only. First of all, what is your age?

1. 18 - 24
2. 25 - 29
3. 30 - 34
4. 35 - 39
5. 40 - 44
6. 45 - 49
7. 50 - 54
8. 55 - 59
9. 60 - 64
10. 65+
11. DK/refused

18. Do you have any children of the following ages currently living in your household: (READ AGE GROUPS, MARK ONE ANSWER FOR EACH GROUP)

Ages	Yes	No	DK
a. under the age of 6?	1	2	3
b. between 6 and 12?	1	2	3
c. between 13 and 17?	1	2	3

19. What is the highest level of education you have completed? (READ LIST ONLY IF NECESSARY.)

1. less than high school
2. high school graduate
3. trade school
4. some college
5. college graduate
6. postgraduate studies
7. (VOL) DK

20. Are you currently (READ LIST):

1. married?
2. single?
3. separated?
4. divorced?
5. or widowed?
6. (VOL) DK

21. Finally, please stop me after I read the category that best describes your household's total annual income, before taxes.

    1. less than $10,000
    2. $10,000 to less than $20,000
    3. $20,000 to less than $30,000
    4. $30,000 to less than $40,000
    5. $40,000 to less than $50,000
    6. $50,000 to less than $60,000
    7. $60,000 to less than $75,000
    8. or $75,000 or more
    9. (VOL) DK

That completes the survey. Thank you very much for your time and cooperation, and have a good (day/evening). INTERVIEWER: BE SURE TO COMPLETE THE REMAINDER OF THE QUESTIONNAIRE BEFORE STARTING THE NEXT INTERVIEW.

22. Respondent's gender: 1. male   2. female

23. Phone # called:_____

24. Elapsed time: _____

AA. Date:_____

National Values Survey

The following interview is a national study conducted by the Barna Research Group on a wide range of issues. This survey lasted an average of 20 minutes per interview.

Hello, this is (NAME). I'm calling from Barna Research in Los Angeles. We're conducting a national public opinion survey and would like to include your opinions. All of your answers will remain confidential and I'm not trying to sell you anything.

To start with, are you 18 years of age or older?

1. yes   CONTINUE
2. no   ASK TO SPEAK WITH SOMEONE 18 OR OLDER; IF
            NOT AVAILABLE, SCHEDULE CALLBACK; IF NONE
            EXIST, MARK AS UNQUALIFIED
3. DK   THANK AND TERMINATE

1. Think about the last 7 days. Please tell me which, if any, of the following activities you have done during the last 7 days. (READ ACTIVITIES)

Activity	Yes	No	DK
[ ] a. attended a church worship service	1	2	3
[ ] b. attended a Sunday School class at a church	1	2	3
[ ] c. read part of the Bible	1	2	3
[ ] d. read part of a book, other than the Bible	1	2	3
[ ] e. volunteered any of your free time to help a church	1	2	3
[ ] f. volunteered any of your free time to help an organization other than a church	1	2	3
[ ] g. watched MTV	1	2	3

2. I'm going to name some aspects of life. For each aspect I mention, please tell me how important that aspect is to you, personally. How important is (READ ELEMENT) to you: is it very important, somewhat important, not too important, or not at all important?

Element	Very	Some	Not too	Not at all	DK
[ ] a. religion	1	2	3	4	5
[ ] b. the Bible	1	2	3	4	5
[ ] c. money	1	2	3	4	5
[ ] d. your time	1	2	3	4	5
[ ] e. living comfortably	1	2	3	4	5
[ ] f. your friends	1	2	3	4	5
[ ] g. family	1	2	3	4	5
[ ] h. your free time	1	2	3	4	5
[ ] i. your career	1	2	3	4	5
[ ] j. health	1	2	3	4	5
[ ] k. your community	1	2	3	4	5
[ ] l. government and politics	1	2	3	4	5

3. I'm going to read some statements about life, in general, and would like you to tell me if you agree or disagree with each statement. (READ STATEMENT) Do you agree or disagree with that statement? Do you (agree/disagree) strongly or moderately?

Statement	Agree		Disagree		
	Str	Mod	Mod	Str	DK
[ ] a. Today's popular music has a positive influence on most people.	1	2	3	4	5
[ ] b. The values and life-styles shown in music videos generally reflect the ways most people live and think these days.	1	2	3	4	5
[ ] c. Abortion is morally wrong.	1	2	3	4	5
[ ] d. Lying is sometimes necessary.	1	2	3	4	5
[ ] e. Nothing can be known for certain except the things you experience in your own life.	1	2	3	4	5
[ ] f. One person can really make a difference in the world these days.	1	2	3	4	5
[ ] g. No matter how you feel about money, it is still the main sign of success in life.	1	2	3	4	5

4. Let's switch the focus just a bit. Now I'm going to read a few statements about your values and beliefs. For each statement, please tell me if you agree strongly, agree somewhat, disagree somewhat, or disagree strongly with the statement. (READ STATEMENT) Do you agree strongly, agree somewhat, disagree somewhat, or disagree strongly with that statement?

	Agree		Disagree		
Statement	Str	Mod	Mod	Str	DK
[ ] a. The Bible is the written word of God and is totally accurate in all that it teaches.	1	2	3	4	5
[ ] b. You have tried Christianity and found it to be disappointing.	1	2	3	4	5
[ ] c. When people pray, it might make them feel better, but their prayers do not have the power to change their circumstances.	1	2	3	4	5
[ ] d. Everyone determines his or her own destiny.	1	2	3	4	5
[ ] e. Horoscopes and astrology work.	1	2	3	4	5
[ ] f. The Ten Commandments are not relevant for people in the 20th century.	1	2	3	4	5
[ ] g. The whole idea of sin is outdated.	1	2	3	4	5
[ ] h. The Bible does not command people to attend a church; that is a man-made requirement.	1	2	3	4	5
[ ] i. All good people, whether they consider Jesus Christ to be their Savior or not, will live in heaven after they die on earth.	1	2	3	4	5

5. There are many different beliefs about God these days. I'm going to read some of the beliefs people have about God. Please tell me which *one* of these descriptions is closest to what you, personally, believe about God. (READ OPTIONS. IF THEY GIVE A NUMBER, REREAD THE OPTION TO BE SURE IT'S WHAT THEY MEANT.)

    1. Everyone is God.
    2. God is the all-powerful, all-knowing and perfect Creator of the universe, who rules the world today.
    3. God is the total realization of personal, human potential.
    4. There are many gods, each with different power and authority.

    5. God represents a state of higher consciousness that a person may reach.
    6. There is no such thing as God.
    7. (VOL) DK

6. Thinking about religion, do you consider yourself to be Christian, Jewish, Muslim, atheist, or of another religious faith?

    1. Christian
    2. Jewish
    3. Muslim
    4. atheist
    5. other: _____
    6. DK

**IF Q6=1, GO TO Q7; OTHERWISE,
GO TO INSTRUCTION BEFORE Q11**

7. What is the denomination of the church that you attend most often?

1. Assembly of God
2. Baptist
3. Brethren
4. Christian/Miss'y Alliance
5. Catholic
6. Church of Christ
7. Church of God
8. Congregational
9. Disciples of Christ
10. Evangelical Free
11. Lutheran
12. Methodist
13. Mormon
14. Nazarene
15. nondenominational
16. Pentecostal/Foursquare
17. Presbyterian
18. Protestant/Christian
19. Reformed
20. Seventh-day Adventist
21. Episcopal
22. other: _____
23. none/don't go to church
24. DK

8. In a typical month, on how many weekends would you attend worship services at a church?

1. one
2. two
3. three
4. four or more
5. none
6. DK

IF Q8=5 OR 6, GO TO Q14;
IF Q8=1-4, GO TO Q9

9. Which one of the following statements best describes your church attendance? (READ EACH STATEMENT; ENTER ONE ANSWER)

   1. You always attend the same church every time you go to church.
   2. You usually attend the same church, but occasionally visit other churches.
   3. You usually divide your attendance between two or more churches that you like.
   4. (VOL) DK

ASK Q10 IF Q9=1 OR 2; OTHERWISE, GO TO Q11

10. How likely is it that during the next 12 months you will change the church that you attend most often to some church other than the one you attend now? Is it (READ OPTIONS):

    1. very likely?
    2. somewhat likely?
    3. not too likely?
    4. or not at all likely?
    5. (VOL) DK

11. I'm going to read some ways in which people might be involved in their church, or in personal spiritual growth. Please tell me which, if any, of the following you are currently involved in (READ ACTIVITY):

Activity	Yes	No	DK
[ ] a. regularly teaching a Sunday School class	1	2	3
[ ] b. participating in a small group Bible study, fellowship group, or prayer group, other than a Sunday School class	1	2	3
[ ] c. serving as a leader in the church, on a board or committee	1	2	3

12. During the past month, which, if any, of the following have you done?

Activity	Yes	No	DK
[ ] a. watched a religious television program	1	2	3
[ ] b. listened to Christian preaching or teaching on the radio	1	2	3
[ ] c. read a Christian book, other than the Bible	1	2	3
[ ] d. donated money to a Christian ministry, other than a church	1	2	3
[ ] e. told someone who had different beliefs about your own religious beliefs	1	2	3
[ ] f. listened to a radio station that was playing Christian music	1	2	3
[ ] g. read a Christian magazine	1	2	3
[ ] h. volunteered your time or money to help needy people in your area	1	2	3
[ ] i. volunteered your time or money to help needy people in other countries	1	2	3

13. In a typical week, during how many days, if any, would you read the Bible, not including times when you are at church?

_____ 1. none   2. DK

14. Have you ever made a personal commitment to Jesus Christ that is still important in your life today?

1. yes   GO TO Q15
2. no   GO TO Q16
3. DK   GO TO Q16

15. I'm going to read six statements about life after death. Please tell me which one of these statements comes closest to describing your own belief about life after death. The (1st/2nd/...) statement is (READ STATEMENT). Which one of these comes closest to describing your beliefs? (IF RESPONDENT GIVES STATEMENT NUMBER, REREAD STATEMENT TO BE SURE IT IS THE ONE THEY MEANT.)

1. When you die you will go to heaven because you have tried to obey the Ten Commandments.
2. When you die you will go to heaven because you are basically a good person.
3. When you die you will go to heaven because you have confessed your sins and have accepted Jesus Christ as your Savior.
4. When you die you will go to heaven because God loves all people and will not let them perish.
5. When you die you will not go to heaven.
6. You do not know what will happen after you die.
7. (VOL) DK

16. Changing topics again, as you may know, 1992 is a presidential election year. In November, we will be voting for president. Are you registered to vote at your current address?

    1. yes   GO TO Q17
    2. no   GO TO Q19
    3. DK   GO TO Q19

17. Are you registered as a Democrat, as a Republican, or are you a registered voter but not registered through one of these parties?

    1. Democrat
    2. Republican
    3. independent
    4. (VOL) other party
    5. DK

18. I'm going to list a few of the issues that might be discussed during the upcoming presidential campaign. Please tell me how important the candidate's position on that issue would be for you in deciding whether or not to support that candidate. The (first/next) issue is (READ ISSUE). Would knowing a candidate's position on (READ ISSUE) be very important, somewhat important, not too important, or not at all important in your decision of which candidate to support?

Issue	VI	SI	NTI	NAAI	DK
[ ] a. women's rights	1	2	3	4	5
[ ] b. abortion	1	2	3	4	5
[ ] c. taxes	1	2	3	4	5
[ ] d. environmental policy	1	2	3	4	5
[ ] e. public education	1	2	3	4	5
[ ] f. crime	1	2	3	4	5
[ ] g. defense spending	1	2	3	4	5
[ ] h. the budget deficit	1	2	3	4	5

[ ]	i. health care	1	2	3	4	5
[ ]	j. welfare and unemployment policies	1	2	3	4	5
[ ]	k. religious freedom	1	2	3	4	5
[ ]	l. drug enforcement	1	2	3	4	5
[ ]	m. human rights protection	1	2	3	4	5
[ ]	n. poverty	1	2	3	4	5
[ ]	o. mass transportation	1	2	3	4	5

19. Finally, I have just a few more questions for classification purposes. What is your age?

_____ DK/refused

20. What is the highest level of education that you have completed?

1. less than high school
2. high school graduate
3. trade school
4. some college
5. college graduate
6. graduate studies
7. DK

21. Are you currently (READ OPTIONS):

1. married?   GO TO Q22
2. single?   GO TO Q22
3. separated?   GO TO Q22
4. divorced?   GO TO Q23
5. or widowed?   GO TO Q22
6. (VOL) DK?   GO TO Q22

22. Have you ever been divorced?

    1. yes
    2. no
    3. DK

23. Are there any children currently living in your home who are under the age of 18?

    1. yes   GO TO Q24
    2. no   GO TO Q25
    3. DK   GO TO Q25

24. Are there any children currently living in your home who are under the age of 13?

    1. yes
    2. no
    3. DK

25. Do you consider yourself to be (READ OPTIONS):

    1. white?
    2. black?
    3. Hispanic?
    4. Asian?
    5. or of some other ethnic origin: which? _____
    6. (VOL) DK

26. Are you currently employed? (IF YES, ASK: Are you employed full-time or part-time?)

    1. full-time
    2. part-time
    3. not employed
    4. DK

    ASK Q27 ONLY IF Q21=1

27. Is your spouse currently employed? (IF YES, ASK: Is your spouse currently employed full-time or part-time?)

    1. full-time
    2. part-time
    3. not employed
    4. DK

28. Would you describe the community in which you live as urban, suburban or rural?

    1. urban
    2. suburban
    3. rural
    4. DK

29. Finally, please stop me after I read the category that best describes your household's total annual income, before taxes. (READ OPTIONS)

    1. less than $20,000
    2. $20,000 to less than $30,000
    3. $30,000 to less than $35,000
    4. $35,000 to less than $40,000
    5. $40,000 to less than $50,000
    6. $50,000 to less than $60,000
    7. $60,000 to less than $75,000
    8. $75,000 to less than $100,000
    9. or $100,000 or more
    10. (VOL) DK

That completes the survey. Thank you very much for your help. Have a nice (day/evening).

==

30. Respondent's gender: 1. male   2. female

31. Region:

    1. New England
    2. Middle Atlantic
    3. East North Central
    4. West North Central
    5. Upper South Atlantic
    6. Lower South Atlantic
    7. East South Central
    8. West South Central
    9. Mountain
   10. Pacific

AA. Interviewer: _____

BB. Date of interview: _____

CC. Length of interview: _____

DD. Respondent's telephone number: _____

APPENDIX 5
SAMPLES OF CONGREGATIONAL SURVEYS

Even more than for community surveys, it is critical that a congregational survey be customized to meet the special needs of a particular congregation. The samples shown below were developed for very different purposes. However, they may help you understand the range of questions you could ask of your people.

Established Church Survey

Please circle the number of the answer you wish to select for each question. Unless otherwise instructed, please circle only one number for each question. Answer only for yourself—not for your spouse, family, or friends. There are no right or wrong answers; we need your honest opinions. Because this survey is completely anonymous, please do NOT write your name on this form. Thank you!

1. What was the first event or activity you attended at Grace Baptist Church? (Please circle one answer.)

   1. 8:00 Sunday service
   2. 9:30 Sunday service
   3. 11:15 Sunday service
   4. house church/small group
   5. Family Fun Night
   6. Adult Children of Alcoholics
   7. youth group ministry
   8. parent lecture series
   9. a dance
   10. a concert
   11. an adult course
   12. other:_____

2. In a **typical** month, how often do you attend a Sunday morning service at Grace?

   1. once a month or less
   2. twice
   3. three times
   4. every week

3. How long have you been attending Grace on a regular basis?

   1. less than a year
   2. 1 year to less than 2 years
   3. 2 years to less than 3 years
   4. 3 years to less than 5 years
   5. 5 years to less than 10 years
   6. 10 years or more
   7. you do not attend Grace regularly, or you're visiting today

4. Before you began attending Grace, were you attending another church regularly?

    1. Yes, you attended another Winston-area church regularly.
    2. Yes, you attended a church in another area regularly.
    3. You attended another church or churches, but not regularly.
    4. No, you did not attend any other church.

5. Do you consider Grace your "home" church?

    1. yes   2. no   3. still deciding

6. Which Sunday morning service at Grace do you attend **most often?** (Please circle only one answer.)

    1. 8:00 A.M.
    2. 9:30 A.M.
    3. 11:15 A.M.

7. Please circle one answer for each statement to indicate how well that statement describes why you usually attend that service at Grace.

Statements	The Main Reason	An Important Reason	Just a Minor Reason	Not a Reason
a. The time of the service is convenient.	1	2	3	4
b. You like the worship style better than in other services.	1	2	3	4
c. The service you attend is more consistent than others; you know what will happen.	1	2	3	4
d. The preaching/teaching are better in the service you attend.	1	2	3	4
e. You prefer the style of music in the service you attend over other services.	1	2	3	4
f. You like how many people there are in the service you attend.	1	2	3	4
g. Most of your friends attend at that time.	1	2	3	4
h. You like the learning center/youth ministry for your kids.	1	2	3	4

8. Think about the worship service you attend **most often** (the time you circled in Question 6). Listed below are various elements of the worship service. Please circle the number that describes whether you think there should be more time devoted to each element, less time, or it should remain the same as it is now.

Elements of the Service	–More Time– A Lot	A Little	Stay the Same	–Less Time– A Little	A Lot
a. the overall length of the service	1	2	3	4	5
b. the preaching and teaching	1	2	3	4	5
c. the overall worship time (not the preaching and teaching time)	1	2	3	4	5
d. the amount of congregational singing	1	2	3	4	5
e. the amount of congregational prayer	1	2	3	4	5
f. silence and time for personal reflection	1	2	3	4	5

9. Still thinking about the worship service you attend **most often,** below are some statements about possible changes that could be made to the worship service. Please circle the number that best describes how you feel about each one.

a. Communion should be served:
   1. much more often
   2. a little more often
   3. as often as it is now
   4. a little less often
   5. much less often

b. The music should be:
   1. much louder
   2. a little louder
   3. left as it is
   4. a little quieter
   5. much quieter

c. The style of the music should be:
  1. much more traditional
  2. a little more traditional
  3. left as it is
  4. a little more contemporary
  5. much more contemporary

d. The amount of musical accompaniment to the singing should be:
  1. increased a lot
  2. increased a little
  3. left as it is
  4. decreased a little
  5. decreased a lot

e. How easy to understand is the teaching and preaching:
  1. much too simple
  2. a little too simple
  3. fine as it is
  4. a little too difficult
  5. much too difficult

f. The teaching and preaching should focus on daily life in today's world:
  1. much more
  2. a little more
  3. as much as it does
  4. a little less
  5. much less

g. How much should the service focus on meeting the needs of people who usually do not attend church:
  1. much more
  2. a little more
  3. as much as it does
  4. a little less
  5. much less

h. The teaching and preaching should focus directly on the Bible and what it says:
1. much more
2. a little more
3. as much as it does
4. a little less
5. much less

10. Which of the following best describes your attendance?
1. You usually attend one service per Sunday.
2. You usually attend both an early service (8:00 or 9:30) and the 11:15 service.

11. If you attend both an early service (8:00 or 9:30) and the 11:15 service once a month or more, please circle the numbers by the statements below that best describe why you attend both services (you may circle more than one number).

1. You get something different out of the teaching in each service.
2. You enjoy the different styles of music and worship in the two services.
3. You have friends in both services.
4. You try to bring your unchurched friends to the 11:15 service, but you attend the earlier service for yourself.
5. Your children are involved in the children's/youth ministry during a time that is different from the service you want to attend.
6. Other reason:_____

12. Have you ever attended the 11:15 seeker service at Grace?

1. yes   CONTINUE WITH QUESTION 13
2. no   PLEASE SKIP TO QUESTION 14

13. Think about the 11:15 seeker service at Grace. Try to see it through the eyes of an unchurched person visiting it for the first time (if you have brought people to the 11:15 service, think about their reactions to it). How do you think a typical unchurched seeker would react to each of these aspects of the 11:15 seeker service at Grace?

Aspects	Would Like It:		Would Dislike It:	
	A Lot	A Little	A Little	A Lot
a. the music	1	2	3	4
b. the content of the teaching	1	2	3	4
c. the style of the teaching	1	2	3	4
d. the atmosphere	1	2	3	4
e. the style of worship	1	2	3	4
f. how many people attend	1	2	3	4
g. the location of the church buildings	1	2	3	4
h. the time of the service	1	2	3	4
i. the drama	1	2	3	4
j. the children's ministry	1	2	3	4
k. the friendliness of the congregation	1	2	3	4

14. Overall, regardless of how often (or whether) you attend the 11:15 seeker service, how valuable is the seeker service to achieving Grace Baptist Church's overall purpose?

    1. very valuable

    3. not too valuable

    2. somewhat valuable

    4. not at all valuable

15. On another subject, have you been to a spiritual gifts workshop at Grace?

    1. yes

    2. no, and you're really not interested in attending one

    3. no, but you'd be interested in attending one

16. Do you feel you know what your spiritual gift or gifts are?

    1. yes
    2. no
    3. you're not sure

17. How helpful has Grace been in helping you develop your spiritual gifts?

    1. very helpful
    2. somewhat helpful
    3. not too helpful
    4. not at all helpful

18. Which of the following best describes your feelings about volunteer ministry work you, personally, might do through Grace? (Circle only one answer.)

    1. You feel a definite call to work with or start a specific ministry within the church.
    2. You feel a definite call to minister through Grace, but are not sure what that ministry should be.
    3. You're not sure how or whether you should be working in ministry through Grace at this time.
    4. You do not feel a call to work in ministry through Grace right now.

19. Which of the following best describes your involvement in a small group through Grace?

    1. You are currently involved in a small group.
    2. You are not currently involved, but used to be.
    3. You have never been involved in a small group through Grace.

20. Please circle all of the activities below to which you have invited a friend who does not usually attend a church. If none are applicable, please circle #13.

1. 8:00 Sunday service
2. 9:30 Sunday service
3. 11:15 Sunday service
4. house church/small group
5. Family Fun Night
6. Adult Children of Alcoholics
7. youth group ministry
8. parent lecture series
9. a dance
10. a concert
11. an adult course
12. other:_____
13. none of the above

21. (Please answer Question 21 only if you circled #13—"none of the above"—to Question 20.) What is the main reason you have not invited any unchurched friends to any of the activities listed above? (Please circle one answer below.)

1. You don't have any friends who don't attend church.
2. You feel uncomfortable or embarrassed inviting unchurched friends to church activities.
3. You don't feel any of these functions are truly sensitive to the needs and perspective of an unchurched person.
4. You don't feel any of these activities are of good quality.
5. You, personally, aren't interested in attending the activities with the friends you would invite.
6. You're not sure how to approach your unchurched friends to get them interested in attending these activities.
7. Other reason:_____

22. Think about your contact with people who are not Christians. In the last 12 months, with how many different non-Christian people have you done each of the following things? (Please write the number on the blank. If none, write "0.")

    a. personally shared your beliefs about Christ and the gospel _____
    b. personally provided Christian counseling _____
    c. taken them to hear someone speaking about Christian topics, other than at church _____
    d. invited them to church or a church activity _____

23. Please circle the number next to the statement that comes closest to your beliefs about life after death:

    1. When you die you will go to heaven because you have tried to obey the Ten Commandments.
    2. When you die you will go to heaven because you are basically a good person.
    3. When you die you will go to heaven by your confession of your sins and acceptance of God's gift of Jesus Christ as your Savior.
    4. When you die you will go to heaven because God loves all people and will not let them perish.
    5. When you die you will not go to heaven.
    6. You do not know what will happen after you die.

24. Before you were attending Grace, would you have answered Question 23 as you just did, or would you have given a different answer to it?

    1. You would have answered in the same way.
    2. You would have answered in a different way.
    3. You're not sure how you would have answered it.

25. If you could change, add, or remove one thing about Grace Baptist Church, what would it be? Please be as candid and specific as possible.

_____

_____

_____

_____

Remember, all of your answers are anonymous. These questions are for classification purposes only.

26. What is your age?_____

27. What is your personal ethnic background? (Please circle one answer.)

　1. Asian/Asian-American/Pacific Islander
　2. black/African-American
　3. Hispanic/Latino/Mexican-American/Puerto Rican
　4. Native Alaskan/American Indian
　5. white/Caucasian
　6. other:_____

28. Are you:　　1. male　　　2. female

29. What is your religious background? (If mixed, circle what you consider to be your primary background—please circle only one number.)

　1. Protestant
　2. Catholic
　3. another religious background
　4. no religious background

30. What is your marital status?

  1. married—first marriage
  2. remarried—not the first marriage
  3. single, never married
  4. divorced or separated
  5. widowed

31. (Answer this question only if you are remarried—circling #2 in Question 30.) Please circle the statement below that best describes your household.

  1. You currently have no children in your household.
  2. You currently only have children in your household from another marriage (either yours or your spouse's).
  3. You only have children in your household from your current marriage.
  4. You have children in your household both from a previous marriage and from your current marriage.

32. How many children do you have in each of the following age categories?

  a. under 5:_____   c. 10 to 13:_____
  b. 5 to 9:_____   d. 14 to 18:_____

33. What is the highest level of education you have completed?

  1. did not graduate from high school
  2. high school graduate
  3. trade school
  4. attended college, did not graduate
  5. college graduate
  6. attended graduate school, did not get a degree
  7. have a graduate degree

34. (If you are married) Are both you and your spouse employed full- or part-time?

    1. both you and your spouse are employed
    2. only you are employed
    3. only your spouse is employed
    4. neither of you is employed
    5. you're not married

35. (If you are married) Does your spouse attend Grace?

    1. yes
    2. no
    3. you're not married

36. (If you are married) To the best of your knowledge, is your spouse filling out this survey?

    1. yes
    2. no
    3. don't know
    4. you're not married

37. What is your household's total annual income, before taxes?

    1. less than $10,000
    2. $10,000 to less than $20,000
    3. $20,000 to less than $30,000
    4. $30,000 to less than $40,000
    5. $40,000 to less than $50,000
    6. $50,000 to less than $60,000
    7. $60,000 to less than $70,000
    8. $70,000 or more

38. In the last 12 months, about how much money, in total, have you donated to charities or ministries (including Grace and any other churches)?

$_____

39. About what percentage of the money you have donated was given to Grace Baptist Church (not including missionaries you support through the church)?

_____%

40. What is the zip code where you live?   _____

41. How many minutes does it take you to travel to Grace for Sunday services (one way)?

_____ minutes

When you are finished, please hand the survey back to an usher. Thank you!

This is the second congregational survey. It was conducted in a smaller church that was preparing to open for its first service. Because of the committed nature of the people involved, the survey was sent to people, rather than handed out during a service.

New Church Survey

Please take a few minutes to complete this questionnaire. It is being sent to those of us who have been active participants in the New Hope Baptist (NHBC) ministry. We need to gain a better perspective of what everyone is experiencing, hoping and praying for regarding this church. Do not write your name on the survey. Please be honest and open in this process. Thanks.

A. Personal Background

1. What is your age group?

    1. under 18
    2. 18-26
    3. 27-35
    4. 36-45
    5. 46 or older

2. What is your gender?   1. male   2. female

3. Do you have any children under the age of 18 currently living with you?

    1. yes   2. no

B. NHBC Experience

1. How long have you been associated with New Hope Baptist Church?

    1. before we began meeting on Sundays at the YMCA
    2. since we started meeting at the YMCA in July
    3. during the last 2-3 months

2. How often do you attend the Sunday night seeker service?

    1. every week
    2. 2-3 times per month
    3. once a month
    4. do not attend it

3. Are you currently involved in a small group through NHBC?

    1. yes   2. no

4. Are you actively involved in the ministry of the church, through the programming, small group, assimilation or administration subministries?

    1. yes   2. no

5. Have you invited anyone you know to visit with you?

    1. yes—was it a positive experience for you?
        1. yes   2. no

    2. no

C. Feelings about NHBC

1. Do you consider NHBC to be your "home" church or primary church?

    1. yes   2. no

2. How well do you feel you understand each of the following elements of NHBC?

Element of the Ministry	Very Well	Some-what	Not Much	Not at All
a. the seven-step philosophy of our ministry	1	2	3	4
b. the meaning of our vision statement	1	2	3	4
c. the leadership structure of the church	1	2	3	4
d. the role of spiritual gifts in your involvement in the ministries of the church	1	2	3	4
e. how to "get connected" to the people of the church	1	2	3	4
f. how to become involved in the NHBC ministry	1	2	3	4

3. Overall, how satisfied are you with each of the following elements of NHBC's ministry to date?

Element of the Ministry	Very Well	Some-what	Not Much	Not at All
a. Bill's messages on Sunday nights	1	2	3	4
b. the music on Sunday nights	1	2	3	4
c. the drama presentations on Sunday nights	1	2	3	4
d. the overall atmosphere at the church before and after the Sunday night services	1	2	3	4
e. the Scripture reading during the services	1	2	3	4

f. the children's program which happens
simultaneous to the adult service   1   2   3   4

g. the consistency of the improvements
made in the services during the past
six weeks or so   1   2   3   4

h. the worship services   1   2   3   4

4. Please circle each of the words or phrases below that accurately describe your experience with NHBC so far. (Mark as many as are appropriate.)

1. fulfilling	11. personally stretching
2. hard work	12. great idea, poor execution
3. an answer to prayer	13. high level of quality
4. challenging spiritually	14. confusing
5. frustrating	15. a friendly group of people
6. a waste of time	16. easy to get involved
7. a unique experience	17. not biblical enough
8. exciting	18. male-dominated
9. inconsistent quality	19. poorly organized
10. spiritually lacking	20. too many surprises/changes

D. Commitment to NHBC

1. Overall, how committed are you, personally, to NHBC in each of the following areas?

Area of Commitment to NHBC	Very Well	Some-what	Not Much	Not at All
a. attending the seeker services	1	2	3	4
b. building relationships with seekers	1	2	3	4
c. consistently supporting the church financially	1	2	3	4
d. attending the worship services	1	2	3	4
e. inviting people to attend the church	1	2	3	4
f. getting involved in a small group	1	2	3	4

g. becoming active in some ministry of
the church, other than attending services
or a small group   1   2   3   4
h. praying consistently for the church   1   2   3   4

2. Think about 12 months from now. How likely is it that you will be an active participant in NHBC's ministry a year from now?

     1. very likely
     2. somewhat likely
     3. not too likely
     4. not at all likely

3. How convinced are you that New Hope Baptist Church will survive the early challenges of being a new church, to reach the point at which it is consistently growing and making a real difference in people's lives?

     1. I'm absolutely certain it will make it.
     2. I think the chances are good.
     3. It's a 50-50 proposition.
     4. I don't think the church will make it.
     5. There is no hope for this church.

4. If you knew several months ago what you know today regarding NHBC, how likely is it that you would have become involved?

     1. would definitely have become involved
     2. would probably have become involved
     3. would probably not have become involved
     4. would definitely not have become involved

5. How well does meeting on Sunday nights work for you?

     1. great
     2. pretty well
     3. not too well
     4. poorly

E. Leadership of the Church

1. If you or someone else in the church truly wanted to get involved in the NHBC ministry, as either a leader or a helper in the ministries of the church, which of the following words would you choose to describe the experience you might have in getting involved. (Choose as many as desired.)

   1. easy to get involved
   2. can't tell opportunities
   3. process is too complex
   4. time commitment expected is reasonable
   5. the leaders seem to want more people to get involved
   6. the training/preparation offered is adequate

   7. difficult to get involved
   8. easy to find opportunities
   9. the process is simple
   10. time commitment expected is unreasonable
   11. leaders don't seem to want more people involved
   12. the training/preparation offered is inadequate

2. Thinking about the leadership of the church, please mark one response to each statement shown below to indicate how strongly you agree or disagree with that statement.

Statement	–Agree– Strong	–Agree– Somewhat	–Disagree– Somewhat	–Disagree– Strong
a. Overall, things seem to be moving smoothly toward our original goals.	1	2	3	4
b. The leaders seem to be confused about what we're doing.	1	2	3	4
c. There is too little follow-through on promises made and efforts initiated.	1	2	3	4
d. I have a sense that things are out of control.	1	2	3	4
e. The leaders provide a strong sense of why we are involved in this ministry.	1	2	3	4
f. It takes too long for the church to respond to different opportunities.	1	2	3	4

g. The leadership seems to be closed
to new or creative ideas.   1   2   3   4

h. There is not enough significant
communication from the leaders about
how we're doing and where we're
going in the days ahead.   1   2   3   4

i. I feel that I can trust the leadership to
provide reliable, competent guidance.   1   2   3   4

j. Sometimes I wonder if the leaders are
spiritually mature enough to lead the
church well.   1   2   3   4

F. Seekers

1. How many seekers do you currently have strong relationships with? _____

2. How many of those seekers do you really feel that you will invite to NHBC within the next six months? _____

3. How aggressively are you planning to initiate and build relationships with unchurched people with a goal of eventually bringing them to the NHBC seeker service?

     1. very aggressively
     2. somewhat aggressively
     3. not too aggressively
     4. not at all

G. Ministry Desires

1. If you could change any aspects of the church at this point, what would you change? Please indicate *how* and *why* you make those changes, too. (Use an extra sheet of paper if necessary. This is important to us!)

2. What do you find to be most satisfying about NHBC for you, personally? (Please be as specific as possible.)

3. What do you find to be most frustrating about NHBC for you, personally? (Please be as specific as possible.)

4. What is the next most important ministry that needs to be developed by NHBC?

Thanks for your help. Please send your completed survey back in the envelope provided, or give it to a member of the leadership team on Sunday.

A BRIEF MARKETING PLAN FOR A CHURCH

Every church exists within a different ministry context and has a different vision for ministry. The marketing plan should reflect those differences. What follows in this section is the portion of the marketing plan that reflects one church's ministry heartbeat, in light of the goals, objectives, strategies and tactics they wish to employ. Other elements of their plan—such as the schedule, assignments, budgets and evaluation procedures—were appended later to their plan. The purpose of including this portion of their plan is not for imitation, but to give a sense of how one church approached their marketing effort.

Goal #1:

- Spread the gospel to those who have not heard it, and lead them to a relationship with Christ.

Objectives:
- Reach at least 300 people in our community before December 31 who have never heard the gospel presented, and play a role in at least 50 of them accepting Christ; budget of $6,000.
- Reach at least 300 people in overseas mission field, through our

resident missionaries, before December 31, and play a role in at least 100 of them accepting Christ; budget of $5000.

Strategies:

- Sponsor evangelistic events in the community.
- Train people to engage in effective relational evangelism with their contacts.
- Study the impact of our existing missionaries in Brazil, India and Kenya.
- Pray consistently and intensively for evangelistic impact in each of our geographic areas of influence.

Tactics:

- Hold a family activities day in Wilson Park, in September, with games, music, and other activities to attract families; have a booth with information about the church; have the ceremonies opened with prayer; have the pastor welcome people and briefly note our sponsorship and desire to meet them.
- Sponsor a debate between an atheist and a Christian apologist regarding the existence of God; promote to the entire community; position as a community social event, with informational overtones; charge a minimal entrance fee.
- Initiate a relational evangelism seminar that will run four consecutive Thursday evenings; hold the seminar each quarter; have a popular, strong teacher from within the church present a hands-on, practical equipping time; provide follow-up and support to those who enroll.
- Have two sermons during the year which emphasize the importance of a strong, coherent verbal witness by believers, encouraging people to intelligently share their faith without becoming overly aggressive.
- Provide a major congregational forum for lay people in the congregation who have played a role in someone accepting Christ this year to share their feelings about the experience.
- Communicate with our missionaries regarding their perception of what is happening in their ministries; get specific answers to spe-

cific questions regarding decisions for Christ, Bible reading, attendance at church services, involvement in cell groups, interest in exploring the Christian faith, images of Christianity.

- Hold a quarterly dedicated offering for our overseas mission work.
- Show a video of the overseas mission work to the entire congregation each quarter, emphasizing the importance of such outreach, the role of each person in that work, the future possibilities related to such outreach.
- Include prayer for evangelism in every leadership meeting, every congregational meeting, every worship service, every small group, every Sunday School class.
- Encourage all people to pray daily for those they know who are not Christians to accept Christ, and to share the good news of decisions for Christ with the Body.

Goal #2:

- Teach God's Word without compromise to an increasing number of people.

Objectives:

- Expand total Sunday School attendance to 300 adults, 250 kids on an average weekend; the aggregate cost of this expansion, for marketing, materials and other resources should be $3,000 or less.
- Increase participation in small groups to 20 adult groups with 200 adults; 10 teen groups with 100 teens; the expansion should cost the church $750 or less.

Strategies:

- Conduct a Sunday School recruitment campaign to encourage people to attend a class regularly.
- Increase the number of adult classes by 2, teen classes by 2, children's classes by 3, to prevent overcrowding and to offer greater variety in the subject matter and styles being taught.

- Enhance the quality of the resources and facilities available for teachers.
- Train a new team of small group leaders in anticipation of new groups being started.
- Encourage existing small groups of 12 people or more to split and seek to grow back to that size.

Tactics:

- Send a mailing to all church households with a schedule of the fall roster of classes, and a strong encouragement from the pastor to participate.
- Closely monitor the quality of the classes, to ensure that people are receiving both quality biblical teaching and personal benefit from their Sunday School experience.
- Make the initial day of the new Sunday School year a major church event, by celebration, marketing and reinforcement of participation.
- Acquire new signs for the campus to help people know where the classes are located.
- Have teachers and their aides contact individuals who attended the class during the first month to thank them and encourage them to continue.
- Identify and train new teachers for new classes.
- Identify potential space for new classes.
- Determine the hottest new topics that might be used in the initiation of each new class.
- Set aside a budget for each school year of $200 per class for materials.
- Determine what types of equipment are necessary for effective teaching, and seek adequate budgets from the elders to purchase such equipment immediately.
- Establish a regular meeting time for training, appreciation and encouragement of teachers.
- Repaint the walls in Rooms 106 and 107; replace the carpet in the basement; repair all lighting fixtures in all rooms; check heating and air conditioning in all rooms to ensure comfort.

- Identify a dozen potential leaders of small groups and begin the six-month training process in anticipation of beginning new small groups.
- Begin two new affinity groups in the second quarter of the year, led by staff until an internal leader emerges.
- Maintain regular contact with current small group leaders to determine problems, weaknesses and new opportunities; have consistent times with those leaders to train and encourage.
- Have associate pastor meet with small groups having 12 or more people to explain the value of splitting and discuss the specifics of the split; to plan a time of celebration; and to pray with them for future growth.

Goal #3:

- Worship God with consistency, intensity and servant hearts.

Objectives:
- Improve the quality of the worship services by comparing people's reactions to worship, as measured in the 1991 survey and a new survey, and improving the areas deemed most deficient; the survey should cost no more than $2,000.
- Try new approaches to worship during the course of the year, toward expressing ourselves creatively to God.

Strategies:
- Conduct a worship-related survey to measure changes in people's response to the quality and depth of the worship experience.
- Have the worship task force prepare a brief synopsis of recommendations for the worship team.
- Consistently have the pastor teach people about worship.

Tactics:
- Conduct a congregational survey, handed out during worship services on the first Sunday in October, using the same questions as

those in the October 1991 survey to gauge people's reactions to the worship services.

- Appoint a team of seven members to serve on the 1992 task force on worship, which would convene each Sunday and provide the worship team with a brief report of recommendations each month.
- Have the pastor, staff and lay leaders consistently seek feedback from people regarding how they meet God in the worship services; what works best for them; what impedes a superior experience of worshiping God; and what ideas they have for the worship team to consider.
- Encourage the pastor and other worship leaders to consistently encourage people to be aware of the presence of God, the purpose of worship, the role of attitude in worship and other critical elements regarding the worship experience.
- Allow church leaders to visit other churches doing significant worship experiences to explore what they are discovering about worship styles and approaches that might be adapted to meet our congregation's needs.
- Encourage the worship leaders to try new approaches in various areas of the worship service, incorporating at least one innovation each month, and evaluating whether or not to continue that innovation on a regular basis, an infrequent basis, or to discontinue the practice.

Goal #4:

- Reflect God's compassion to mankind by helping the needy people in our midst with practical assistance.

Objectives:

- Enable three adults with families to gain jobs after a significant period of unemployment; the cost to the church should be up to $3,000.
- Subsidize the rent for three young families that are working but unable to make their payments; up to $100 per month subsidy per

family, a one-year obligation, toward enabling them to become self-sufficient; the aggregate budget for this program is $3,600 for the fiscal year.

- Enhance the educational abilities and achievement of minority children by establishing an after school tutoring program that will assist at least 30 young people from low-income households in the community; the church will spend a maximum of $7,000 on this program.

Strategies:

- Identify three young men or women with children living with them who are under 12 years of age, and have been unemployed for 12 months or more despite seeking work, and prepare them for a successful job search.
- Identify three families with young children in which the adults are employed but unable to afford a reasonable rent and enter a contract with them to subsidize their payments in return for the commitment to seek higher paying employment.
- Establish a tutoring program at the church for elementary school children who live in the low-income section of the community and who are struggling academically despite promise or desire to improve.

Tactics:

- Work with the YMCA, Salvation Army and local social workers to identify unemployed adults meeting our criteria.
- Interview the adults to ascertain their circumstances.
- Select three adults which the church will assist in job preparation skills: preparing a resume, interviewing techniques, personal grooming, identification of possible positions, etc. Have the training process conducted by Almonson Employment Services at the church's expense with a designated church representative for each adult sponsored.
- Once the person has secured a position have a weekly check-in time to encourage and support as possible.

- Work with the YMCA, Salvation Army and local social workers to identify families struggling to make their rent payments despite regular income.
- Set up a time to review their family budget and help them work through a leaner budgeting process if appropriate.
- Arrange with their landlord to make the monthly subsidy payment directly to the landlord.
- Set up counseling sessions to prepare the heads of these households for a job search that may result in a higher paying position and the ability to make ends meet without subsidy.
- Identify 15 volunteers who will work two or more afternoons per week to tutor academically needy children.
- Establish the schedule and location for the tutoring program.
- Recruit qualified students by working with Johnson Elementary and St. Mark's Christian School to identify students meeting our criteria; contacting the parents regarding the nature and purpose of the program; and establishing a maximum of three students per tutor, per day, for a two-hour time block.
- Purchase the textbooks for the tutors that the students are using, which will be kept in the church library for future reference.
- Hire a credentialed teacher to oversee the program and all tutoring activities, who will be on site during the entire process.
- Measure the impact of the program by keeping in contact with the teachers of the students enrolled in the program and ascertaining if progress is being made academically.

EXAMPLES OF CHURCH NEWS RELEASES

Sample 1:

News Release
For Immediate Release
January 6, 1993
Contact: Mark Wilson, 344-7926

Community Arts Festival
Scheduled for April

Rev. Jim Mueller, pastor of St. Matthew's Christian Church, announced today that the fourth annual Community Arts Festival will be held in Pottsville on Saturday, April 6.

The festival provides local artists a forum for displaying their creative talents. The festival is held outdoors, in East Square, from 10 a.m. to 4 p.m., offering people the chance to examine the work of dozens of area artisans. At the start of each hour, in the center of the square, a performing artist will provide entertainment. There is no admission charge to peruse the displays and events during the festival.

Rev. Mueller explained that the church began the festival as a means of bringing the community closer together. "We have a growing community which includes literally hundreds of very talented people whose works of art and handmade crafts never get the recognition they deserve. Our desire was to serve the community by providing a means of recognizing their talent and sharing it with a wide range of people."

Police estimate that the festival drew about 8,000 people during the day last year. The organizers of the festival, led by Michael Peterson, an elder at St. Matthew's, are expecting a minimum of 10,000 people this year.

"The festival has gained widespread recognition as a unique and appealing event," explained Peterson. "The perceived value of the festival is evidenced by the fact that we do not do any advertising or other type of paid promotional activity. People come because they hear about the festival from people who have attended in the past and enjoyed the experience."

Unlike past years, artists and craftspeople will be permitted to set up booths to sell their items this year. A portion of the revenue from the licenses sold to artists purchasing a temporary sales license from the city will be transferred directly to the city's schools.

For further information about the festival, call the Community Arts Festival Hotline at 246-3467. If you would like to help with the planning or administration of the festival, contact Michael Peterson at St. Matthew's Christian Church, 344-7926.

—end—

Sample 2:

News Release
Date: August 15, 1992
From: Portland Community Church,
        1346 East Oak Street, Portland
Phone: 771-9200
Contact Person: Rev. Harold Lindsay
Subject: Music Director hired
For release on August 21, 1992

Portland Community Church Hires
New Music Director

Portland Community Church is proud to announce the hiring of a new Director of Music, Mrs. Shirley Tan. Mrs. Tan will fill the vacancy created by the passing of Mr. James Cristell, who had filled the post for 41 years.

Mrs. Tan has been the Director of Music at Mt. Zion Baptist Church in Chloe, IL. She served in that position for 12 years before accepting the post at Portland Community Church. In her new position she will direct all music programs at the church, which includes three choirs and two instrumental groups.

"We are excited to have a person of Shirley's experience, competence and vision join our ministry. Music is such a critical part of the Christian experience. We look forward to new and adventurous musical experiences under her gifted leadership."

Mrs. Tan is a graduate of Trenton State Teacher's College, where she received a Bachelor's degree in Music Education, and Westerly Conservatory, where she earned a Master's Degree in piano. Upon graduating from Westerly, she studied for several years at the Lysees Institute in Paris. Upon returning to America, she served as choirmaster at the Wadsworth School, then assumed her recent position as Director of Music at Mt. Zion Baptist Church. She has been married for ten years and has a son, Jeffrey, who is six, and a daughter, Anna, who is two. Her husband, Zachary, will be an associate professor of biology at Portland Community College.

Mrs. Tan expects to encounter many changes from her experience at Mt. Zion Baptist. "The PCC congregation has expressed an interest in expanding the scope of the music ministry, and I am anxiously awaiting the chance to take part in that growth. During my visits to the church I have met many people who are interested in participating in a larger music ministry. This will be a great opportunity and a great challenge to take advantage of the wide range of talents represented in this church. My dream is to make PCC a church known for great music that brings people closer to God in worship and exploration."

Mrs. Tan will begin at Portland Community Church on September 1.

(PHOTOGRAPHS AVAILABLE UPON REQUEST)

30#

SAMPLE #3:

News Release
For Immediate Release
Date of Release: March 14, 1993
Contact: Phil Jeffries (888-0901)

Church Leader Charges City with Neglect of Youth

Speaking at the Full Gospel Business Men's monthly meeting last Tuesday, Dr. Richard Grant, pastor of First Baptist Church of Richmond, charged that recent decisions by the City Council reflect a disregard for our children.

"Allowing the Cloverleaf Family Planning Center to locate in our community is just one more instance of a city council that lacks the moral integrity to take a stand against abortion. On the one hand, the council members campaign for office with statements about the importance of family services and family programs within our community. Then, when we're not looking, they approve the operating license for an abortion clinic in our community. This certainly does not promote solid family values."

During the presentation, Dr. Grant stated that his research shows that approximately 230 youths from the community have an abortion each year. "Having an abortion clinic right in their backyard not only sends the message that abortion is apparently acceptable, but also makes this act of irresponsibility and murder more convenient for our children."

The Council measure referred to by the minister was a bill passed by unanimous voice vote during the March 2 City Council meeting, in which an operating license was granted by the Council to Hillsdale Family Planning Centers, Inc. Hillsdale is the parent company of the Cloverleaf Family Planning Center. They are located in Nyack and own and operate a chain of eight abortion clinics. The

Cloverleaf facility will open in April and will be located at 241 Tulane Street.

Dr. Grant warned that the city had not heard the end of protests against permitting an abortion clinic to operate in Richmond. "The City Council must know by now that parents and all people who believe in the sanctity of life and the importance of protecting our society from undesirable temptations will do whatever is necessary to revoke that license. We anticipate lawsuits, advertising campaigns, and acts of civil disobedience to send a clear warning to the people of this community. Our goal is to represent the community by informing the City Council in no uncertain terms that the people who voted them into office do not approve of abortion or any organization that performs such acts of medical homicide."

Representatives of the Cloverleaf Family Planning Center refused to comment on Dr. Grant's charges.

(PHOTOGRAPH AVAILABLE UPON REQUEST)

30#

OTHER RESOURCES RELATED TO MARKETING

Books by Subject Matter

New books are constantly being released regarding all aspects of the marketing process. Most of these works are not targeted to the Christian market, but the techniques described are applicable to ministry activities. Here are some of the best books, by marketing subject, which you might find to be of use.

Vision

The Power of Vision, George Barna, Regal Books, 1992.
Vision Building, Peter Brierley, Hodder & Stoughton, 1989.

Qualitative Research

Focus Groups, Jane Farley Templeton, Probus Publishing, 1987.
Focus Groups, Richard Kreuger, Sage Books, 1988.

Quantitative Research

Mail and Telephone Surveys, Don Dillman, Wiley & Sons, 1978.
Asking Questions, Norman Bradburn and Seymour Sudman, Jossey-Bass, 1982.

Survey Research Handbook, Pamela Alreck and Robert Settle, Irwin Books, 1985.

The Art of Asking Questions, Stanley Payne, Princeton Univ. Press, 1980.

Basic Marketing Research, Gilbert Churchill, Dryden Press, 1988.

Using Secondary Information

Demographic Know-How, Penelope Wickham, Probus Publishing, 1988.

The Clustering of America, Michael Weiss, Harper & Row, 1988.

Trend Tracking, Gerald Celente, Wiley & Sons, 1990.

Trend Watching, John Merriam and Joel Makower, Tilden Press, 1988.

Marketing

Marketing the Church, George Barna, NavPress, 1988.

Strategic Marketing for Non-Profit Organizations, Phillip Kotler and Alan Andreasen, Prentice-Hall, 1987.

Guerrilla Marketing, Jay Conrad Levinson, Houghton-Mifflin, 1984.

Ogilvy on Advertising, David Ogilvy, Crown Publishers, 1983.

Strategic Marketing

Mind of the Strategist, Keniche Ohmae, Penguin Books, 1982.

Guerrilla Marketing Attack, Jay Conrad Levinson, Houghton-Mifflin, 1989.

Positioning, Al Ries and Jack Trout, Warner Books, 1981.

Market Segmentation, Art Weinstein, Probus Publishing, 1987.

Why They Buy, Robert Settle and Pamela Alreck, Wiley & Sons, 1986.

Marketing Plans

Marketing Planning Guide, Robert Stevens et. al., Haworth Press, 1991.

Developing a Winning Marketing Plan, William Cohen, Wiley & Sons, 1987.

The Marketing Plan, William Luther, AMACOM, 1982.

Communications

Media Planning, Jim Surmanek, Crain Books, 1980.

Contemporary Christian Communications, James Engel, Thomas Nelson Publishers, 1979.

Tested Advertising Methods, John Caples, Prentice-Hall, 1974.

The 27 Most Common Mistakes in Advertising, Alec Benn, AMACOM, 1978.

Confessions of an Advertising Man, David Ogilvy, Atheneum, 1963.

APPENDIX 9

OTHER RESOURCES FOR MINISTRY FROM BARNA RESEARCH GROUP, LTD.

Barna Research Group exists to help ministries understand their context for ministry more precisely, toward making better decisions for ministry. The company provides the following resources for churches. New resources are consistently being added to the list.

Newsletter
Ministry Currents, published quarterly.

Books (by George Barna)
The Barna Report 1992-1993, Regal Books, 1992.
The Power of Vision, Regal Books, 1992.
What Americans Believe 1991, Regal Books, 1991.
User Friendly Churches, Regal Books, 1991.
The Frog in the Kettle, Regal Books, 1990.
Marketing the Church, NavPress, 1988.

Reports
The Church Today: Insightful Statistics and Commentary, 1990.
Today's Teens: A Generation in Transition, 1990.

Church Growth: New Attitudes for a New Era, 1989.
Never on a Sunday: The Challenge of the Unchurched, 1990.
Born Again: A Look at Christians in America, 1990.

Audiocassette Study Guides

"Current Trends" 1991.
"Creating a User Friendly Church" 1991.

Other Resources

The User Friendly Church Inventory (100-question, self-adminis-
    tered test to determine how user friendly your church is).

Forthcoming Resources (tentative titles)

Reviving Dead Churches—a book regarding research on how churches
    that were declining or dead were revived and have since
    become growing, vibrant, impactful churches.
Baby Busters: The Angry Generation—the boomers get the media
    attention, but the busters are the new generation of young
    adults. Discover what makes them tick, why they are angry
    about life, how the church does (or does not) fit in their
    future, and how we might reach out to this group.
The American Family: A Status Report—results of a national research
    regarding changes in structures, attitudes and activities of fam-
    ilies, and the role of the church in influencing family behav-
    ior.
Devastating Deceptions—we know that most Americans do not have a
    philosophy of life or an articulated worldview. Yet we make
    decisions based upon a series of key values and basic assump-
    tions about life. In this book, learn about these assumptions
    and values, and how they impact your attempts to minister to
    people.
Ministering to Women—women are the most devoted of the sexes to
    Christianity and to the work of the Church but they also have
    unique needs and expectations regarding their faith and their
    church. This book will outline our findings of research con-
    cerning the special desires, needs and hopes of women related
    to their faith and their life.

A View from the Pulpit—a continuation of the tracking study by Barna Research Group concerning the experiences, the dreams, the disappointments and the plans of pastors in churches around the nation.

Penetrating Hispanic America—a study of the nation's rapidly growing Hispanic population and how the Christian community can be more intimately tied to the life of this special population.

Penetrating Asian America—a study of the nation's rapidly growing Asian population and how the Christian community can more effectively impact the life of the Asian-American population.

Ministering to the Black Community—the second largest people group in America are the blacks—yet so little is known about the nature of their religious commitment. This study will reveal what they believe, the impact of their faith on their life-styles and how we might minister more effectively to and with black Americans.

For additional information about the resources, the research or other services of the Barna Research Group, please contact them at P.O. Box 4152, Glendale, CA 91222-0152.